SIDELIGHTS
ON
QUEEN VICTORIA

MACMILLAN AND CO., Limited
LONDON · BOMBAY · CALCUTTA · MADRAS
MELBOURNE

THE MACMILLAN COMPANY
OF CANADA, LIMITED
TORONTO

Queen Victoria

SIDELIGHTS
ON
QUEEN VICTORIA

by

THE RIGHT HONOURABLE
SIR FREDERICK PONSONBY
G.C.B., G.C.V.O.

MACMILLAN AND CO., LIMITED
ST. MARTIN'S STREET, LONDON
1930

COPYRIGHT

First printed September 1930
Reprinted October 1930

PRINTED IN GREAT BRITAIN
BY R. & R. CLARK, LIMITED, EDINBURGH

PREFACE

ALTHOUGH the majority of my father's letters are stored either in the archives at Windsor Castle or in the muniment rooms of the descendants of eminent Victorians, he kept a certain number of so-called private letters himself, and these at his death in 1895 he left to me. When I looked through these I found, mingled with letters that never could be of general interest, letters from politicians, soldiers, sailors, civil servants and other eminent public men. While it was impossible to knit into a coherent narrative these spasmodic letters, I felt that they might be utilised to supplement contemporary biographies. Therefore, whenever a biography of an eminent Victorian has been undertaken, I have invariably sent any relevant letter that happened to be in this collection to the biographer and often they have been found useful in filling gaps in the life or correspondence. Although this method of dealing with the majority of letters seemed quite satisfactory, there were certain incidents which concerned so many people that it was difficult, if not impossible, to decide into whose biography they should go. In the case of letters from Gladstone and Disraeli, whose biographies have already been amply written, it was of course a matter of deciding whether these further details concerning them were of sufficient importance to the public or whether they should go for ever unrecorded.

These incidents seem to bring out very clearly Queen Victoria's dominant personality and to illustrate so well the tenacity with which she pursued any line of policy once she had arrived at a decision. The means were immaterial; it was the end that mattered; but as there is naturally no record of her conversations with Ministers or of the verbal instructions she gave to her private secretary, these can only be inferred.

In deciding to publish these incidents I fully realise the difficulty of attempting to interpret to the present generation the political and social atmosphere of the middle of the last century. It is, in fact, almost as difficult as endeavouring to make the modern, short-skirted, hard-hitting lawn-tennis girl of the present day understand the psychology of the lady with voluminous flounces, bustle, chignon and ringlets playing croquet with a gentleman with long whiskers, an eye-glass and a pork-pie hat.

Future generations will doubtless deride the present age for its unscientific handling of post-war problems, but we for our part can only wonder what the Victorians would have made of them and smile at the kind of problems with which they were confronted. It is the custom now to speak with a sneer of Victorian security and self-satisfaction, but seeing the sort of issues on which politics then turned, security was only natural. Governments could rise and fall on such questions as the establishment of an Irish University, the

vi

increase of the beer duty, or the supply of cordite; fierce political campaigns could rage over the agricultural franchise or the Straits of Malacca.

In spite of this, intense earnestness was expected of a statesman and was essential to his success. A wit like Bernal Osborne might aspire to Westminster but never to Downing Street, and the flippancy and free-and-easy ways of modern politicians would have horrified the House and the country. All members cultivated the grand manner and adorned their speeches with quotations from the classics. But political life was pure, and as everyone was interested in politics, parliamentary debates were not ignored as they are now in the more popular press, but were read as eagerly as the reports of test matches and football finals are to-day.

About the middle of the last century there were two outstanding figures in politics, Gladstone and Disraeli, and these two, so sharply opposed in political expediency, personal characteristics and psychological outlook, attracted a warmth of admiration and of detestation perhaps unparalleled in history. Disraeli, the sphinx-like leader of the Conservative party, the Machiavellian diplomat, thought Gladstone a designing politician—a Tartuffe "inebriated with the exuberance of his own verbosity"—out for the furtherance of his own sinister ends: while Gladstone confessed when Disraeli died that even a mild tribute "cost him much searching of heart". The country seemed more or less equally divided between the two, and the political pendulum swung fairly evenly between the two parties they led.

SIDELIGHTS ON QUEEN VICTORIA

Apart from politics, life swept grandly along century-old grooves. To read the letters of that time is to be transported not indeed into the lavender-scented days and ways of Quality Street, but at least to Rotten Row in its glory, to balls, dinners and assemblies quite unlike anything to-day. Dinners, skirts and sermons were long, and shrift for social transgression very short. Comfort, and a carriage and pair, were the outward and visible signs of progress. Coachmen still wore wigs and most footmen were powdered. Taxes were light; drinking was heavy. The only new things were the Crystal Palace and the crinoline. And at the apex of this placid pyramidal England sat, supremely royal in her seclusion, Queen Victoria.

In such a world, the political waters were so unruffled that a small ripple was often mistaken for a storm. The question of who should fire a gun, as the first chapter will relate, or ride a pony, as the second chapter of this book will tell, were matters of tremendous import that caused endless perturbation in the Royal household and even in the Cabinet.

CONTENTS

CHAPTER I

The Fatal Gun, 1872 . . . . . PAGE I

CHAPTER II

The Pony Row, Balmoral, 1869 46

CHAPTER III

The Visit of the Grand Duke Wladimir, 1871 . 65

CHAPTER IV

Gladstone, Disraeli and the Irish University Bill, 1873 88

CHAPTER V

The Visit of the Shah of Persia, 1873 . . . 118

CHAPTER VI

The Queen's Speech, 1881 136

CHAPTER VII

The Franchise Bill, January to July 1884 . . 159

CHAPTER VIII

The Franchise Bill, August to October 1884 . 189

SIDELIGHTS ON QUEEN VICTORIA

CHAPTER IX

THE FRANCHISE BILL, OCTOBER TO DECEMBER 1884 . PAGE 244

CHAPTER X

MR. GLADSTONE'S RETIREMENT, 1894 . . . 280

INDEX 299

ILLUSTRATIONS

QUEEN VICTORIA. Photogravure reproduced from a portrait by W. and D. Downey, Ltd. . . . *Frontispiece*

FACE PAGE

THE ROYAL YACHT, *Victoria and Albert* 8

" PERSIA WON ! " Cartoon by Sir John Tenniel, reproduced by kind permission of the Proprietors of *Punch* 72

" COME TO GRIEF." Cartoon by Sir John Tenniel, reproduced by kind permission of the Proprietors of *Punch* 100

" COME A CROPPER." Cartoon by Sir John Tenniel, reproduced by kind permission of the Proprietors of *Punch* 164

GENERAL THE RIGHT HON. SIR HENRY PONSONBY, G.C.B. 278

CHAPTER I

THE FATAL GUN, 1872

QUEEN VICTORIA had little love for London: she disliked its noise, its fogs, its fierce unbridled materialism. By contrast she loved the moors and braes of Balmoral, the sunny freshness of Osborne, and even the dignified feudalism of Windsor, where she held many state functions. But where Windsor could be reached easily by train and almost by carriage drive, and Balmoral by a comfortable railway journey, Osborne, in the Isle of Wight, required a short sea trip. For this purpose Queen Victoria used the second largest of the two Royal yachts, the *Alberta*, while the smallest, the *Elfin*, was utilised to carry messengers, members of the household and officials whose social standing was not high enough to entitle them to use the *Alberta*. The largest Royal yacht, the *Victoria and Albert*, a dignified paddle-wheel steamer picked out in black and gold, with deck cabins of gleaming white and funnels of light buff, was intended for Queen Victoria's more public appearances at sea, for naval reviews, Royal welcomes, etc., but as a matter of fact she was very seldom used.

In 1872 there were held the usual manœuvres of the Channel Fleet. The Queen never attended them, but it was agreed that the Prince of Wales (later Edward VII.) should represent her and should utilise the *Victoria and Albert*, whose captain, Prince Leiningen, was a half-nephew of Queen Victoria by the Duchess of Kent's first marriage. The presence of the Royal yacht at manœuvres was quite an innovation, and a precedent—that stronghold of the red-tape mind—did not exist regarding its function or position.

According to the usual naval routine an evening gun is fired every day by the officer in command of the fleet. This firing of the gun is not a simple ceremony: it indicates to the assembled fleet who is the Senior Flag Officer, where he is to be found, and where to look for orders. It also gives the time to the fleet or squadron, denotes the setting of the watch and the time for placing the guard boats and look-outs. Similarly, the morning, or daylight gun, sanctions the relief of the watch and look-outs, and is the signal for the recall of the guard boats. Thus the gun signal was of no little importance.

It was on the 10th of August 1872 that the firing of this gun caused such an explosion that its reverberations made even the Cabinet shake in their shoes, for it was fired, not at the order of Rear-Admiral Hornby, who was in command of the Channel Fleet; nor of Admiral Sir Sydney Dacres, the First Sea Lord, who was there for the manœuvres; nor even of Mr. Goschen, the First Lord of the Admiralty, but at the order of that very junior captain, Prince Leiningen. Worse still, it was fired a few seconds too early, as if to emphasise his right to fire the gun.

At the moment, Admiral Sir Sydney Dacres was on board the Royal yacht. The outrageous conduct of Prince Leiningen he considered to be so serious that, instead of remonstrating with him verbally, he sat down in his cabin and indited the following semi-official letter:

My DEAR PRINCE LEININGEN—I beg leave to inform you, to avoid mistakes, that the Daylight Gun to-morrow morning will be fired by the *Minotaur* bearing the flag of the officer commanding the Channel Fleet. I am quite sure you must be well aware that the yacht firing an evening and morning gun is quite an innovation under present circumstances, more particularly when the Admiralty had informed Rear-Admiral Hornby that he was to conduct the duties of the fleet in the usual manner. I think I may frankly say that the Admiralty are much surprised at having a gun fired from the Royal yacht as they are quite unaware of any regulation of the Service that would authorise it, and they see how very much inconvenience would attend on such a departure from custom.

Yours sincerely,

S. DACRES.

Prince Leiningen, being only a captain, had to be careful in what he said to so exalted a personage as the First Sea Lord, and his reply, delivered a few minutes later, ran:

DEAR SIR SYDNEY DACRES—I am excessively sorry you should think I had done anything unusual in firing a gun at 9 o'clock. It has *always* been the custom to do so ever since I have been in the yacht when the Royal Standard is flying. An instance of this occurred only five months ago in Portsmouth harbour, and I am

3

sure Sir Rodney Mundy[1] himself will bear me out in what I say.

Believe me to remain, Very sincerely yours,

LEININGEN.

I shall be much obliged to you [he added] if you kindly will let me know your decision on the matter in question, so that I may know what to do to-morrow morning.

Sir Sydney Dacres, as he sat in his cabin, must have been relieved to find that the incident had ended so satisfactorily. He had kept up his end and successfully remonstrated with Prince Leiningen. He could, there-fore, unbend a little since there was now no prospect of paper warfare; so he wrote this time to "My Dear Leiningen" a letter which he thought would close the whole incident.

In answer to your note [his reply ran] the precedent you quote at Portsmouth is not a point. The Queen was on board, and if I may quote my own experience, it was then a novelty. But here we have a large fleet—the Admiralty themselves are present, and the question is one far more of responsibility than ceremony—and nothing must be done to lessen the authority of those who are held responsible. Rear-Admiral Hornby must therefore, as has been ordered, fire the gun.

Yours sincerely,

S. DACRES.

---

[1] Commander-in-Chief at Portsmouth.

The Queen's Regulations [he added as a postscript] confine the firing of a gun to flag officers and commodores. (See Page 2. Article 10.)

The marine orderly who was acting as messenger, having had a busy evening taking letters from one cabin to another, was now to spend a restless night. First of all Sir Sydney Dacres thought it prudent to send an account of the incident to the First Lord of the Admiralty on board the *Enchantress*, together with copies of the letters that had passed between him and Prince Leiningen. Then there must have been a conference on the *Victoria and Albert* between the Prince of Wales, Prince Leiningen and Colonel Grey (father of Viscount Grey of Fallodon), at which the decision was reached that Prince Leiningen should continue to fire the gun.

The marine orderly, having already delivered Sir Sydney Dacres' packet of letters, had therefore to go a second time to the *Enchantress*, this time from the *Victoria and Albert*, with the following letter for Mr. Goschen, the First Lord of the Admiralty:

August 10th, 1872.

Sir—I am desired by His Royal Highness the Prince of Wales to inform you that Prince Leiningen has placed the correspondence between Sir S. Dacres and himself in His Royal Highness' hands, and as His Royal Highness' Standard is flying on board the Royal yacht, and as moreover His Royal Highness is here as the Queen's representative, he has ordered Prince Leiningen to fire the morning and evening

5

gun according to the usual custom of the Royal yachts.

I have the honour to be, Sir, Your obedient Servant,

G. GREY,

Equerry-in-Waiting.

The question was now posed for Mr. Goschen to answer. He, as First Lord of the Admiralty, represented the Government as the civilian head of the Navy. He, or his predecessor, had been responsible for appointing Rear-Admiral Hornby to the command of the Channel Fleet, and could therefore delegate to him the duty of firing the gun. But the Prince of Wales was there as heir-apparent, representing the Queen, and furthermore quite determined to exercise all Royal privilege. Naval manœuvres were Greek to Mr. Goschen, who was enjoying a pleasant sea holiday at the Government's expense, but constitutional precedents he felt to be his own particular territorial waters. He probably agreed with Lord Fisher that while every member of the House of Commons is a heaven-sent Army reformer, the Navy is little more to them than "a huge mystery hedged around by sea-sickness".

Colonel Grey's letter reached the *Enchantress* at 2 A.M., but no one dared disturb a sleeping First Lord, and seven o'clock came, the time for the firing of the daylight gun, before the civilian "ruler of the Queen's Navee" had had his morning cup of tea or the morning's mail. Meanwhile, the Prince of Wales had given orders to Prince Leiningen to fire the gun from the *Victoria and Albert*, while Sir Sydney Dacres had sent similar instructions to Admiral Hornby to fire it from the flagship. Suddenly the placid morning air of the Solent was rent by two explosions—two morning guns

6

had been fired! They awoke Mr. Goschen, who probably wondered what all the row was about. A few minutes later he opened Sir Sydney Dacres' and Colonel Grey's letters and realised that something unpleasant had happened; what it was exactly he was unable for the moment to grasp. Breakfast was soon despatched and he hurriedly summoned to a consultation the Sea Lords and Admiralty officials, whose apoplectic countenances made it clear that he was expected to take a very serious view of the matter.

The consultation resulted in so bewildering Mr. Goschen that he decided to lay the whole matter before Queen Victoria, and his letter to her, dated August 11, ran:

Mr. Goschen presents his humble duty to Your Majesty and much regrets to feel it incumbent upon him to lay before Your Majesty the following particulars of an incident which occurred yesterday evening in connection with the Royal yacht.

What is technically called "the evening gun" was fired from the *Victoria and Albert* by Captain His Serene Highness Prince Leiningen, under what the Admiralty believes to be a misapprehension of the regulations known as "The Queen's Regulations for the Government of Her Majesty's Naval Service". Under these regulations the right of firing a gun on certain occasions is limited to Flag Officers and Commodores, and when more than one are present, the senior only can exercise the right (Mr. Goschen encloses the words of this regulation in question). Consequently the firing of the gun is not a simple ceremony. It indicates to the assembled vessels who is the Senior Flag Officer present and therefore in command.

The Lords of the Admiralty, being officially present in Portland and having had delegated to them by Your Majesty's gracious commission the supreme authority over Your Majesty's Naval Forces, had directed Rear-Admiral Hornby, the Commander-in-chief of the Channel Squadron, to carry on the duties of Commander-in-chief during their stay at Portland.

The Lords of the Admiralty were distinctly of opinion that it was Rear-Admiral Hornby who, under the regulations, was alone entitled to fire the evening gun, and that the step taken by the captain of the Royal yacht was contrary to the regulation. Had there been a question of ceremony, no difficulty whatever would have been raised, but the important point involved was who was entitled to command of the fleet assembled.

It was thought that H.S.H. Prince Leiningen had acted under a mistake, and Admiral Sir Sydney Dacres, the Senior Naval Lord, pointed this out to him in writing. Prince Leiningen in reply pointed to a precedent which he believed to be applicable, and asked to be informed of Sir Sydney Dacres' decision so as to guide him with reference to the morning gun. Sir Sydney Dacres then informed Prince Leiningen that the precedent did not apply as Your Majesty had been present in person on the occasion in question, and that the morning gun would be fired by Admiral Hornby. Mr. Goschen begs to add that as the regulation prescribes that only Flag Officers should fire these guns

THE ROYAL YACHT, *VICTORIA AND ALBERT*

from their ships it was not known to the Lords of the Admiralty that they had been fired from the Royal yacht.

Mr. Goschen most humbly ventures to point out to Your Majesty that it is a very serious question in every point of view under what circumstances the supreme command over ships of war (and the consequent responsibilities) should be exercised by any of those to whom Your Majesty has delegated it by Royal Commission, and that the flying of the Royal Standard on any ship, especially if Your Majesty is not on board in person, cannot in itself be held to derogate from that delegated power, or to transfer it to any other quarter.

Mr. Goschen should add that the letters of Sir Sydney Dacres were written to Prince Leiningen in his capacity of a Naval officer on questions arising out of the Queen's Regulations, and that the Lords of the Admiralty had no information as to any personal intervention in the matter.

After the last letter of Sir Sydney Dacres to Prince Leiningen, His Royal Highness the Prince of Wales caused Mr. Goschen to be informed that he had given an order (as the representative of Your Majesty) that the gun should be fired from the Royal yacht, but Mr. Goschen, deeply as he regrets that any such question should have been raised between His Royal Highness and the Admiralty, feels bound to point out that in his humble opinion His Royal Highness the Prince of Wales did not obtain authority over the ships of war present by the fact of the Royal Standard flying on the yacht, or by being deputed by Your Majesty to act as

9

her representative on the occasion of a ceremonial. Mr. Goschen humbly hopes that Your Majesty will pardon him for placing this matter before Your Majesty. The point at the moment might be considered of less importance if it did not carry with it ulterior questions, as to the authority of members of the Royal Family over Your Majesty's Forces on other occasions.

The letter written to Mr. Goschen by command of the Prince of Wales, of which he encloses a copy, was not brought to him till seven o'clock this morning, though it was brought on board the *Enchantress* at two in the night. Had Mr. Goschen had any notice of His Royal Highness' personal intervention in this case, Mr. Goschen would have at once asked permission to wait on His Royal Highness and to explain to him the difficulties of the position. As it was, Rear-Admiral Hornby fired the morning gun in accordance with the notice which had been sent to Prince Leiningen, and the latter also fired the gun, possibly in consequence of no reply having arrived to the letter sent to Mr. Goschen by His Royal Highness' command, but which did not reach him till the gun had been fired.

Mr. Goschen need scarcely assure Your Majesty that he deeply laments any annoyance which may have been caused to His Royal Highness in the course of proceedings in which His Royal Highness had graciously consented to take part.

Mr. Goschen still desires to mention for the information of Your Majesty that the Standard flying on the *Victoria and Albert* was that of H.R.H. the Prince of

Wales, though Mr. Goschen has spoken of it in this letter simply as the Royal Standard.

The Queen received Mr. Goschen's letter just before breakfast on the morning of the 12th August, and with it the following explanatory memorandum which had been prepared for her by the Naval Secretary at the Admiralty:

Memorandum

The firing of the Evening Gun in any port or roadstead denotes the presence of the flag officer in command of a fleet or squadron, to whom, during the night, the several commanding officers will look for instructions by signal in any emergencies which may arise.

It is accompanied by the hoisting by the flag officer of the top light and the uncovering of the stern lights, which are invariably shown at sea and in harbour or roadstead in addition to the position light on the fore stay.

It also gives the time to the squadron, and denotes the setting of the watch, the rowing of guards and placing look-outs.

The firing of the morning gun in like manner denotes daylight and sanctions the relief of the look-outs and watch who in war-time are kept at their guns or under arms on the quarter-deck in readiness for immediate action, and it is also the signal for the recall of the guard boats.

The words used in the Queen's Regulations and Admiralty instructions clearly indicate that the firing of the gun is left to the discretion and judgment of the Admiral in Command.

In war-time it might frequently be considered inexpedient to fire the gun as it might apprise a watchful enemy, not only of the position of a fleet or squadron, but it would also denote that the force was sufficient to be under the command of an admiral or commander.

In war-time, moreover, the daylight gun is not fired by the officer commanding the fleet until by careful observation it has been ascertained that no approach of the enemy has been made under cover of the darkness and that the watch may be safely relieved.

The above considerations lead to the conclusion that the firing of the evening and morning gun is a token of the command exercised by an admiral or other officer responsible for the charge and duties of a fleet or squadron, that it is a military observance, and could not be set aside without impairing the authority of the admirals, and departing from the regulations and usages of the service founded on long experience.

The point in dispute had now been magnified into a big constitutional problem. The question who should fire a gun seemed so trivial that it could with a little common sense have been decided on the spot, but when it became symbolic of the rights of the Lords of the Admiralty, and when the Queen's supremacy at sea was questioned, it seemed a serious matter.

Queen Victoria asked her private secretary, Colonel H. Ponsonby, to draw up a memorandum on the subject, and his opinion was as follows:

The Admiralty question must be separated into several heads:

(1) The question of the Queen's supremacy at sea. I scarcely think this will be disputed. William IV. by an Order in Council in 1833 directed that when the Sovereign was on board any vessel of war, the Royal Standard, the flag of the Lord High Admiral and the Union Jack should be displayed. Now I conceive that this implies the Sovereign and the minister are both on board and that all orders emanating from that ship are law to the Navy.

As to compliments, when these flags are flown all honours are paid from all ships and forts. But it is ordered in the Queen's Regulations that when the Royal Standard alone is flying, ships salute but forts do not —thereby implying there is a difference. The Prince's Standard is treated with the same respect as the Royal Standard.

I think, therefore, that no contention can be raised as to the Queen's right at sea, and that on this point the reply will chiefly be addressed to the remark made in the Queen's letter on the ignorance of the Admiralty respecting the custom which has been invariably observed.

If they admit the Queen's supremacy they cannot of course object to the Queen's right to order the gun to be fired from the yacht, but they will deny that the custom was known. It has been so seldom put in force that only one well-authenticated case can be proved before this year, and the custom can of course only be invariable since the time the yacht has had guns on board.

This, however, would only be a sort of remonstrance against the charge brought against the Admiralty of ignorance of custom. I repeat I do not think they desire to dispute the Queen's undoubted supremacy.

(2) The position held by the Prince of Wales at Portland has been defined as representing the Sovereign. But in what way he represented the Queen is not so clear. It may be agreed that he was entitled to all the compliments paid to the Sovereign, but he held no warrant, nor was there any public notification of his so representing her, nor was it probable that the Queen intended to invest him with any power whatever. At any rate, he appears with his own standard flying, so that no announcement was made to the fleet that he was anything more than the Prince of Wales, entitled hereby to every honour and respect from the ships but invested with no command or responsibility.

Would it not be advisable that on public occasions when any of the princes represent the Queen, a notice to this effect should be made known?

The Prince, on this occasion, flew his own standard, which was entitled by the regulation to the same compliments as the Royal Standard, but not the same as the Royal Standard and the other two conjoined.

(3) The Admiralty, having received the Queen's warrant to command the Navy, refuse to admit the right of any other person to command the Navy without a similar warrant from the Queen. There cannot, of course, be two commanders. Therefore, while according all respect and honour to the Prince of Wales,

14

they steadfastly maintain the right as derived from the Queen to command the Navy, and no one else.

They cannot allow the Queen's warrant to them to be disputed.

The Admiralty only could command the fleet at Portland. They alone, without any other order, ordered the fleet to Portland, and ordered the fleet away. Without touching the question of courtesy, they maintain as a right that they had the right to order all the ships away while the Prince was there. Of course, this is pushing the question to the extreme, but they are most firm on the rights which belong to them by the Constitution. This being so, they consider that any order given by the Prince of Wales was an infringement of their rights. Either he or they must have the power. They maintain that they have, and therefore that the order given by H.R.H. that the gun should be fired was unconstitutional.

(4) On writing to Prince Leiningen the Admiralty received a reply from him in which, after touching on the above-mentioned subject, he asserted a claim which they entirely deny. They evidently lay great stress on this point, and he does so equally. He claims the right of the Royal yacht—with the Royal Standard flying—to be Senior Officer. Therefore, whenever the Royal Standard is hoisted on board the *Victoria and Albert*, all commands issuing therefrom must be obeyed. The Admiralty emphatically deny such right, and deny also that the Royal yacht is entitled as a ship to any precedence over any other ship, except by reason of the flag it may display.

And the rules as to these flags being already stated, it does not appear that any special claim can be put forward on behalf of the Royal Standard alone to exercise command.

HENRY F. PONSONBY.

Colonel Ponsonby thus tactfully gave it as his opinion that the Prince of Wales and Prince Leiningen were in the wrong, and this opinion he expressed even more frankly in a letter to his wife written that day from Osborne (August 12, 1872); in fact he averred that their action was "subversive of discipline" and "a direct incitement to mutiny":

In the afternoon Otho Fitzgerald[1] came to see me. He apologised for interfering in a matter in which he really had no business, but said he felt this naval question might really lead to something serious, and he was anxious to let me know the feelings of the admirals. They were unanimous in affirming that the conduct of the Prince of Wales was so utterly subversive of discipline that he would not be surprised if the Admiralty Lords resigned if they were not supported. Leiningen had been ordered by the Lords of the Admiralty not to fire the gun. He had done so and was guilty of insubordination, for which some wished to try him by court-martial. "But", I said, "all the Navy don't agree with you." "Ah", said Otho, "I know you mean Rim Macdonald [a retired admiral] and others. The Prince went round the fleet canvassing officers to take part in

---

[1] Lord Otho Fitzgerald, brother of the Duke of Leinster, and a retired naval captain.

16

his view and secured Rim and one or two others. He has foolishly given their names. This is a direct incitation to mutiny, and no authorities can allow such a proceeding. The Prince, by ordering officers to disobey the Lords of the Admiralty to whom the Queen has delegated her power, has committed a grave act, and if the Queen supports him she gives these lords a snub they cannot stand. Goschen will stand or fall with them." All this, of course, was discussed at length and I could not well make head, so I changed to my strong point. "Do you mean to tell me that Goschen supports the junior lords who tell the Queen she has no right to fire this gun, that she was under a misapprehension in having ordered it, and that the practice was an innovation."

I must say Otho stuck well up even for this—saying that command and responsibility must go together, and that the Queen, having confided the Navy to the care of the lords, could not withdraw it capriciously. He also maintained it was an innovation. He then turned back to his strong ground, the Portland affair, and said it had been grossly mismanaged, and that Leiningen had given the Prince bad advice. "Well", I said, "that is hard on Leiningen." "If he didn't", replied Otho, "who did advise him? Was it his Privy Council consisting of Charles Beresford, Clonmel and Arthur Sumner? If he represents the Queen, who represents the Queen's advisers? It is absurd to say that the Navy is to obey the caprices of a Prince advised by a German prince and a knot of gay, giddy boys." I felt unpleasant and so got back to Dacres, and

C

Otho persisted in getting back to the Portland row. He ended by entreating me that no hurried action should be taken as consequences might be serious. Bids,[1] in the meanwhile, had written a letter for the Queen, very strong. I suggested moderation because: first, are we sure of our facts that the Queen has always fired this gun? second, had we better not fight solely the Queen's right? and third, above all things don't let us advance to any position which we should have to retire from with shame. Bids thereupon said he would keep the answer till to-morrow. But he says he won't allow the Queen to sacrifice any right. I quite agree, but we must clearly see it is a right. Cowell[2] won't listen to any doubt about the Queen's right, and says any question of it is legal quibbling, but, on the other hand, he thinks the Prince of Wales quite wrong. He says that flags are everything. The Prince exhibited his own flag alone, which (for all purposes of compliment only) is entitled to be treated as the Queen's Standard. His advice is throw the Prince over and maintain the Queen's right. Now, throwing the Prince over is a serious matter, and if we abandon that point the Admiralty will follow up their victory by insisting on their demands about the Queen. I seek for some mode of an amicable settlement, but don't see it yet. I lay awake half the night. I think the Queen should take a judicial tone, something like this: "You, Goschen, complain to me of the Prince of Wales. You, Prince of Wales, complain to me of Goschen. You say

[1] General Sir Thomas Biddulph, Keeper of the Privy Purse to Queen Victoria.   [2] Sir John Cowell, Master of the Queen's Household.

18

you did so because I did, and you, Goschen, say I was wrong when I did so. Let us clear that up first." But in any case I don't want the Queen to enter into controversy if it can be avoided, but to be above it. Besides, we can't fight from Scotland.

How tired you will be of all this, but it is a small thing that if not carefully judged may swell into a large one, so that it requires most careful handling. Of course, if I were the Queen I would send for Goschen and have it out with him. But that cannot be.

Queen Victoria, on receiving Mr. Goschen's letter, must at first have thought it was merely a trivial matter relating to naval etiquette. The fact that her son had come to loggerheads with the Admiralty left her singularly cold, but when she read Colonel Ponsonby's memorandum and found that her supremacy at sea was being disputed, she at once plunged into the fray. Without going into the niceties of the technical arguments and the interpretation of the nebulous regulations, she put the controversy on a higher plane and wrote to Mr. Goschen from Osborne on August 13:

OSBORNE,
August 13th, 1872.

The Queen has received Mr. Goschen's letter respecting the misunderstanding which occurred at Portland, and has also seen copies of the correspondence which took place between Sir S. Dacres and Prince Leiningen and a letter from the Prince of Wales' equerry.

The circumstances have given the Queen considerable annoyance, particularly as it appears to her that great misapprehension exists in the Board of Admiralty as to the custom of the Service with regard to her position, when on board the Royal yacht with the Royal Standard flying.

In his second letter to Prince Leiningen Sir S. Dacres observes, in reply to Prince Leiningen's observation that he had always fired the gun when on board the Royal yacht with the Royal Standard flying and once within a few months at Portsmouth, that, quoting his own (Sir S. Dacres') experience, such a proceeding was then a novelty, though the Queen was on board. Mr. Goschen also observes that it was not known to the Lords of the Admiralty that such was the custom.

The Queen must express her surprise at this. The custom has been invariable during the Queen's reign, and she has no intention of dispensing with the mark of respect to the Sovereign which it indicates.

The Prince of Wales' (and the Prince Consort's) Standards are entitled by a special order to the same respect as the Queen's, and the Queen thinks, on the occasion of his visiting Portland as her representative, every respect should have been shown to him. No command or interference with the fleet is intended, but the Sovereign and the Prince of Wales can hardly be placed in the position of a private person on board, so that the ships of a squadron or fleet, accompanying the Royal yacht, might leave the harbour without announcing their intention to do so.

The Queen by no means desires, nor would she allow, the Prince of Wales to introduce any alteration in the regulations of the Service on these points. Nothing can be further from her wish than to deprive the Board of Admiralty of the authority they should exercise. All the Queen desires is to maintain the proper dignity of the Sovereign, or of the Heir Apparent representing her, and not to allow innovations to be introduced.

The circumstance of two morning guns having been fired appears to have arisen from misapprehension, owing to Mr. Goschen not having received the letter addressed to him as intended, and the circumstances which led to it having occurred in the middle of the night, all personal communication was prevented, which, no doubt, would have removed the misunderstanding.   VICTORIA, R.

The Queen thus appeared to support the action of the Prince of Wales and Prince Leiningen. Mr. Goschen, however, was determined not to let the matter rest here, and he instructed the Secretary of the Admiralty to call for a report of the incident from Prince Leiningen, whose report ran as follows (August 18):

SIR—In compliance with the request contained in your letter of the 17th inst., I have the honour to inform you:

(1) The morning and evening guns have not been fired since I have had command of the Royal yacht, with the Queen on board, except at Portsmouth in the month of March of the present year, both on leaving for and returning from Cherbourg.

Her Majesty has not stayed on board on any other occasions in the presence of a flag officer. A morning and evening gun was fired at Cherbourg in 1858 in the presence of both the Admiralty and Lord Lyons' squadron. I was then commander of the Royal yacht. The Admiralty flag was flying on board here on both occasions. A morning and evening gun was fired in 1868 at Kingstown (Ireland) with the Prince of Wales' Standard and no other flag flying. A flag officer (Rear-Admiral Warden) and a squadron was present at the time.

(2) No intimation has at any time been sent by me to any senior or flag officer of my intention to fire the gun, nor did I do so at Portland.

Ever since I have known the yacht, now nearly eighteen years, she has always been considered as senior officer in every case whenever the Royal Standard was flying with or without the Queen herself being on board.

(3) I did not inform the Commander-in-Chief at Portsmouth in March last of my intention to fire the gun. The Admiralty flag was flying on board here at that time, whilst at Portland it was not.

Then the matter simmered for over a month, ostensibly on account of the death of Princess Hohenlohe, but really because each side wanted time to strengthen their case.

But Colonel Ponsonby was determined to pour what oil he could on these troubled waters and suggested privately to Mr. Goschen that, if the Portland incident could be dismissed as a misunderstanding, it would then only be necessary to discuss the new regulation that would obviate further trouble. His letter to Mr.

Goschen, written from Balmoral on September 26, runs:

> The Queen inquired to-day about the memorandum and I said that you had not wished to trouble Her Majesty at the present moment with it.
>
> As I had said I had spoken to you on the subject, the Queen expressed a hope that you did not intend to contest her undoubted right to supremacy afloat. I did not undertake to represent your views accurately, but repeating them to the best of my power assured her that I did not think you intended to question her rights and privileges, but only to explain that the infrequency of the custom of firing the gun at night from the Royal yacht justified the Admiralty in their ignorance that such was usual.
>
> But if the Queen's supremacy is admitted the Admiralty should not have doubted her right to fire the gun.
>
> The Regulations, however, are not so clear on this point as they might be, and the Queen thought that perhaps you would assure her of her rights and if necessary propose some addition to the Queen's Regulations that would put the matter beyond doubt.
>
> I did not enter into the details of the question of the Prince of Wales beyond remarking that I felt sure I was not misrepresenting you in saying you thought the Queen's Regulations very obscure on that point also, and that, although you believed that Prince Leiningen was wrong both in what he did at Portland, and what he afterwards claimed on behalf of the yacht, you

admitted there was ample room to allow of the mis-understanding.

Will not any controversy on this point in its present form assume to a certain extent a personal tone in so much as it may condemn the acts of individuals who may have considered themselves justified by custom and by portions of the Regulations?

If so, would it not be better that the incident at Portland should be considered entirely as a misunder-standing, and, being treated as such, be no further alluded to?—but that new rules founded on the case should be drawn up by you and submitted for the Queen's consideration—and that the discussion should then take place on the proposed rules?

This proposal is only mine, so that you are quite at liberty to reject it, and, at the same time, I should scarcely like you to accept it before I have consulted the Prince of Wales, but I have taken the liberty of suggesting this, as a cold and dry discussion of rules would, I think, be preferable to a hot controversy on the acts of individuals.—Yours very truly,

HENRY PONSONBY.

The Prince of Wales, who was now at Abergeldie Castle, close to Balmoral, followed the discussion closely, and to Colonel Ponsonby he wrote on September 28:

Many thanks for sending me all the correspondence relative to the "incident at Portland". I should be very glad to have some conversation with you on the sub-ject—perhaps the Queen would give you permission to lunch here to-morrow—so that I may speak to you afterwards.

Colonel Ponsonby thought it well to keep Prince Leiningen also informed about the proposal he had put forward to Mr. Goschen.

It was unlucky [he wrote on September 28] that the illness and death of Princess Hohenlohe prevented Mr. Goschen from communicating with the Queen on the Portland incident.

I cannot help thinking that there are innumerable difficulties in the case arising from the want of pre-ciseness in the regulation and that the discussion as to what each individual did must degenerate into a personal dispute. I think it would be undesirable that the Queen and the Prince of Wales should be mixed up in anything that is personal, and I imagine that Your Serene Highness would much prefer that the argument should take place on the merits of the case.

The question of the Queen having supreme authority when she is afloat on any vessel of war with the Royal Standard, the flag of the Lord High Admiral and the Union Jack flying is, I imagine, beyond dispute, though it must be affirmed now more clearly.

I venture to suggest, therefore, whether it would not be as well that the Portland incident should be treated as a misunderstanding by all parties, and that no further discussion should take place on the acts of individuals on that occasion, but that new rules or amended regulations, founded on the necessity arising for such rules from the obscurity of those which exist, should be framed by the Admiralty and submitted to the Queen, and upon these a discussion may fairly take place. Do you think this would be advisable?

Mr. Goschen, feeling that the Portland incident strengthened his hand, was loath to drop it. A cut-and-dried discussion on future regulations might place him in a difficult position and he might be forced to give way. On September 30, he wrote to Colonel Ponsonby:

Let me proceed at once to the main point of your letter of the 26th, which I received at the Admiralty to-day.

You say: "Would it not be better that the incident at Portland should be considered entirely as a misunderstanding, and being treated as such be no further alluded to."

I quite concur in the desirability of treating the question in the abstract. But how does it stand now? That the Queen has written a very strong letter to me officially, in which the action of the Admiralty is strongly commented on. That letter I can, of course, scarcely treat as other than a letter directed to me officially in the character of the First Lord of the Admiralty. I cannot leave that letter unanswered or unexplained. It would be unjust to my colleagues and myself.

If the whole correspondence were withdrawn it would be a different matter, but I do not think it can possibly close with the last letter I have received. That letter cannot remain as the final record of the incident at Portland.

With regard to the other part of your letter, it is always a most difficult matter to report a long conversation to another person in a few sentences.

I admitted that the regulations as to the hoisting of the flag were not as clear as they might be, but I certainly did not intend to convey that any ambiguity in the Regulations afforded "ample room to allow for the misunderstanding" as regards the action of Prince Leiningen when the Prince of Wales was on board— nor was there any ambiguity which in my judgement could justify the giving of an order by the Prince of Wales as to a matter connected with the fleet.

You appear to have misunderstood me to mean that while I thought Prince Leiningen was wrong there was great excuse for him on account of the Regulations. I was far from meaning that. The difficulty in the Regulations is with regard to the hoisting of the three flags, and what is the position of the Sovereign when the three flags are not hoisted, but only the Royal Standard? But that does not exculpate Prince Leiningen on the particular occasion in question. I think that the officers of the yacht have created some customs on a very narrow basis without the knowledge of the Admiralty, in the teeth of the Regulations. Then they plead these alleged customs against the Regulations, and the poor Regulations are then to be condemned.

I have delayed further action till I had really gathered all the facts together and I have now done so. As to your first suggestion, you will have understood what I mean. I should prefer a dry correspondence as to *future* rules and would most gladly hail a release from the necessity of dealing with the past, but so long as the last letter is in full force, you will agree with me that I have no alternative but to deal with the points it raises.—Yours very truly,   G. GOSCHEN.

Prince Leiningen, who was a junior captain, while perfectly willing to support the Prince of Wales, did not like the idea of the Queen and the Admiralty deciding the larger issues in a spirit of amicability, while leaving him to be the scapegoat on the minor issues. He therefore wrote to Colonel Ponsonby on October 2:

I quite agree with you that the discussion of the Portland business should not become a personal dispute and that, as you suggest, new regulations on the subject should be submitted to the Queen. Whatever decision is then arrived at will be a guidance for myself on future occasions. Moreover, it can be a matter of perfect indifference to me whether Her Majesty is pleased to give in to the Admiralty or not, which really and truly is the point at issue. I only have to obey and to do as I am told.

But there is another side to the question, entirely separate from the "Standard" business in itself. I mean the way my own case has been prejudged by their Lordships. I have been pitched into, privately, by Sir Sidney Dacres, and in his letter to the Queen, Mr. Goschen very considerately tried to throw all the blame on me. Moreover, there has been a very nasty article in the *Army and Navy Gazette*, abusing myself, who, from being on full pay, am not allowed to open my mouth in self-defence.

28

Now if, as you suggest, I drop the matter altogether, I admit myself snubbed, although "right or wrong", I merely have carried out the routine of the yacht such as it is and has been for the last thirty years.

Besides, people will say the matter has been hushed up because I am the Queen's nephew, etc., etc. I think, instead of being told on official foolscap that I ought to have known "better", I have a right to expect a *letter* to say I have acted to the best of my judgement. That is the mildest way I can put it.—Sincerely yours, LEININGEN.

As Leiningen indicated, the story leaked out and the "very nasty article" of which he complained appeared in the *United Services Gazette* on September 28, 1872. It was a travesty of the incident in the form of a letter headed "The Fatal Gun". The key to the principal characters is as follows:

ALBERTO, PRINCE OF ASTURIAS	The Prince of Wales.
QUEEN JOANNA	Queen Victoria.
DON ERNESTO	Prince Ernest Leiningen.
DON VIEJO ACRES Y LIMPET	Admiral Sir Sydney Dacres.

The letter was addressed to the Editor of the *United Services Gazette*, and ran:

SIR—Having been in Spain, studying the language, in order to qualify myself for the post of interpreter, I unearthed the following curious manuscript in the public library of Valladolid. As it is a valuable picture

29

of nautical manners and customs 350 years ago, I trust it will be interesting to your readers. . . .

I am, Sir, etc. TRITON.

THE ARGUMENT

Alberto, Prince of Asturias, Infante of Spain, proceeds to Ferrol, to open the breakwater there. He is surrounded by a numerous suite, and as he represents his mother, Joanna, Queen of Castile and Aragon, he travels in the Royal yacht, and a fleet is assembled at Ferrol to do him honour. The weather is not propitious, but blows a heavy gale. In the first scene the Royal yacht has just arrived at her buoy, and has been duly saluted by the fleet.

ACT I.—SCENE I

The deck of the Royal yacht abaft the mainmast. Officers on the quarter-deck. DON ERNESTO, *the captain of the yacht, at the gangway. To him enter up the ladder* DON JOACHIM GOSCHENO, *the Minister for Naval Affairs.*

DON JOACHIM GOSCHENO. Upon my word, Ernesto, I'm not at all well; sea passages don't agree with me. I'm not like my predecessor, who, I am told, was bold enough even to take charge of the fleet. But where is his Royal Highness?

ERNESTO. Your Excellency does not look well; his Royal Highness is in the Pavilion.

(*Enter up the ladder* DON VIEJO ACRES Y LIMPET, *in a white hat, and laughing all over his face.*)

DON VIEJO ACRES. Ah, ha! Ho, Ho! Ernesto, good day, you're looking well (*pokes him in the ribs*). Good-day, you fellows (*to officers of yacht*): you see I'm still the hearty, bluff old admiral.

> (*Enter successively*, DON HOUSTON STUARTO, *of the Admiralty;* DON IMAGO D'ORO,[1] *the Com-mander-in-Chief at Cadiz;* DON HENRICO LONGSHANKO,[2] *Commander-in-Chief at Barce-lona;* DON G. P. HUMBI,[3] *the Admiral com-manding the Armada; the* LORD OF THE NORTHERN ISLES,[4] *second in command of the Armada;* DON G. G. PANDOLFO, *third in command;* DON RAMSI Y DALHOUSI, *his flag-lieutenant;* CAPT. VAN DEVELSKIN,[5] *the senior captain of the fleet; and others. They all go aft to the Pavilion door.* DON ERNESTO *presents them to the* PRINCE OF ASTURIAS.)

PRINCE OF ASTURIAS. I hope you are well, Don Joachim. We've had rather a stormy passage. (DON JOACHIM *bows.*)

DON JOACHIM GOSCHENO. Yes, Your Royal Highness. I've suffered from it.

PRINCE OF ASTURIAS. So it seems. (*Waits a little, as if expecting something, then aside to aide-de-camp.*) Oughtn't he to give me a list of the ships?

AIDE-DE-CAMP. Yes, sir, but he doesn't know what he's about.

PRINCE OF ASTURIAS (*to* DON VIEJO ACRES). Admiral, I see you're looking well. There's no chance of Her Majesty losing your services, I can see.

---

[1] Admiral Mundy.
[2] Admiral Codrington.
[3] Rear-Admiral Hornby.
[4] Admiral Macdonald.
[5] Captain Vansittart.

DON VIEJO ACRES Y LIMPET. No, Your Royal Highness; I mean to serve Her Majesty under any Government and under any circumstances, whatever. I am connected with the Limpets of Biscay, sir.

PRINCE OF ASTURIAS (*to* LORD OF NORTHERN ISLES). Ah! Mac, how are you? Dine with me at eight to-night, and bring Don Ramsi with you?

DON ERNESTO (*to* PRINCE OF ASTURIAS). Your Royal Highness's barge is ready.

PRINCE OF ASTURIAS. Thank God! (*To Aide-de-camp*). Dismiss the rest of them, and tell Van Develskin to dine; he's good for whist.

(*Goes to open breakwater. Exeunt Omnes.*)

ACT I.—SCENE 2

(*In the Admiralty barge.* GOSCHENO, VIEJO ACRES Y LIMPET *and the rest are being pulled on shore.*)

DON VIEJO ACRES Y LIMPET. By jingo, Goscheno! did you hear? he asked the Laird to dinner and that fellow Van, and left us out!

DON JOACHIM GOSCHENO. I'm very glad, I'm very sick, I couldn't eat, I wish I was back in my counting-house—office, I mean.

DON VIEJO ACRES Y LIMPET. But I could eat, though, and I don't like it. Both those fellows junior to me, and I the rough-and-ready old man of the sea who rules the Navy!

(*Scene closes.*)

32

Act II.—Scene 1

(*In after-cabin of Admiralty yacht,* Don Viejo Acres, Don H. Stuarto, Don Imago D'Oro, Don H. Longshanko, Don G. P. Humbi, *and* Don G. G. Pandolfo *seated at table.* Time, 8.45 p.m.)

Don H. Longshanko. Where's Goscheno?

Don Viejo Acres y Limpet. Sick and gone to bed.

(*A burst of laughter is heard across the water.*)

Don Imago d'Oro. They seem merry on board the yacht. I think it is so wrong of the Prince to let those fellows laugh like that. I never let my flag-lieutenant even smile at my official dinners. I'm afraid in these days dress and dinners are not thought such important matters as they really. . . .

Omnes. Oh, shut up! (*He shuts up.*)

Don G. P. Humbi. Admiral, who fires the 9 o'clock gun?

Don Viejo Acres y Limpet. Oh! you'd better do it; it will show our independence.

Don H. Stuarto. But won't it be uncivil to His Royal Highness? He represents the Queen, and she always does it when she's afloat. I know it, because I was at Cadiz when she went to France, and she did it then, didn't she, Imago d'Oro?

Don Viejo Acres y Limpet. Don't bother yourself, Stuarto; I'll take the responsibility. That will be enough for you, I know.

Don Houston Stuarto. Yes, I always want to do the right; I like to be safe on both tacks.

DON G. P. HUMBI. I'll go and give direc——

(*The Fatal Gun fires from Royal yacht.*)

OMNES. The Fatal Gun! Let us write letters.

DON VIEJO ACRES Y LIMPET. Yes, I'll rub Ernesto down first.

DON G. G. PANDOLFO. Good. Quite my style. Make as many people's lives miserable as you are able.

> (DON VIEJO ACRES Y LIMPET *and* DON HOUSTON STUARTO *retire with huge volume of regulations and instructions. In* 35 *minutes they return with their composition, which is sent to* ERNESTO *on board the yacht.*)

ACT II.—SCENE 2

(*The Royal Bedroom.* PRINCE OF ASTURIAS *and* DON ERNESTO.)

PRINCE OF ASTURIAS. Well, Ernesto, I never yet came across such men; not content with insulting me more than ever I was insulted before, they must correspond with me at half-past 2 on Sunday morning. Take this letter: it tells Goscheno that as it's always been customary to fire the morning and evening gun when the Royal Standard is flying here, I shall do so, and refer the matter to the Queen.

DON ERNESTO. Very good, Your Royal Highness; then we'll fire the morning gun at 4 A.M.

PRINCE OF ASTURIAS. Yes, please. I hope they won't send any more letters. Those officers must be tired taking them.

34

THE FATAL GUN, 1872

ERNESTO. Yes, three letters between 10 P.M. and 2.30 A.M. *is* rather strong. Good-night, sir.

PRINCE OF ASTURIAS. Good-night, Ernesto.

(*Exit* ERNESTO. *Scene closes.*)

ACT III.—SCENE I

(*The deck of the Royal yacht. Time, just after* 4 A.M. *Officer of middle watch walking the bridge, expecting Officer of morning watch. Enter Officer of morning watch*).

OFFICER OF MORNING WATCH. Well, what's the news? How did your morning gun go?

OFFICER OF MIDDLE WATCH. Oh! pretty right. Don G. P. Humbi fired his morning gun at 3.45 A.M., we fired ours at 4 A.M. A pretty quarrel, isn't it?

OFFICER OF MORNING WATCH. Yes, good-night, old fellow!

(*Scene closes.*)

THE SEQUEL

The correspondence continued for twenty years, at the end of which time My Lords apologised, but acquainted the maker of gun-tubes to the Royal yacht that he had fallen under their grave censure for supplying tubes which *would* go off at inopportune moments.

FINIS

The *United Services Gazette* was eagerly read by the fleet, and even Colonel Ponsonby received two copies. The first, from Prince Leiningen, was accompanied

35

by the following letter from the commander of the Royal yacht, dated October 14, 1872:

DEAR COLONEL PONSONBY—Prince Leiningen has asked me to send you a copy of the *U.S. Gazette* of the 28th September, which I forward by this post. You will see a beautiful account of the Portland business under the heading "The Fatal Gun" on page 6. I think the names of the characters are easily understood, except:

DON IMAGO D'ORO	Admiral Mundy
DON H. LONGSHANKO	Admiral Codrington
CAPTAIN VAN DEVELSKIN	Captain Vansittart
LORD OF THE NORTHERN ISLES	Admiral Macdonald

We have been unable to discover who wrote it, and I expect some of the characters would be glad to find out.

I should have sent it before, but have had some difficulty in procuring a copy.

Believe me, very faithfully yours,

H. F. STEPHENSON.

The second was from the Prince of Wales, who wrote from Abergeldie Castle:

MY DEAR PONSONBY—I enclose the article out of the *United Services Gazette*—called the "Fatal Gun"—which I think will amuse you. Please return it when you have done with it.

I remain, yours very sincerely,

ALBERT EDWARD.

Meanwhile Queen Victoria had no intention of following Mr. Goschen's suggestion that she should withdraw her letter, and the Prince of Wales seemed opposed to the proposal to drop the Portland incident. There was, therefore, nothing to be done but to carry on the discussions. Consequently Colonel Ponsonby wrote to Mr. Goschen on October 5:

I am sorry I did not clearly comprehend your meaning about there being room for misunderstanding in the Portland incident.

But I only repeated in very general terms to the Queen my impression of what I supposed to be your opinion. As the Queen is very tenacious of her rights at sea, and as her letter to you was almost entirely devoted to the assertion of her rights, I scarcely think I could propose to her to withdraw that letter. I may as well mention to you that I spoke to the Prince of Wales and made my suggestion to him. He did not seem to think it was possible to obliterate the Portland incident for reasons which are too long to enter into here. But ultimately he seemed ready to listen to my proposal. As the matter at present stands you will, I suppose, send the Queen the memorandum you have prepared.

The suggestion I made was merely mine and its non-adoption simply leaves the question as it was.

Since the question might be referred to the Prime Minister, Mr. Gladstone, and the Cabinet, Colonel Ponsonby took the precaution of enlisting the sympathies of Lord Halifax, the Lord Privy Seal, a member of the Cabinet and a *persona grata* with Queen Victoria, but while Lord Halifax liked the proposal to drop the Portland incident, he took a serious view of the Prince of Wales having given an order to an officer of the Navy. To Colonel Ponsonby he wrote on October 7:

I have read over your letter since I came here and I am quite sure that the first step which you suggest, *i.e.* treating what has happened at Portland as a *misunderstanding*, is the wisest and best course.

The Prince cannot really suppose that Sir S. Dacres was *intentionally* guilty of disrespect. Mr. Goschen cannot suppose that P. Leiningen committed an act of insubordination. Captain Tryon, Mr. Goschen's private secretary, whom I met at Drummond Castle, seems to me to be of this opinion, though it is fair to say that whilst he knew all about it, I do not know that he represented Mr. Goschen's opinion.

I will not now enter into the question of the Queen herself being on board the yacht. It does not arise here, and we should only complicate the present matter by going into it.

I hold it to be indisputable that the Prince of Wales can give no orders to any public officer in the administration of public affairs.

He has no authority of his own—he can only derive it from the Queen.

It is impossible to say, when he goes down to act for the Queen in a matter of ceremony, that this gives him authority over any part of the administration of public departments.

Certain persons are entrusted with the performance of certain duties and functions by formal commission, patent or authority from the Queen, and such authority cannot be superseded except by similar authority as formally conveyed.

It is essentially for the interest of the Sovereign that this should be so. If any public official was bound to obey a Prince who could show no formal authority from the Sovereign, it would in old times have gone far to warrant officers in aiding rebellion by an undutiful son.

I am going up to a Cabinet to be held on Thursday, and I will speak to Mr. Goschen on the subject.

Yours truly,   HALIFAX.

The whole question was now before the Cabinet, of which Mr. Gladstone was the head, and of which Lord Halifax, as Lord Privy Seal, was one of the most important members. The task of explaining to an apathetic and possibly soporific Cabinet the enormity of the crime that had been committed by the Prince of Wales and the implied insults that had been levelled at my Lords of the Admiralty must have taxed Mr. Goschen's powers to the utmost. Possibly he may have made some impression on a few Cabinet Ministers who were not too much occupied with their own departmental affairs to listen to him, but he appears to have made little impression on Mr. Gladstone who only wanted to settle the matter in a manner that would satisfy Queen Victoria. It must have been pure Greek to Mr. Gladstone, and probably the other Cabinet Ministers were totally unable to understand what the controversy was about, but Mr. Goschen had to support the Lords of the Admiralty and make their point of view clear to the Cabinet. A few minutes before the meeting (October 14) Lord Halifax wrote to Colonel Ponsonby:

DEAR PONSONBY—We have been so busy that I have not been able to see Mr. Goschen till this morning, and here I am in the Cabinet room with the Cabinet meeting to take place in five minutes, so I have no time to write to you to-day.

There is no hurry and there are one or two matters to be looked into, and whatever is done should be done thoroughly.—Yours truly,   HALIFAX.

A few days after the Cabinet meeting, Lord Halifax raised the whole constitutional point again, and even suggested that the Queen should relinquish her right of precedence at sea. To this Colonel Ponsonby replied on October 24, 1872:

DEAR LORD HALIFAX—I was very sorry to get your letter disputing what I had understood to be beyond dispute.

I sincerely hope you will not ask me to submit it to the Queen, as I feel certain it would not help us to a quiet solution.

You ask that the Queen should withdraw her letter and that she should relinquish her right of precedence at sea.

When I privately inquired if the past could be forgotten I was reminded that the Queen's letter was the

40

last recorded, and that it would not be just to the Admiralty that it should remain unanswered. I quite saw the truth of this argument, and I cannot conceive now why the Queen is to withdraw her letter and leave on the last recorded document the complaint of the Admiralty and the accusation brought against the Queen by the First Naval Lord that Her Majesty had been guilty of introducing an unauthorised innovation. Surely you would not advise the Queen to take no notice of this. As to the point itself, it is a question of fact whether it was correct or not, and I think you will find the custom has been sanctioned by the Lords of the Admiralty. You ask me what I mean by the Queen's supremacy and what Prince Leiningen means. I cannot say what Prince Leiningen means for I have never spoken to him on this part of the question, and have only seen that part of his letter which Mr. Goschen showed me. What I mean by supremacy is entire precedence in command, honour and dignity. You ask if the Sovereign sent away a ship that was wrecked, would he not be responsible. I cannot conceive such a case, for a sovereign who exercised his power in this way would soon cease to be a sovereign. If you push arguments to absurdity, I would ask whether you mean that an admiral could order off the Royal yacht at any moment. These are straining the Constitution and must snap the delicately arranged machine. But the form of command, it seems to me, must belong to the Queen, for you would never advise she should be under some admiral.

Mr. Goschen asked me if a Royal Standard alone

could be considered equal to the Royal Standard and two other flags. No more can the Admiralty flying a jack be equal to all three. The Standard and an Admiralty flag conjoined imply the Queen is there with the Lords of the Admiralty. G. will say this is a fiction, but not more so than hundreds of fictions in everyday life and in our Constitution.

I have asked First Lord to look at the papers and should be glad of some mode of settling the difficult question, but I do really think that your proposal would light up a flame and not allay one.

You say there would be no difficulty in firing the gun, but it was the difficulty of firing the gun that raised this controversy.

Two days later (October 26) Colonel Ponsonby wrote to Mrs. Ponsonby:

I sat up some time writing on Thursday and considering whether I should send Lord Halifax the semi-chaff letter in which under cover of chaff I could say a great deal, or the serious letter which you thought was treating the subject too much *au sérieux*. But I thought the chaff might offend, and I thought also it was as well he should know that the Queen will be pretty determined if he demands she shall withdraw the letter of censure on the Admiralty for not knowing she always has fired the gun—as she has—and that she shall give up her privilege at sea. So I sent the stiff letter. Of course if it came to a fight it must end in her giving up these rights, but it will be a very ugly thing for the Government to demand, placed in the light it has been done. And Forster[1] will certainly not join in doing anything that has the appearance of discourtesy.

Mr. Goschen now took up the argument again, and with almost exaggerated deference wrote to the Queen on December 9, 1872, and made it clear that nothing was further from the thoughts of the Lords of the Admiralty than any want of respect either to her or to the Prince of Wales, but he politely insisted that the gun must be fired from the flagship. Therefore the only solution he could suggest was that a gun should be fired from both the Royal yacht and the flagship, the latter taking time by the former.

The peacemaker, Lord Halifax, was pleased his efforts were now bearing fruit, and on December 19, 1872, wrote to Colonel Ponsonby:

DEAR PONSONBY—I am very glad indeed to get your letter, and to see the prospect of a solution *à l'amiable* of the Portland affair. I told Mr. Goschen you and I had agreed on the wisest thing being to consider all that passed at Portland as *non avenu*—and he quite agreed.

If the Prince of Wales concurs, then the most awkward part of the business is got rid of.

Nobody ever dreamt of putting the Queen under the order of the Admiral, and as to the ceremony of firing the gun, it ought to be provided for in the Queen's Regulations, and there need be no difficulty about it.

Queen Victoria didn't seem to mind how many guns

---

[1] Generally thought to be the probable successor to Mr. Gladstone should he retire.

were fired, or where they were fired, so long as the Royal yacht fired one first, and her letter to Mr. Goschen, on January 3, 1873, bears the truly regal imprint:

The Queen has given due consideration to Mr. Goschen's letter of the 9th ult., in reply to hers of August last, respecting an incident which occurred when the Royal yacht with the Prince of Wales on board was in the harbour off Portland.

The Queen is willing to accept Mr. Goschen's explanation that no intention existed of treating the Prince of Wales with disrespect, and desires to pass over that circumstance, and is also willing to believe that the Lords of the Admiralty present on that occasion were unaware of the custom, which has for so long a time prevailed, of the evening and morning gun being fired from the Royal yacht when the Royal Standard is flying. Still, the custom has prevailed, and the Queen believes no instance of the non-observance of it can be found. Mr. Goschen observes that Prince Leiningen can only state two instances, in 1858 and 1872. These will be found to be the only occasions since 1857 when the Queen has remained on board at night in the presence of an admiral. In 1858 the Board of Admiralty were also present. The Queen has no objection to a regulation being inserted that when she is on board the gun shall be fired from the Royal yacht, or other ship on which the Royal Standard is hoisted, and that the Flag Officer present may follow the firing of the gun . . . taking the time from the

44

Royal yacht, and that the same practice shall prevail as Mr. Goschen proposes when the Prince of Wales represents the Queen, of which notice should be given.

The Queen has no wish to interfere with the proper responsibility which should rest on an admiral, but trusts Mr. Goschen will feel that at no time can the Queen place herself under the order of an admiral, or the Board of Admiralty.

The Queen thanks Mr. Goschen for the manner in which he has treated the question, and well knows he is incapable of acting discourteously to her or any of the Royal Family.

This incident, which began so mildly as a slight difference of opinion between sailors with regard to the interpretation of nebulous regulations, ended in the Cabinet discussing the Queen's supremacy at sea. At one time the controversy threatened to become acute, and on one side were the Prime Minister, the First Lord of the Admiralty, the Cabinet and the Sea Lords of the Admiralty, while on the other side there was only Queen Victoria quite determined not to give away any of her rights at sea.

Finally, in the spring of 1873, the Lords of the Admiralty very solemnly issued a circular in which they "desired it to be understood" that whenever the Queen or the Prince of Wales were on board the Royal yacht or any of Her Majesty's ships, with Standard flying, "the regulation firing of the morning and evening gun is to be adhered to . . . but the time is to be taken from the gun which will be fired from the Royal yacht. . . ."

CHAPTER II

THE PONY ROW, BALMORAL, 1869

LIFE at Balmoral was distinctly quiet in 1869 when Queen Victoria was in retirement and visitors were rare. A minister or two might come and go; a painter or sculptor might be wanted to execute some memorial; but otherwise there were only the members of the household. Dullness and a sense of ennui grew until a storm in a teacup seemed inevitable, and such a storm sprang up over the bestriding of ponies by a clergyman, a sculptor and a German secretary. Queen Victoria, although in retirement, kept a very firm hand on all that concerned the household, and her love of animals made her particularly interested in the kennels and the stables at each of the Royal palaces. Dogs she adored and was rarely unaccompanied by one, but horses and ponies she was also very fond of, and always alluded to them by name. Among her favourites at Balmoral were several sturdy Highland ponies. These ponies are not difficult to ride: in fact no knowledge of horsemanship is necessary, and therefore a man who would never think of attempting to ride a horse or an ordinary pony, mounts a hill pony with the greatest confidence. All he has to do is to sit still and the sure-footed animal will take him up and down precipitous places without the slightest trouble.

The man, however, who has had no experience of

horses and ponies is no judge of what a pony should and should not do. He may unmercifully urge the panting pony up a steep hill, quite unconscious that he is straining the animal's powers. He may hold on by the reins and impede its movements just as it is going over a difficult bit of ground. He may treat it like a machine and tire it out without imagining for a moment that he is doing anything wrong. It was, no doubt, for these reasons that Queen Victoria decided to restrict the pony-riding to those who understood horses, probably having been told stories about the inconsiderate manner in which the ponies were treated. But while she wished to prevent the ponies being ridden by bad riders, she did not wish to hurt her guests' feelings by letting them know that any restrictions emanated from her. This unpleasant duty, therefore, devolved upon the equerry-in-waiting, who had charge of all the stables, and it was his duty to see that no carriage, horse, or pony was taken out by people who had not been given the privilege of using them by the Queen. The equerry-in-waiting was Colonel Ponsonby, who was not appointed Private Secretary till two years later.

Among the guests at Balmoral in the autumn of 1869 were Canon Duckworth, a friend of the Prince of Wales, who was probably staying at Balmoral because the Queen wished to consult him about the Prince's future, and Mr. Edgar Boehm, an eminent sculptor, who was often employed by the Queen.[1] In addition,

---

[1] Mr. Boehm, by birth a Hungarian, settled in London in 1862 and became naturalised. He was elected A.R.A. in 1878 and was created a baronet in 1889. His most notable statues in London are Lord Beaconsfield, Dean Stanley (in Westminster Abbey), Lord Napier of Magdala, Carlyle and William Tyndale, while among his innumerable busts are those of Gladstone, Huxley, Rosebery, Russell, Wolseley and Shaftesbury.

there was Mr. Hermann Sahl, the German secretary, whose principal work consisted of drafting official letters of condolence and congratulation to foreign sovereigns. The Queen always did the private telegrams herself, but the official ones were drafted for her approval by Mr. Sahl. His duties also consisted of docketing and filing all the Queen's correspondence and preparing it for its eventual destination in the archives, which were also entirely under his management. Mr. Sahl was the successor of Baron Stockmar, who had played the part of adviser and mentor to Queen Victoria years earlier, but unlike Baron Stockmar, he was incapable of giving any advice on foreign politics, and merely did the routine work day by day and acted as librarian at Balmoral and Osborne.

All these three considered themselves capable of riding hill ponies, but there were members of the Royal family who did not hold this opinion, and late in the August of 1869, Colonel Ponsonby received an intimation that Canon Duckworth, Mr. Boehm and Mr. Sahl were no longer to be allowed the freedom of the Royal stables. His note of what happened when he informed these gentlemen of this decision runs as follows:

On August 21 I received a message from the Queen to say that irregularities having crept into the stables, she hoped I would give orders as from myself that none were to have ponies except by my especial orders, and that I was not to allow them to be overworked. Next day I received a "confidential" memoranda saying that Duckworth and Sahl were only to ride on occasions. I told them so. They asked, "Is this the Queen's order?" I replied, "You must take it as my order, but you can well understand I give no order without being desired". This is the point of the controversy. It is said I took on myself to give these orders suppressing the Queen's name. I understood I was not to give her name, but I fully made D. and S. understand that the order came from the Queen. D. accordingly spoke and wrote to me saying he hoped I would protest against this restriction, thus showing by this that he perfectly understood it was the Queen. As D. could ride but seldom, I saw no difficulty in his applying through me as always used to be the case, and that I did not think there was much possibility of his being refused a pony. I know that Duckworth has felt sore about it, as he considers it a withdrawal of one of his privileges, but I never heard anything more from him. Sahl spoke to me in a half jolly sort of way about it, showing that he understood it was the Queen's order, not my own idea.

On the 31st August I was going out in a hurry and met Sahl, who asked me whether he might have a certain pony, which had always been out, as he was on his way to order ponies for himself and Boehm. I said, "You know that you must not order ponies for yourself and they will not give them to you without and under orders from me. Neither you nor Boehm can take a pony by right." Sahl said, "I assure you, you must have made a mistake about Boehm. The order you received could not be intended to apply to him. Let me submit the question." I replied, "By all means if you think it will do any good". I then gave him an order for the two ponies, but I believe he did not take them.

This, I maintain, also proves he knew it was not my order but the Queen's. What he wrote I don't know. But we went to the Gelder Shiel, and there Lady Churchill [1] told me there was a trouble about the ponies, that someone had complained of this order, and that the Queen had been told that Boehm, who was accustomed to live in a gentleman's house and to have always ponies there, would go home if he had not one at Balmoral. I told Lady Churchill I had seen enough of Boehm to see he was a gentleman and had never sent such a message, and Lady C. quite agreed with me. She then told me the Queen was afraid of Sahl's riding, that he damaged the ponies, but if anyone went with him, he might join expeditions, etc. But he was not to take out Boehm. In view of the above, Boehm might ride out with us sometimes, and I had better ask him to do so. Duckworth might come with us occasionally, when convenient.

Early in September I returned to Balmoral. I asked Boehm to ride, but he was busy and could not. On September 28 I received another message from Lady C. urging me to be very particular in impressing these rules upon people. After luncheon I sent out an order for a dogcart. Sahl came to me and said, "As you are seeing to the stables, order 'Maude' and 'Clyde' for me and Boehm". I have since heard that he came to me after having been told in the stables that ponies were not given without an order. His style was dictatorial, but not suspecting he was wanting a row, I thought it chaff and said, "My dear Sahl, I am not supposed to

[1] One of the Queen's favourite ladies-in-waiting.

grant you these ponies". A row followed and he said Duckworth did not mean to protest against this order. Surely these words show he understood the order was the Queen's, not mine. He got angry and voluble and rushed away. It is quite true, however, that I did not introduce the Queen's name, because as the instructions respecting Sahl and Boehm were confidential, I could not do so. This is the weak point. As Prince Christian [1] says, if you keep the order a secret the blame is applied to you; if you publish it Sahl will be more furious than ever.

On Monday, Sahl sent the most outrageous letter to the Queen, first three pages full of invective about the insolence of Colonel Ponsonby, who refuses him a pony in the ordinary way. Both complain of "Colonel Ponsonby's manipulating the household" (Boehm says this is fiction), and Sahl says that ponies are given to footmen and these servants sniff at him, and that he is called in to write the Queen's letters. He concluded by dictating an order that he was to have any pony that was available.

Duckworth does not agree about the annoyance, but he does about the ponies, and says that my manner to Sahl annoyed him.

I begged Prince Christian not to consider me in the matter as Sahl, having written the letter, need not be considered as having offended me. I had no feeling on the subject, for what I had done was to execute the Queen's order to the best of my power.

[1] Son-in-law of Queen Victoria.

Sahl wrote, just as I was going, the enclosed letter. By "the others" I presume he meant Biddulph.[1]

The "enclosed letter" from Sahl, to which Colonel Ponsonby refers, must surely be one of the most surprising missives ever received by the Queen's equerry. Although the military autocracy in Germany was only in its infancy, Mr. Sahl had evidently at his home suffered from the fact that he wore no uniform and was unconnected in any way with the Army, but in England such a thing as a military caste was unknown. · Still, under the delusion that Colonel Ponsonby had intended to inflict a snub on him personally, he came to the conclusion that this could only be because he was not a soldier, quite oblivious to the fact that neither the canon nor the sculptor was tainted with militarism. It was dated Balmoral, September 30, 1869, and runs as follows:

MY DEAR PONSONBY—Hearing from Duckworth that you are evidently under some misconception regarding my "*outrageous*" letter to the Queen, I cannot help calling your attention to the following points:

You (personally) refused to me (personally) the use of a pony, although you had—as Prince Christian, by the Queen's command, last night assured me—the right and power to grant it, and when allusion was made to the fact that *others* freely obtained *your* permission, your answer was: "Well, all I can tell you is that I shall not allow it to you". The *others* happening to be military officers, I could only find one clue to this unsympathetic treatment, viz. a certain military

[1] Lieut.-General Sir Thomas Biddulph, Keeper of the Privy Purse.

52

exclusiveness and jealousy towards *non-officers in the Army*; and I maintain up to the present hour that if I had been, *e.g.*, a major—I should have obtained your permission.

I therefore strongly disclaim a translation and interpretation which is not at all justified in using the terms *"military arrogance and insolence"* which I earnestly beg to substitute by the words *jealousy* and *exclusiveness*.

Further on, as my *soreness* on this *ground* was only a personal one, I cannot possibly allow your version, which speaks of the *whole household annoyance* at your military arrogance as you say! as, besides the ladies, I am (with Duckworth) the only civilian concerned!

But, as to your withholding *your permission to me*, I *beg* to say I *have* the *fullest sympathy* of all those with whom I already spoke on the subject, and am perfectly sure I shall obtain it equally from all who get a fair statement of the facts.

As I shall have no opportunity in all probability to see you before your going, I avail myself of this opportunity of saying good-bye to you and Mrs. Ponsonby. —Yours sincerely,
HERMANN SAHL.

P.S.—There is no objection against showing this reply to Prince Christian.

Prince Christian now found himself in a very difficult position. Being an independent-minded man who was fearless in expressing his opinion, he naturally came to the conclusion that Canon Duckworth and Mr. Sahl had been badly treated when he heard their version of the story, but being too much a man of the world to commit himself entirely without hearing the other side, he approached the equerry, Colonel Ponsonby. He then learnt that it was really the Queen behind all this, and while sympathising with their complaint he naturally felt it his duty to support Her Majesty's authority.

To people of the present day who are accustomed to have their squabbles settled by telegraph or telephone it must seem curious that the principal actors in this comedy should have found it necessary to write long letters to each other, more especially when they happened to be in the same building. The writing of carefully worded letters which would be delivered by a footman presented no difficulty and was probably the safest way of avoiding a mistake, but it must have been extremely awkward after inditing one of the following lengthy epistles for the writer and recipient of the letter to meet at luncheon or dinner and treat the missive as never having been written or received.

It was about this date (September 30) that Colonel Ponsonby received the following letter from Canon Duckworth:

MY DEAR PONSONBY—I can assure you that I have been entirely misrepresented if it has been insinuated that I have the slightest complaint to make of *you personally*, or that I have ever found your manner other than thoroughly courteous and kind to me. I am exceedingly sorry that Sahl should have conveyed such an impression to you.

My sympathy with him extends to this recent restriction in the use of the ponies, of which, of course, I am at liberty to form my own opinion, and, as you

54

know, I did not shrink from expressing it frankly to you at the earliest moment.

I can assure you that against yourself personally I have not the slightest feeling; and Sahl is utterly mistaken in quoting me as one aggrieved by "military arrogance". He himself appears to have been deeply affronted by the manner of denial of a little privilege which I can testify he has been as careful as myself not to abuse, and which I do think it was a very great mistake to withdraw. The harmony and comfort of those who are serving the Queen from year's end to year's end is surely worth while, with stables full of ponies.—Yours very truly,   R. DUCKWORTH.

Meanwhile, Colonel Ponsonby had sent "the soft answer that turneth away wrath", and Mr. Sahl's reply (dated October 1, 1869) runs as follows:

MY DEAR PONSONBY—I have to thank you for your lines—written at the moment of your departure. After I had read them over, I ran down to the door, but I found that your carriage was already twenty yards off; so I must give you a short reply by letter.

I am pleased to see that you always looked upon me as a *friend*; I may add in return, that it was also my constant endeavour to prove to you and Mrs. Ponsonby that I fully appreciated your friendship—any interruption of it I greatly regret. But with regard to this miserable matter of the *ponies* and your speaking of my *accusations*, I must, first of all, remind you that *by your own advice* given to me in August "to protest if I chose", I was justified in stating to the Queen the facts of

55

your refusing me the use of a pony, and your failing to give me the reasons for doing so.

You give a denial to my version of the exact words used, and to my *conjecture* as to the possible *reason*, but in your hurry you omitted to correct both points by a positive statement. Never mind! although I might have expected that as a *friend* you should have spoken with me on this matter openly and unreservedly, I can now quite understand that you may have found it too inconvenient or painful openly to state the real reason of your refusal, and I was consequently, of course, at liberty, seeing who enjoyed and who did not enjoy the privilege, to *conjecture* and to say *"it almost looked like as though* this refusal was due to military jealousy working against civilians, etc."* But I will confess to you that I was *most anxious not to believe* that this could be true of you.

My deep and thorough irritation was less the result of *your* denying me what I maintain I was justified in considering a sort of right, than of being denied it at all. Therefore you need not fear that I consider your manner such as you chose to designate it in your letter.

The deeper cause of my irritation has to do with a matter far too delicate to be treated in a letter; perhaps a mere *allusion* is intelligible; if not, I trust I shall, at some later period, have an opportunity to talk the matter over with you.

Meanwhile I may perhaps hope that your and Mrs. Ponsonby's opinions of my conduct may be less severe —as I did not move in this distasteful matter without

56

having first consulted a number of persons whose opinion I shall ever hold in high esteem up to the last hour of my life.

Let me conclude by saying that when making my protest I strongly felt that what I did was done in the interest of the *whole Household* certainly as much as in my own! All who know me here are aware that I have no private aims in view. HERMANN SAHL.

The next day (October 2) the excellent canon, as became his cloth, tried to smooth matters without, however, weakening in his support of his co-equestrians, the German secretary and the sculptor. The amusing part of the squabble was that if either of these three had been asked to mount a *horse* none of them would have dared do so. The sculptor seems to have been singularly silent; whether it was from apathy or from a shrewd suspicion that he was up against a far higher authority than the equerry-in-waiting can only be surmised. Canon Duckworth's letter ran:

MY DEAR PONSONBY—Sahl had written to you yesterday before your letter from Ballater reached me, or he would have explained to you what is now apparent to him, that you have been much misinformed as to a large portion of his letter to the Queen. The letter was written in *German*; and it seems to him from the terms in which you speak of it that you cannot have seen it, but must have got your impression of its contents from some loose and not too friendly version of them. I myself, as you know, greatly regret that Sahl did not confine himself, as I hoped he would, to a simple petition to the Queen against the restriction complained of: avoiding *all personality*, and *everything irrelevant* to the matter in hand. However, he maintains:

(1) That nowhere in the letter does he use an expression which can fairly be translated into "arrogance", "coarseness", or "rudeness". Where he speaks of military assumption, he says it only "looks as if" this had something to do with it, as it happens that the persons specially aimed at are *civilians*.

(2) He nowhere charges *you* with having given the use of a pony to the sergeant footman, or to any other servant, but he maintains as a glaring instance of *inequality* of treatment (which, after all, is the real ground of annoyance) that the sergeant footman and others in similar positions had been known to make free use of the ponies.

(3) He does *not* say that Boehm had made any complaint against you. He puts it (very unwisely I think) to the Queen that Boehm, accustomed to be treated with the utmost consideration in great houses, cannot fail to be making comparisons damaging to this establishment, when he notices what arrangements with regard to the use of ponies you are willing to carry out.

Sahl declares he had not the remotest thought of being *dictatorial* in asking you to order ponies for Boehm and himself. And as you had *volunteered* to supply Boehm with a pony, he thought there would be no difficulty. And when you absolutely declined to grant his request, he says he did not ask you if you *would* protest against the order, but expressed his astonishment and disappointment that you *had not done so*, supposing, what he says you declined to admit, that the order was not your own, but imposed from a higher quarter.

Certain it is that, whatever may have been the nature of your interview, I never saw Sahl so irritated and excited in my life as when I met him by chance downstairs a few minutes afterwards. I asked in amazement what had happened, and he then told me with strong indignation of the rebuff he had received. What annoyed him was nothing "rude" or "coarse" in your manner, he assures me, but the *marked personal exception*, which you were at no pains to disguise, made to *his* case, and which you would not account for.

I am quite sure that Sahl is the last person who would wish to interfere with the equerry's prerogative, and I would also support the equerry to the utmost against any interference with his rights.

Perhaps it is no business of mine to hint at what I humbly think might have prevented this unhappy affair: but I know you will not take offence if I say that had you been willing to act on the suggestion I ventured to make, and to plead *at first* on behalf of all concerned, much pain might have been spared in every quarter. Had you found it impossible to alter things for our comfort, then we should have acquiesced in the Queen's pleasure, and you could not have come into collision with anybody. For this is the *withdrawal* of a privilege long enjoyed, and which gave some little occasional variety to a life much in need of it, a withdrawal of which, if ever so delicately managed, was sure to cause unpleasant feeling. I am perhaps less affected by the change than anybody in the house, as it is very rarely that I have leisure to ride. Yet I feel that such an order can only be tolerable if enforced in *the Queen's own name* and on *all alike*, and that any individual must stand in a position very invidious and unfair to himself in carrying it out by his own authority. As you are aware, I have this season never asked you for a pony, because, after you had assumed the entire responsibility of the change, I saw that I must run the risk of a refusal doubly disagreeable because of the sincere regard which I have always felt for you.

Sahl is very much cut up by this whole affair. As he is a most kind-hearted man, and has always been on very friendly terms with you, I am sure that estrangement from you is deeply painful to him. Whatever may be thought of his letter, I am confident that, though written with wounded feelings, it was not intended as the *personal attack* it has appeared to be. So I earnestly hope that this unhappy business may be forgotten, and good feeling restored.

With many apologies for the length of this letter, believe me, yours sincerely,   R. DUCKWORTH.

To this letter Colonel Ponsonby replied on October 5. Unfortunately, the actual letter he sent is not available, but from a rough note left by him it is evident that he took up the cudgels with vigour. "The persons aimed at", he wrote, "were not civilians—the order was applied to all; hence there was no inequality of treatment. If footmen have given orders I will, of course, investigate." But he added that he did not "know any house where any man may take any pony at any time without the leave of the Master of the house. You say it wasn't my manner. Before, you said it was, hence my Ballater letter. How can you think that the order is a personal one when you say that it is against civilians? In any case, I am the Queen's servant, and the order was that no one should have a pony without my permission. Generally speaking, I should have given you one if you had asked me.

"Sahl claims the right to take any pony at any time out of the stables without reference to equerry. I say according to rule he cannot do so."

Three days later (on October 8), Canon Duckworth, finding he was on a bad wicket, had recourse to a verbose and intricate explanation of what he meant in his first letter:

MY DEAR PONSONBY—I must thank you for your kind letter from Hampton Court. I cordially join with you in the hope that this misunderstanding between Sahl and yourself is at an end, and that you may be friends as of old. I need not explain again *my* share in the matter, as you are well aware that there has been no interruption in my friendly feeling towards you, and I trust there never will be.

You will see, if you happen to have kept my last letter, that the statements I make in the first part of it, including that about the use of ponies by the sergeant footman, etc., are explanations furnished to me *by Sahl* and sent to you by me on his behalf, to correct misconception of his letter. *I* have not seen the sergeant footman riding during your waiting, though I certainly have seen him riding in former times, whether by permission or not I, of course, cannot say.

You have put into a brief postscript what you suppose to be the point of dispute. I assure you, you quite misconceive it, unless I am greatly mistaken. You say "Sahl claims the right to take any pony at any time out of the stable without reference to the equerry".

If Sahl claimed such a right he was very wrong to represent *me* as sympathising with him, for I have not disputed for one moment the propriety of the rule that the equerry's sanction should be given, nor would I think of interfering in the slightest with the equerry's control of the stables.

No, I do not believe Sahl was the least aggrieved by this perfectly reasonable and intelligible rule. What aggrieved him was the refusal of a pony *when he applied to the equerry* for one—a refusal for which no reason was given—and which was therefore certain to wound even a less sensitive man than Sahl. Prince Christian, in talking the matter over with him, said that he, in Sahl's place, would have felt deeply hurt by it.

Suppose that Sahl, whose control of the library corresponds to the equerry's control of the stables, had said to me, "I am going to be very strict about the use of the library: the books are to be much less used than they have been, and I shall only give leave to take them out under the most exceptional circumstances". I should have felt no little disgust at such an announcement. And if, on applying to him for a book, he had absolutely declined to let me have it, and refused to give his reason for doing so, I think I should then have

62

addressed the Queen on the subject, and should have asked her whether *she* really intended to withdraw from me a privilege which I had for my part been careful never to abuse.

I would not have you think that I asked you to take a course disrespectful to the Queen when I suggested to you to "protest" at first. Of course, I did not mean that you should do more than ask to have the order reconsidered for our sakes. You can easily imagine that I have had some experience by this time in receiving orders from Headquarters. Again and again I have deemed it my duty to get things reconsidered which I felt to be very inexpedient. I don't dispute for one moment your right to judge for yourself of the expediency in this case. I only wish to assure you that I had no thought of asking you to do anything either disrespectful or impracticable. And I was perfectly sure that you were little likely to have had any hand in bringing about the change deprecated. I hope you won't imagine that there is any feeling of antipathy towards you here, for there is nothing of the kind.

With my kind regards, believe me, dear Ponsonby, yours very sincerely,   R. DUCKWORTH.

The matter now seemed to be settled in the most amicable manner, but its real funeral dirge was sung three weeks later, on November 1, 1869, when Mr. Hermann Sahl, in writing to Colonel Ponsonby about the Librarian's post in the Royal Library, took occasion to add an apology. It is curious to note that Sahl was never told that it was the Queen's order, and was therefore left under the impression that Colonel

Ponsonby had taken upon himself to forbid people to ride. His letter ran:

My DEAR PONSONBY—I am ashamed to say that I have received a letter from you, without having replied to the first—which solely referred to the miserable pony question. I daresay you hardly expected an answer and are (as much as I am) anxious to bury the squabble. I will therefore say nothing more, but correct *one incorrect* statement of *mine*, to which you call justly my attention. I was wrong in speaking of *others* who had obtained *your* permission to ride; I ought to have spoken simply of *others* (if I chose to use the plural form at all) *having obtained the equerries'* permission.

I am very sorry for having made this mistake, but I trust this frank confession and correction will persuade you to forget the original error, and help to convince you, that in the whole of this matter there was *no* animosity on my part against you, as I shall be able —I hope soon—to show you when you give me an opportunity to *talk* the subject over.

HERMANN SAHL.

Queen Victoria, who undoubtedly was kept fully informed by Lady Churchill of all that had passed, must have been very much amused at this storm in a tea-cup, but she had saved her dear hill ponies from any possible harm, and that, to her, was far more important than the wounded feelings of her guests.

CHAPTER III

THE VISIT OF THE GRAND DUKE WLADIMIR, 1871

THE preceding chapters have referred to two storms in Royal tea-cups, but perhaps this account of a Royal visit to these shores can more accurately be described as a humorous breeze. These letters are only interesting because they give such a good picture of Mid-Victorian life and incidentally shew what a strenuous programme a foreign prince was expected to carry out even when paying an incognito visit to this country.

At this time, Queen Victoria occupied a unique position in Europe. Quite apart from her position as Queen of England, her dominant personality made her the person who counted most among the Royal families of Europe: in fact in any ordinary family she would have held an exceptional position. So it happened that in addition to the official State visits that were paid to her by the Emperor of Russia, the Sultan of Turkey, the Shah of Persia and the Emperor Napoleon III., only to name a few, it was customary for all Princes who were of any importance in their own country to come "incognito" to London and pay their respects to her. Among such was a scion of the Russian Imperial House.

It was in the May of 1871 that the Grand Duke Wladimir, the second surviving son of Alexander II., the Tsar of Russia, arrived in England, under the

F

none too veiled incognito of a Russian Count, for a month's stay. He was accompanied during his stay by Count Brunnow, the Russian ambassador to England, Admiral de Bock, Count Schouvaloff and a galaxy of officers and officials.

In the case of State visits it was customary for the Queen to attach to the visiting sovereign's or prince's suite one of her lords-in-waiting, an equerry and a gentleman usher, in addition to a distinguished admiral and general; but when the visit was a private one no special suite was attached. An exception appears to have been made in this case, no doubt because of the inability of the Russian suite to speak English.

Queen Victoria attached one of her equerries, Colonel the Hon. Arthur Hardinge, to the Grand Duke to make all the necessary arrangements for his comfort and edification, but as so much depended on the Prince of Wales, His Royal Highness also attached one of his equerries, Lieut.-Colonel Arthur Ellis, to the Grand Ducal suite. Colonel the Hon. Arthur Hardinge had been one of the equerries to the Prince Consort and was later appointed equerry to the Queen. He had served with distinction in the Crimean War as Assistant Quartermaster-General; subsequently he became Commander-in-Chief at Bombay, 1881–85, and Governor of Gibraltar, 1886–89, and was eventually promoted to the rank of General and awarded the K.C.B.

What this distinguished soldier thought of the Royal visitor may be gathered from the following letters addressed by him to Colonel Ponsonby, which need nothing in the way of comment to make them intelligible or to add to their humour. The first letter, dated May 28, runs as follows:

My opening chapter of the Diary of a Grand Duke need not be long.

So soon as I had received the Queen's commands to attend upon H.I.H. I went to the Russian Embassy, but finding "The Count" out, left word that Colonel Ellis (who is attached to the Grand Duke on the part of the Prince of Wales) and myself would call upon His Excellency on Friday at noon.

A. Ellis was detained on military duty, so that at the appointed time I was left to a *tête-à-tête* interview, commenced on Brunnow's part by many flowery acknowledgements of the Queen's consideration in appointing one of her own gentlemen to the service of his young Prince. My explanation of the reason of Colonel Ellis' absence was cut short by a playful poke into my *weak side* as, with an indescribable expression of triumphant penetration, and diving his chin into his special black satin, the astute ambassador exclaimed, "He is at the Oaks!" to which I replied with looks of injured candour, "Excellence, pour cette seule fois votre diplomatie dépasse le fait actuel".

Resuming more serious topics, I touched inquiringly upon the probable bent of H.I.H.'s inclinations.

"C'est, cher General, un jeune Prince avec d'excellentes dispositions, qui aime ... assez boire et manger ... et la science, et les beaux arts, et j'abdique avec une confiance toute parfaite mes fonctions, à son égard, dans vos mains."

Ellis and myself went down yesterday to Dover by an early train. Lord Sydney[1] had ordered a Guard of

[1] The Lord Chamberlain.

67

Honour to receive H.I.H., and I was authorised to provide a special train if the arrival of the Ostend boat did not fit in with the ordinary express. At Dover I found the General Novitzki, who has been for many years Military Attaché in England, who had come from Torquay to meet the Grand Duke.

The latter landed about two, when luncheon was immediately served, General Rupell and the Commanding Officer of Engineers being invited to join the party.

At a quarter to six we arrived at Victoria, the Russian suite consisting of Admiral Le Comte Bock, Comte Schouvaloff, General Novitzki, and were met by the Prince of Wales, who conducted the Grand Duke to Claridge's Hotel. H.R.H. had to go to a regimental dinner of the 10th Hussars, so the Russians dined at their hotel, and Ellis and myself took them to the Queen's Box, Covent Garden.

To-day they lunch at Marlborough House, and I shall propose to them the Zoological as the only relief to a London Sunday. The Prince of Wales attends the Cosmopolitan this evening, and to propose a change from their yesterday's dinner, I asked H.I.H. with his gentlemen to dine with me here, which he seemed glad to accept. In appearance the Grand Duke is *Plon-Plon*[1] *rajeuni et embelli*—rather stout for so young a man; he speaks English very fairly and is affable and pleasant in conversation; his earliest requisition upon English

---

[1] Son of Napoleon's youngest brother, Jerome, King of Westphalia, and therefore first cousin of Napoleon III. He earned the nickname by his rotundity.

industry has been in the tailoring department, which I hope will be creditably displayed at Ascot, as he is to be at the Prince's party at Titness.

Two days later, May 29, Hardinge sent his "Second Chapter" to Colonel Ponsonby:

On our way to the Zoological on Sunday we pulled up at Gloucester House, where H.I.H. was very cordially received by the Duke.[1]

The Gardens after the rain were in their brightest verdure, the ladies in their smartest frocks and the beasts on their best behaviour: the bears unusually complacent, the lion pompous but peaceful, and the Bengal tigers alone just a little restless. The elephant of Assam was conciliated by buns from Imperial hands and the chimpanzee barked with delight in belief that the pre-Adamite race had recovered the missing link in Monsieur Poulostioff, a little personage of Kalmuck type, who has great wealth, having picked up for wife a foundling who turned out by some romantic combinations an immense heiress. He is connoisseur *de bric-à-brac,* and accompanies the Grand Duke *à la recherche des objets de vertu.*

In the evening the cook of the Marlborough was fully appreciated, having risen to the occasion of my humble entertainment of so critical a Prince.

On Monday in carriages and four to White Lodge to give the Imperial accolade to Princess Mary (of Teck), and adopting a suggestion I had let drop, after

---

[1] The Duke of Cambridge.

exploring *le Richmond Parc*, sat down before a pyramid of Wenham ice, to a beautiful view of winding Thames and an excellent luncheon at the "Star and Garter", thence back to Claridge's to consult our tailor, and again to Marlborough House, from which, with a large party, including the Tecks, we visited Islington and witnessed in the leaping section some innocent tumbles in soft sawdust.

Their Royal Highnesses had a dinner party in the evening, but the Grand Duke preferring the Stabat, in H.M.'s box, at Albert Hall, we dined (Colonel Scott and Cole Junior being also the guests of the Russians) in a room of the building fitted up for the occasion. A somewhat too ambitious feast was served by Spiers and Pond, whilst for noble music we heard the harmonies of unceasing industry.

The Hall was admirably lighted and upholstered by the variegated colours of a well-dressed audience, filled, too, with impressive harmonics, it was, as Lothian might express it, the sublime eulogy of sweet refinement, before which the Russians stood speechless.

Between acts the Grand Duke examined every portion of the galleries, and later, resuming the veil of incognito, by exchanging at Hyde Park Corner, Royal Clarences for popular hansoms, we drifted to Cremorne Gardens, in time to be present at the pyrotechnic display representing the storming and fall of Strasbourg.

I enclose for the Queen a sketch by A. Ellis of H.I.H. which I have told the artist will establish his character rather as a Court painter than a caricaturist.

For to-day our arrangements are in the embryo state. I am off to Claridge's to hatch them.

Thursday, June 1, saw "the Count" at the South Kensington Museum, where from Hardinge's account he found the Duchess of Inverness more interesting than ethnological and archaeological specimens. Hardinge's letter (June 3) runs:

MY DEAR PONSONBY—You will have seen it!

Pass incognito to the Gardens, far from being preserved, was advertised as an interesting transparency by that fashionable tattler, the *Morning Post*. I read out its revelation to my Telemachus (at the propitious hour of luncheon) with a tremulous emphasis of caution, but his modesty had only to rejoice that the publicity of an inquisitorial trip should shed a broad light upon Imperial decorum! Science and beaux arts!

To the Kensington Museum. Mr. Owen did the honours and we could not have desired a more accomplished cicerone.

He crammed the Grand Ducal brain with Cinque Cento delicacies, faïence by Master Giorgio, Henri Deux Limoges enamels, ranging world-wide through Japanese conceits and Oriental glitter to the last barbaric trophy of an Abyssinian crown.

Turning his back upon *les antiquités de Musée*, H.I.H. inscribed himself upon the Duchess of Inverness, followed by the same courtesy at the house of Prince Edward—then home for a limited siesta, denied at the Marlborough Club "qui lui est énormément sympathique", afterwards joined our Royalties at the

Haymarket, and I made my bow to him after the opera.

As a study of customs it seems worthy of note that his suite speak of him and to his face in terms of patriarchal familiarity. Bock says "Vis-à-vis de mon Wladimir, je suis des fois trop partial, des fois trop sévère", but then the admiral's sensibilities have no common wing.

My wife happening to be also at Covent Garden with Mina Ellis, I took the count into a small box on the pit tier, and as we re-ascended to a more exalted neighbourhood he stopped me by the arm on the stairs, and brushing out his fierce moustache with a pocket brush, which is his peculiarity, when about to be sententious, said very slowly, "Do you know what I shall do, sir? I will light twelve candles to your two wives!" How would you have understood and acknowledged this mystic compliment?

Yesterday I went out with Wladimir, a day's work, that tested speed and endurance.

We began with the British Museum, Mr. Winter Jones leading the first gallop through the books, manuscripts, autographs and Raphael drawings. It was Lady P. Lewis who uttered her despair when the volumes were numbered to Sir Cornewall from a presentiment he would never come away till he had devoured the whole of them!

My anxieties to carry out the Queen's commands for the entertainment of her guest did not assuredly take that form, but it would be injustice to H.I.H. to imply that Birch, on Egyptian Hieroglyphics, and

"PERSIA WON!"

NASSR-ED-DIN. "Enjoyed my visit, dear madam?—Enchanted!—
Charmed! and—by the beard of the prophet—you may rest
assured I will allow no trespassers to cross *my grounds* into
your child Indiana's garden! Bismallah!"

Reproduced by kind permission of the Proprietors of "Punch."

Professor Owen, upon Antediluvians, failed to sustain his interest.

The Grand Duke is himself patron of several scientific societies, and our visit to the library enabled me to put him in the way of certain publications he wished to acquire for them.

After the midday repast we perambulated the flags and did a little shopping.

The next notability the Russians elected to call upon was—The Lady in duplicate, springing from an unique torso. She danced before us with quadrupedal grace, warbled a duet, and in affable conversation expressed the contentment of single-mindedness.

Here also the great man made friends with the greatest giantess, Miss Swan, aged 19, and 8 feet high, born of parents neither of them remarkable in stature.

Then I took H.I.H. the rounds of the clubs, many of which have done the civil to him, and presented F.-Marshal Gomm as a specimen of the seniors, finishing a long day at the French Gallery, where I called his attention to a remarkable picture by Gérôme of an Eastern nautch girl, but more remarkable as the only picture the Duke of Wellington has ever been known to buy.

Again indebted to *la main légère* of the cook here, we sat through some somewhat heavy French acting at the Lyceum, listening from *entr'acte* to Monsieur Felix's lachrymose recital of the conflagration of Porte St. Martin, and his diatribes against the too successful rivalry of the Opéra-Comique—then to a ball at Lady Rendlesham's and to bed (not sorry) about 3 o'clock.

The visit continued smoothly, a smoothness only marred from the point of view of Colonel the Hon. Arthur Hardinge by the fact that Admiral Bock, one of the distinguished and bearded Russians of the Grand Duke's suite, showed his whole-hearted appreciation of Hardinge's effort by kissing him. Hardinge's letter, after this unexpected embrace, runs as follows (June 5):

Anything for the Queen's service, but . . . I have been kissed by Bock! Without mistake, a palpable hirsute embrace upon my unexpecting cheek, seconded by the fervent assurance that I was in all things the director of his innocence!!

I tried to look grateful, and had just presence of mind left to suggest that in future such gratifications should be reserved for the higher officials of the Crown, so I pray the Lord Chamberlain may intercept the next benefit of this too flattering kind, though you, indeed, most deserve it, as having provoked the effusion by your message about H.M.'s box at the Albert Hall, which I reported as an instance of the Queen's solicitude.

The Grand Duke telegraphed to the Empress: "Qu'il était écrasé par la splendeur du Théâtre, retentissant d'un chœur de neuf cent personnes—et capable de contenir dix mille auditeurs".

On Saturday morning H.I.H. went, by underground, for modern history, to Madame Tussaud.

After luncheon (preceded by "hors-d'œuvre, et le petit verre de Kimmel", under the orthodox title of Zakouska) to Marlborough House, and with the Prince on to Hurlingham. We were late for the handicap, in which the Prince had proposed to shoot, so Their Highnesses refrained from handling their Lancasters, and were only accessories to the slaughter of many blue-rocks, hardly bluer than the gunners, for the wind was at times more piercing than their shots and the muster of London beauty quite as trembling as the doves.

We all dined again at Marlborough House, again went to the opera, the presence of the Duke of Edinburgh affording the admiral *d'eau douce* a splendid field for his maritime reminiscences as a "sailor of the old canvas", which he declares still the only school for discipline. His startling affection for me places him ever in my foreground. In politics decidedly Conservative, his patriotism is tempered by progress. In religion a devout Greek, he crosses himself repeatedly before eating substantially, but is fond of calling the Pope *Un vieux Jupon.*

Wladimir rather more *l'enfant du siècle*—Schouvaloff an Hussar with killing eyes, whilst *l'amateur de bric-à-brac* has very properly only a profound regard for "The Old".

Sunday after the Greek service H.I.H. gave us early luncheon, his "Paphos" also breaking bread at Claridge's. A saloon carriage transported us to Windsor, where Prince Arthur and Prince Christian met the Duke at the station. After his visit to Prince Christian, I took him to say prayers under the *Pavillon de l'Empereur* in St. George's. Mrs. Wellesley poured out his tea, and the Dean hurried him into the Wolsey Chapel, with a view to his conversion, interrupted, however, by the announcement of our carriages; the Royalties dined at Lionel Rothschild's. Thirty-six guests sat down to an interminable banquet. The house was resplendent with Hebrew gold, and the Darwinian principle of selection was perfectly developed in a matchless cluster of English beauty.

This morning (as a corrective) I take H.I.H. to Westminster Abbey, having asked its Phil-Hellenic Dean to display all his erudition upon the time-honoured relics of English Gothic.

During the following week, the Grand Duke "qui aimait assez boire et manger, et la science et les beaux arts", was given his fill of these worldly things.

On Saturday, June 10, Colonel Hardinge wrote to Colonel Ponsonby:

MY DEAR PONSONBY—I have just deposited the Grand Duke at Claridge's Hotel, after an Ascot week that was only dull in point of weather. The party at the House (Marlboro' House) was limited by the accommodation, but none the less agreeable, the Dukes of Edinburgh and of Cambridge, Duke and Duchess d'Opura, Lady Hamilton, Lady E. Kingscote, Mrs. Grey, being the Prince of Wales' guests.

On Wednesday H.I.H. abjured racing for the worthier sight of Windsor, lunching at the Deanery, and lionised over the castle, kennels, dairy, by the Lord Chamberlain in person. He was especially gratified by the Queen's permission that he should visit the mausoleum.

On his way back from the racecourse on Thursday

Cook took him over the Buckhounds establishment, with which he seemed very much struck. There was a ball last night at Titness, and I think that everything that was hospitable has been done to return the civilities that the Prince of Wales himself met with in Russia.

To-night he dines with the Duke of Edinburgh, to-morrow I take him in the afternoon to Cliveden, on Monday he pays a visit to Prince Arthur at Woolwich, and up to the 22nd he has engagements of one sort or another that will skim the cream from the large part of English sights and English hospitality.

Hitherto everything has gone most smoothly, and the Russians are profuse in their acknowledgements of the facilities that have been put at their disposal.—Yours sincerely, A. HARDINGE.

Hardinge's "Fourth Chapter", written three days later (June 13), runs as follows:

Thanks to the Royal mews, everything continues to run smoothly. On the Saturday that landed us from Ascot the Grand Duke dined privately with the Duke of Edinburgh, who took him to the Haymarket, whence he returned delighted with Sothern and the National Drama. Sunday's ever-dismal atmosphere to the foreign element was gladdened by an excursion to the lights, and shades, and silvery sheen of Cliveden.

The Duke of Sutherland, always so good-natured, went down with us. Lord Westminster sent carriages to the station, and Lady W., bringing strawberries in a "goodly dish", invited our whole party to tarry for dinner in her enchanted domain, but as Stafford was dining in town, we followed his lead along the banks of the dark flowing river, and came into dangerous collision with the Prince and Princess of Wales, but without more serious accident than the interchange of royal courtesies.

A dinner at the Travellers released me from further attendance.

Claridge's has become reanimated, but metropolitan attractions and hospitality have a decentralising influence, and the obsequious waiters have not *once* had the honour of a dinner at home.

Monday was a very surprise of compliments.

We went down to Woolwich, and H.I.H. was received at the Arsenal Station by Prince Arthur in uniform, as belonging to the Rifles that furnished a very smart Guard of Honour, and by Sir David Wood, commanding the garrison.

We had luncheon in the Artillery mess-room—to the melodious playing of their band—a national potpourri discomfited my postprandial moments as it included the unhallowed strains of *La Marseillaise*.

The time we employed in food and banter was utilised by the Horse Artillery, who turned out perfect in every respect on the parade opposite our windows —from three to six we wandered in amazement through the din of machinery and the searching glow of diabolical furnaces. On our way back to town the Grand Duke intimated a wish to dine at the Marlborough Club and go to the opera. I drove off, therefore, to

Biddulph's house,[1] to find him out, and the Queen's box given to the Duchess of Roxburghe: on, therefore, to the Clarendon to consult with Her Grace how this difficulty could best be met. She was invisible, but we resorted to diplomatic notes, couched on her part in the most delicate terms of surrender, though her capitulation was embarrassed by the extended position of her allies—so finding from Mitchell that H.I.H. could have a box next to H.M.'s, and interpreting his sentiments in the chivalrous sense, I left the Duchess in undisturbed possession of the higher honours, and took the Prince into the box, to confirm gracefully the responsibility I had thus taken upon myself.

After the opera we went to Captain Shaw's fire brigade in Watling Street, where the Dukes of Edinburgh and Sutherland joined us. *Ventre à terre* we made the circuit of the different stations, but as *les pétroleuses de Paris* enjoy a monopoly for the present, were *unlucky* in our search for flames. Then we descended into a fire brigade steamer, and under the clouds of hazy night steered through the black arches of many bridges. Remounting our clattering car we halted at the head of Southwark Bridge and by telegraph summoned a cohort of engines, to an imaginary point of distress, ending a late but interesting entertainment with a supper at Captain Shaw's.

This morning at 9.30 we underwent a long process of purification at the Turkish bath, which was closed to the public for the Prince's use. This was followed by a visit to Princess Louise at Argyll Lodge—on our

---

[1] Sir Thomas Biddulph, Keeper of the Privy Purse.

way back we crossed the Park, lunched with Edward Baring[1] (*bons plats, jolies assiettes*), thence under the auspices of Lord Ashburton to Bath House and Manchester House.

Thursday, June 15, was the occasion of a magnificent banquet and ball at Chesham House given by the Count and Countess Brunnow. Of this affair Hardinge writes (June 17):

My DEAR PONSONBY—Thursday's exhaustive programme continued with a banquet at Brunnow's, and was carried over to another day by a ball following the feast, that made light of the inroads of rosy-fingered morn.

The Grand Duke gave us punctual rendezvous at Chesham House, as H.I.H. wished to receive all the guests and do all the honours of "his father's house".

The ambassador, with a promptitude surpassing I fear our means of army organisation, mobilised a formidable reserve of able-bodied footmen, powdered and pomatumed to the single hair, and perfectly turned out in decorative plush.

Exotics arranged by the delicate experience of the hostess exhaled an insidious fragrance, midst floods of splendour, and of music, and Augustus Lumley, revived by the occasion to freshest youth and absolutely entangled in hoops of calico flowers, led the cotillon, with more than the energy of former years.

On Friday morning, Lord Sydney conducted H.I.H. over Buckingham Palace. The Gun Club gave him a

---

[1] Afterwards Lord Revelstoke.

déjeuner at Hurlingham (previous to the contest between Lords and Commons), the Duke of C. a dinner
at Gloucester House, and Henry Lennox the finishing
stroke of kindness in a crush at the Kensington
Museum. M. Schouvaloff has succumbed, having
sprung a vein, which keeps him to his bed, and the
Admiral is suffering from a swelled face. His mind
seems not so much confused by the whirl of our actions
as stupefied by our national peculiarities. He has not
yet recovered his surprise at Captain Shaw returning
him £10 he had enclosed as a gratification to the
firemen, and says in daily bewilderment of our engagements "Cher Général, quand est le dîner chez
Lord Vane—dois-je porter plaque et cordon?" On
Saturday, Mr. Tom Baring spread a luncheon for his
Imperial guest in his picture gallery and invited Sir
Francis Grant and some artists. Thence to the Botani-
cal Gardens, *jour de Fête*, under the Presidency of Prince
Teck, and to be graced by the presence of the Princess
of Wales. It rained cats and dogs, so that the huddle of
female apparel in a steaming tent, allowing only an
avenue of Royalty to pass, left the flowers to blush
unseen.

We had an early dinner in shooting jackets at Stafford House, as, sated with the West End, we were to
seek scenes of lower life in the town's eastern extremity,
carried in cabs beyond Islington, under the protection of Captain Hams of the police. We looked in to a
succession of music halls and theatres, ending in a
"Penny Gaff" where there was no better accommodation than the pit, crammed with the extreme youth

of both sexes; then we stopped at several police stations, and crossed a bridge in the direction of the docks, where a sinister policeman was posted to wrest the unfortunate from the desperate temptation of its black pool of Lethe. Walking through horrid streets to the Chinese quarter where we found some natives of the Celestial Empire, crouching like animals in their small dens, but happy as kings, smoking opium.

Then we disappeared into the refuges of the fraternity of talent, but could only be presented to the lower classes of thieves, as the ornaments of the profession have habitations of their own. We saw one ruffian, who had that day been enriched by a reward of £100 for giving some information about the Stratford murder. If this ever oozes out, his life will not be worth a minute's purchase. As a lamentable study of human life, all these sights were worth seeing—but some of us were not sorry to get back to the better-lighted and better-ventilated West End at about 2.30.

To-day we are going to the Crystal Palace.—Yours very sincerely,   A. HARDINGE.

Two more letters (dated June 25 and June 28) served to narrate the events of the last week of the Royal visitors' stay:

June 25th.

The newspapers keep you pretty well *au courant* of Imperial activity that shows no symptoms of abatement.

After H.M.'s breakfast, the Grand Duke was entertained to dinner and ball at Stafford House. All our own Royalties honoured the Duke by their presence. The artillery band played in the hall and the princely style of the reception was in harmony with the illustrious rank of the guests. On Saturday morning we paid a visit to Piccadilly, to a quaint Mr. Barker. He is a retired bootmaker, who, free from any family cares, has employed in his old age a sudden fortune that had poured in upon the mid-career of his trade in amassing a wonderful collection of fine old furniture and manifold objects of art, finding comfort in the polish of Louis XVI. for the discontinuance of humble varnish.

His establishment consists entirely of light-handed housemaids, with cambric dusters, who would seem to neglect their master's clothes in their preoccupation for his more sightly chattels.

He exhibited his treasures in excruciating French, and his last proposal was to appear before his own door, mounted on a pony whose merits consisted in its resemblance to a lion, but H.I.H. declined this Van Hamburgh spectacle, as the shaggy mane of the king of beasts would have collected the "Roughs".

We went on afterwards to Dorchester House, back to Claridge's for luncheon, dined at the M. Club, and went thence to *Nurcadet le faiseur* where H.I.H. seemed thoroughly to enjoy the excellence of Balzac's wit.

To-morrow, the Prince of Wales and the Grand Duke are to dine at the Crystal Palace, to witness the fireworks, a pyrotechnic compliment being arranged for the Russian Prince, so if only the weather permits it, we shall see Wladimir coruscating against his will in the vault of heaven, which he seems in no immediate impatience to exchange for his present planet.

In the afternoon to-morrow he has luncheon at Apsley House; on the 29th (of June) he takes his departure.

June 28th.

MY DEAR PONSONBY—Not to drop one single thread in the web of Imperial narrative.

On the Sabbath, that blank commencement of crowded weeks, a dinner excursion up, or down, the river was conditionally debated, but, as in lieu of balmy zephyrs, the inexorable east wind was still clouding the streets with dust, the patriotic tendencies of the Grand Duke elected to discharge the vapours of the uncongenial day in a second visit to the Turkish bath. For more than an hour I enjoyed the honour of what may be termed a formal interview—in sweltering crescendo. Then two slim and lissome Hindoos noiselessly led away their powerful captive to a marble slab, and treated him to a superlatively rigorous process of scientific mangling and loud thumping, which he endured like an orthodox martyr.

Next he dived into the plunging bath, and bade me follow, which indeed I did, but there was no need of a Cassius to support that Caesar's buoyant body in the glassy flood. Then, in turban and flowing robes, he smoked his pipe like a great Mogul, and released me to return to the bosom of my family whilst (for the first time he had dined at Claridge's) he entertained some fellow-countrymen of literary repute.

84

GRAND DUKE WLADIMIR, 1871

On Monday we had luncheon at Apsley House.

Amongst the trophies of the Iron Duke, Russian eyes dilated upon the Grand Cross of St. George which no one of the present generation is licensed to wear save the Emperor of Germany, who has certainly chalked down more big guns to his score than any conqueror since the time of Alexander of Macedon, who captured none.

At 4 P.M., we started from Marlborough House for the Crystal Palace. Three carriage loads, reinforced in the Royal Gallery by a sum total of about fifty.

The distinguished party first listened to the dilated crash of innumerable fiddles and blended voices. Then the great fountains of the gardens—and the greater band of the Coldstream—played. So we sat down to dinner, till Belshazzar's feast was interrupted by an innocent explosion of a hundred 50-lb. shells which moved up Royalties to the front of a red balcony.

Wladimir's special illumination inspired a popular tumult of cheers, but notwithstanding physical press-ure, so backward was he in coming forward that a sub-manager of the victualling department in irre-pressible enthusiasm waved a hat from a side window, a demonstration that ignorantly, but sympathetically, commended itself to the crowd below.

The weather was propitious and the fête a grand success.

On Tuesday the Grand Duke, attended only by the Admiral, visited the ex-Emperor at Chislehurst.

In the evening the Queen's ball.

This morning was devoted to photography.

85

I will send you a copy of the result—single portrait and groups, in case the Queen might care to see them.

At 1.30 we were unctuously received by the Earl of Dudley in Park Lane. He did the honours of his pictures and his Sèvres, in didactic detail, so glibly that after the luncheon, which was aldermanic (Lady Dudley as hostess throwing into the shade all the old masters), I can only remember one incident, that of an American vocalist, who innocently asked whether a Venus by Titian was not the portrait of Mdlle. Titiens.

We dine with H.I.H. to-night at Claridge's.

He takes leave of the Prince and Princess of Wales at Chiswick to-morrow and we re-conduct him to Dover by the 8.30 P.M. train.

The final letter of the series (written on June 29, the day of the departure of the Grand Duke to join the Emperor and Empress of Russia at Ems) sheds a soft light upon the ability of the *amiral d'eau douce* to counter a fresh breeze:

Shortly after nine two open carriages conveyed the Grand Duke and suite entire to Fenchurch Street, there to meet the Prince of Wales, who had arranged that Alfred Paget's yacht should take us a cruise to sea to see the Thames Regatta. We made this point through the Park, Constitution Hill and Thames Embankment, as I thought this route would conscientiously clear off some of the obligatory sights of London. At Gravesend we found Alfred, flying his pennant as Vice-Commodore and looming large on the bridge of his steamer, and surpassing in grandeur all other river captains in the "ease her", "stop her" business. He was an enigma, even to the Russian *amiral d'eau douce*, but his vessel, like himself, an imposing example of Naval enterprise.

Wide-awakes and monkey jackets being the indispensable appanage of an aquatic excursion, the sudden adoption of this costume by the illustrious visitors was not attended with that picturesque effect I should have desired. The Grand Duke was, at the last moment, only able to obtain as head-gear an inverted soup plate, the ill fashion of which, I fear, somewhat distressed the hospitable anxieties of the Prince of Wales.

A moderate interest in the sailing match, varied by inquiries whether the band of the Rosherville Gardens was not that of the Royal Blues, was sustained till the more satisfactory hour of luncheon.

The breeze freshened as we imprudently got out to the open sea, and "going about" we shipped a sea, which, as good humour prevailed, was but an enlivening catastrophe, fortunately not followed (of which at one moment there was a suspicion, my colleague, the Admiral, being the first to retire to a berth) by any more disagreeable results. At seven we got back.

Thus, on the 29th the Grand Duke Wladimir left London and returned to Russia, leaving behind him many good stories of curious events.

CHAPTER IV

GLADSTONE, DISRAELI AND THE IRISH UNIVERSITY BILL, 1873

THE duties of the private secretary to the Sovereign are often of a very delicate nature, but at no time do they require more tact and judgement than when a change of Government is either in process or a dissolution is threatened. The Sovereign then becomes the intermediary between the leaders of two great parties who are determined to extract as much advantage for their party as they can from any critical situation, and when, as in this case, the Sovereign has to be represented by her private secretary in the conversations with the opposing ministers, it becomes a matter of great difficulty to repeat accurately what each great man said and make the Sovereign's point of view unmistakably clear to them.

It is unfortunate that some of the instructions given to Colonel Ponsonby by Queen Victoria in these instances should have been verbal, and that therefore no accurate record of them should exist, and that equally very little should be known of what she said in her difficult interviews with Mr. Gladstone and Mr. Disraeli. But from the notes that have been made in different biographies, there is no doubt that, perplexing as the situation undoubtedly was, her instructions to her private secretary were always clear, and that once having decided on what was the best line to pursue she never hesitated or went back on her decision.

In 1868 Gladstone entered on his first premiership after a general election fought on three main issues—franchise reform, public economy and the Irish question. The Irish question was like a hawthorn tree, and one of its prickliest branches was the question of a university for Ireland. For five years Gladstone did not touch it, and then, on February 13, 1873, he submitted the Irish University Bill, which was an ingenious attempt to reconcile higher education with the irreconcilable aspirations of Catholicism and Protestantism. He proposed to make the University of Dublin and Trinity College entirely distinct and separate bodies, and by way of placating religious temper he laid it down that the university should not have chairs of Modern History, Philosophy or Theology.

At first the measure was favourably received, but suddenly opposition arose. The Irish priests disliked it, scientific men derided it, and the Protestants of Trinity College denounced it with a vigour only equalled by that of the Roman Catholics the measure was supposed to benefit.

The Cabinet had given careful consideration to the measure, for, as Mr. Gladstone reported to Queen Victoria on January 31:

The Cabinet to-day has spent many hours in examining and settling the clauses of the Irish University Bill which they propose to introduce into Parliament. The Bill is in a state in which a print of it could be submitted to Your Majesty, should Your Majesty be disposed to take the trouble of examining it.[1]

[1] For full text see *Letters of Queen Victoria*, vol. ii. p. 239.

Queen Victoria in reply (February 1, 1873) announced that she would "certainly desire" to see the Bill "as it is not right or fair that the Sovereign should be expected to give her support and consent to measures which she knows nothing of". Gladstone duly forwarded "the last secret print" of the Bill.[1]

Rumours early began to reach Queen Victoria at Windsor that there was a possibility that the growing opposition to the Bill might result in a Government defeat, and early in March she instructed her private secretary, Colonel Ponsonby, who had just succeeded General Grey, to find out what was going on in London. "It would be well", she wrote, "if Colonel Ponsonby could hear all he could as to the prospects of Friday (when the Bill came up for the second reading). Would Mr. Gladstone resign if he was defeated? Perhaps the Queen had better write and ask him to state how affairs stand."

At the same time she inquired of Mr. Gladstone "if anything particular took place at the Cabinet to-day with regard to the present state of affairs". On March 8 Mr. Gladstone replied—very fully—and hinted that a difficulty might arise if the Bill were passed with too small a majority.[2] The following day Queen Victoria wrote to Mr. Gladstone, thanking him "very sincerely" for "so fully explaining the present state of affairs, which is very critical", and adding:

She regrets much the difficulties which have so unexpectedly arisen, and still hopes that the Government will have such a majority as will enable them to go on. The Queen trusts that Mr. Gladstone will not let any

---

[1] For full text see *Letters of Queen Victoria*, vol. ii. p. 240.
[2] For full text see Morley's *Life of Gladstone*, vol. ii. pp. 336 *seq.*

natural annoyance and disappointment weigh more with him than he can help when he has to come to a decision after the vote which is expected on Tuesday. What would Mr. Gladstone call a too small majority?

She would be grateful if he would let her know to-morrow what he learns of the feelings of the House of Commons, and prospects of the Government. She entirely approves of Mr. Gladstone's decided expression of opinion that nothing more can be done for the Roman Catholics, who have *no* right whatever to complain.[1]

In reply, Mr. Gladstone wrote that "the Cabinet would probably now decide upon going on with any majority, however small, to the next stage of the Bill".

Through Colonel Ponsonby, the Queen passed on Mr. Gladstone's letter to the Prince of Wales (afterwards King Edward VII.), who showed his keen interest in the crisis by replying to Colonel Ponsonby that evening:

My DEAR PONSONBY—I received your letter whilst dining with Charlie Prosser, for which many thanks. Will you also thank the Queen for letting me know all she can at the present state of affairs.

I presume that there will be another Cabinet to-morrow and that an announcement will be made to both Houses of Parliament as to the course the Government intend to pursue.

I should be much obliged if the Queen would excuse my coming to see her to-morrow morning, as I have

[1] *Letters of Queen Victoria*, vol. ii. p. 245.

an engagement between twelve and one I cannot well put off, and between one and two I must be at the House of Lords to attend the fourth meeting of the "Select Committee on Horses", where some important witnesses have to be examined.

Any time after six I shall be quite ready to see the Queen should she wish it.

Believe me, Yours very sincerely,

ALBERT EDWARD.

The second reading of the Bill was put to a division at 2 o'clock in the morning of Wednesday, March 12. Irish Liberals and Home Rulers went almost tearfully into the Opposition Lobby, and the Government was defeated by three votes. The following day, Gladstone, equally tearfully, if one of his earlier biographers is to be believed, decided to resign.[1] This is borne out by the following note of Colonel Ponsonby, which is dated March 12:

The Queen went to Buckingham Palace on Wednesday morning, and saw Mr. Gladstone before and after the Council, when he told her the division was postponed till the following day.

At the time Lord Granville told me the three courses each member of the Cabinet was to give his opinion on were: immediate dissolution, prospective dissolution, or resignation. Much would depend on what Mr. Gladstone said. Charles Villiers thought the Government owed its defeat to its own obstinacy. General Peel ridiculed the idea of the Tories coming in. E. Taylor

[1] Mr. Forster's Diary, quoted in Sir Wemyss Reid's *Life of Gladstone*.

[Tory whip] assured me the thing would pass and matters return to as you were. Brand [Speaker] told me there was no advantage, perhaps almost the contrary, in being in power when a dissolution took place.

In the result, Gladstone decided to resign.

The Queen lost no time in summoning the leader of the Opposition in accordance with constitutional precedent, and her method was to send Colonel Ponsonby, on Thursday, March 13, to find Mr. Disraeli in the House of Commons. Curiously enough, at the moment when the Government was defeated, Mr. Disraeli was not in the House, nor was there any particular reason why he should have been, it would appear, for the Government defeat was due to Liberal defections rather than to Conservative machinations. Colonel Ponsonby's note on the interview runs as follows:

On Thursday, March 13, Mr. Gladstone came to Buckingham Palace at 3 o'clock in the afternoon after the Cabinet and resigned. The Queen told me what he had said and desired me to go to Mr. Disraeli with her letter of summons. I went to the House of Commons just as it was assembling and told Lord Charles Russell my mission. He placed Captain Gossett and Colonel Forester at the two entrances to stop Mr. Disraeli. When he arrived, I went with him into a waiting-room and gave him the Queen's letter. He said, "I am sorry it has come to this. I did not expect it." He read the letter and I told him what I had just heard in the lobby, that Mr. Gladstone had just announced his resignation. He said, "Oh, that is over; then I won't go into the House and am glad you stopped me first. I

93

will be at the Palace at the hour named—6 o'clock."
It was then a quarter to five. I returned to the Palace
and reported to the Queen.

The letter the Queen had written to Mr. Disraeli
and which Colonel Ponsonby handed to him ran as
follows (March 13):

Mr. Gladstone has just been here and has tendered
his resignation and that of all his colleagues, in consequence of the vote on Tuesday, which the Queen has
accepted.

She therefore writes to Mr. Disraeli to ask him
whether he will undertake to form a Government.

The Queen would like to see Mr. Disraeli at six, or
as soon after as possible. She sends this letter by her
private secretary, Colonel Ponsonby, who can be
the bearer of any written or verbal answer from
Mr. Disraeli.[1]

An hour later, as Colonel Ponsonby noted:

Mr. Disraeli came to the Palace at 6 o'clock and saw
the Queen. He told her he was ready to form a Government but not in the present Parliament. I did not
quite understand whether this meant an absolute refusal, but the Queen said that, coupled with the rest of
his conversation it did, and sent me to communicate
this to Mr. Gladstone, which I at once did. I was at
Carlton House at 7 o'clock.

[1] *Life of Disraeli*, vol. ii. p. 208.   Mem. by Queen Victoria on interview
with Mr. Disraeli.

Colonel Ponsonby's notes for the Queen's information on his interview with Mr. Gladstone (March 13) give some indication of the perplexity in which Mr. Gladstone found himself:

Colonel Ponsonby saw Mr. Gladstone at his house in the evening and gave him the Queen's message that Her Majesty had asked Mr. Disraeli if he could form a Government and that he had replied he could, but not with the present Parliament, that he did not ask the Queen to dissolve, that he advised Her Majesty to ask Mr. Gladstone for advice how to proceed and to tell Mr. Gladstone what Mr. Disraeli had said.

Mr. Gladstone replied to Colonel Ponsonby that he considered the message came to him as Chief Minister of the Crown, whose duty it was to give Her Majesty his best advice till she had accepted the services of a successor. That he did not clearly understand the purport of what Mr. Disraeli had said to the Queen, and thought it would be desirable that it should be put in writing by Mr. Disraeli. Till he saw it in writing he scarcely felt justified in forming any opinion upon it.

Colonel Ponsonby, in the private notes which he made for future reference, gives an account of the interview he had with the two statesmen. First of all, Mr. Gladstone in Downing Street, who was most convincing in his arguments, and under the impression that Mr. Disraeli had taken up a position which he would find it impossible to maintain. Then Mr. Disraeli, who had already been Prime Minister in 1868 for ten months. It must have been a curious interview in a London Hotel, the leader of the Opposition being intent on smashing the

95

Government and being asked by the Queen's private secretary not only to explain his Delphic utterances but to write down on a piece of paper what exactly he had said.

When I saw Mr. Gladstone and gave him my message he said it was the most extraordinary proceeding he had ever heard of. That Mr. Disraeli, at the head of a party which had used every effort and had succeeded in defeating his Government, should summarily and without any consultation with his political friends refuse to attempt to form an administration was an unheard-of proceeding. He begged leave to consider my message as one from the Queen asking for advice from him, who still was first Minister of the Crown, but he was quite unable to form any opinion on what Mr. Disraeli had said unless he had it in writing. Mr. Gladstone seemed very much in earnest and determined.

Having returned this message to the Queen, Her Majesty sent me to see Mr. Disraeli in Edward's Hotel, George Street, Hanover Square. He at once acceded to the Queen's wish, and getting pen and ink, said, "There. Let me see, I can easily put down what is wanted; that is very nearly what I said." I observed that I did not quite understand it and hoped he could forgive me if I asked him whether he meant it as a refusal to take office while this Parliament sat, or whether he refused entirely, whether the Queen consented to dissolve or not. He said he meant it as a refusal, that he could not carry on the Government in a Parliament where there were eighty votes of majority against him.

But, I said, "Would you take office and dissolve?" He said, "I thought the Queen would not agree to this". I replied I thought she would not object, in fact, I felt certain she would not. But, he said, there is an idea that this not being my Parliament it cannot be dissolved by me. Then, I remarked, the Queen could offer you a dissolution, though of course you would be responsible for advising her to do so. "Of course", he said, "I well understand that, but I decline altogether to accept office." He went on: "How could I proceed. For two months at least Parliament must continue while the regular Estimates, Mutiny Act, etc., are passed. The Conservatives are gaining favour in the country, but these two months would ruin them. They would be exposed in a hostile House to every insult which the Opposition might choose to fling at them, and the party would be seriously damaged, while the business of the country would suffer. The only possibility of carrying any measure would be by allying myself to the Irish lot, whom I detest and disagree with, and who would throw me over whenever it suited their purpose."

I said, "You have defeated the Government—ought you not therefore to undertake the responsibility of forming one?" "No", he replied, "we did not defeat the Government. We threw out a stupid blundering Bill which Gladstone in his *tête montée* way tried to make a vote of confidence. It was a foolish mistake of his, but he has condoned for it by resigning. He can now resume office with perfect freedom." During the first part of the interview, Disraeli sat at a table, and as he spoke with eagerness there was something in his

over-civil expression about "the Queen", or "My dear
Colonel", which made me think he was playing with
me, and I felt once or twice a difficulty in not laughing,
but when he developed the reasons of his policy he
rose and stood much more upright than I have ever
seen him, spoke in a most frank and straightforward
manner and with a sharpness and decision which was
different from his early words. Yet, probably he had
measured the length of my foot and had been more
sincere and honest in his message to the Queen than
when he made me believe in his frank exposition of
policy.

He was far easier to speak to than Gladstone, who
forces you into his groove, while Disraeli apparently
follows yours and is genial, almost too genial, in his
sentiment. He concluded by begging me to ask the
Queen's permission, though it was merely a matter of
form, to repeat the substance of the audience he had
had the honour of having with her.

I returned at once to the Queen, who desired me to
communicate the result of my visit to Mr. Gladstone.[1]

Queen Victoria had had thirty-six years of experience of political crises. Brought up by Lord Melbourne
in the Liberal school, she had successfully dealt with
the various clashes of the Whigs and Tories, and after
negotiations with men like Peel, Derby, Aberdeen,
Palmerston, the disputes between Disraeli and Gladstone must have seemed to her child's play.

At that time Disraeli had not yet gained her confidence; neither had he poisoned her mind against

---

[1] Previously published in Buckle's *Life of Disraeli*, vol. ii. p. 212.

Gladstone. Therefore, she was quite prepared to hold the balance evenly as far as their personalities were concerned.

Colonel Ponsonby early next morning sent a précis of Disraeli's letter to Mr. Gladstone, with the following covering note, on March 14:

DEAR MR. GLADSTONE—The enclosed contains the substance of what Mr. Disraeli has written to the Queen. May I call on you at ten?

Yours very truly,   HENRY F. PONSONBY.

Sent at 8 A.M., on 14th.

The enclosure ran as follows:

The Queen informed Mr. Disraeli that Mr. Gladstone had resigned and that his resignation had been accepted and that Her Majesty asked Mr. Disraeli if he were prepared to form a Government. In answer, Mr. Disraeli said he was prepared to form an administration which he believed would carry on H.M.'s affairs with efficiency and would possess her confidence, but he could not undertake to carry on H.M.'s Government in the present House of Commons.

Subsequently Her Majesty remarked that Mr. Gladstone was not inclined to recommend a dissolution of Parliament, and Mr. Disraeli stated that he himself would not advise Her Majesty to take that step!

Another general election suited no one, and neither statesman was prepared to recommend this solution. Disraeli was reputed to be so shrewd and cunning a parliamentarian that Colonel Ponsonby appears to have had some doubts as to whether he had correctly reported their conversation to the Queen, and on the following day he wrote to Disraeli (March 14):

DEAR MR. DISRAELI—As I am most anxious not to have conveyed any erroneous message, I have put down the substance of the conversation I had with you last night, which I repeated to the Queen. If there is anything wrong in this, I will lose no time in correcting it. I gave the Queen your memorandum. Her Majesty desired me to extract the substance from it, which in fact was almost the whole of the words, and let Mr. Gladstone see what I had written, which I said you had told me you had no objection to.

I also told the Queen what you had said to me as to the reasons of your declining office in the present state of affairs with a hostile majority.—Yours very truly,

HENRY F. PONSONBY.

To this Mr. Disraeli replied the same day:

DEAR COLONEL PONSONBY—Your memorandum is quite correct. I should have liked to have kept it, but fearing you might not have a copy I think it best to enclose it.

I have enclosed also a note for the Queen. It does not relate to public affairs, or of course it would not have been written.

Yours faithfully, B. DISRAELI.

That day Colonel Ponsonby saw Mr. Gladstone again. Gladstone, who mistrusted Disraeli entirely and

"COME TO GRIEF."

"Boo-hoo! they've been an' tore my new dress all to ribbins, and
I'll just go and tell my big Fo(r)ster Brother."

Reproduced by kind permission of the Proprietors of "Punch."

who had no intention of falling into any trap Disraeli wished to lay for him, was still in the throes of perplexity, as the following letter from Colonel Ponsonby to the Queen (dated March 14) shows:

Colonel Ponsonby presents his humble duty to Your Majesty.

Mr. Gladstone said he would ask leave to consider for a short time the memorandum sent by Colonel Ponsonby of what Mr. Disraeli had written.

He thought it was without precedent that the leader of a party which had done its utmost to defeat a Government should refuse without any consultation with the other members of that party to accept the responsibility of forming an administration.

He would, however, examine the previous cases and would write to Your Majesty in a few hours. Should Your Majesty at any moment desire to see him, Mr. Gladstone would readily await upon Your Majesty, but at the present moment he had nothing further to say till he had studied previous cases.

Colonel Ponsonby said he thought it was clearly impossible Your Majesty could again call on Mr. Disraeli after his positive refusal. Mr. Gladstone said it could scarcely be called a positive refusal, as it simply said Mr. Disraeli could not form a Government in the present Parliament, and he asked Colonel Ponsonby whether he did not think Your Majesty could point out to Mr. Disraeli that Mr. Gladstone could make a serious case against him in Parliament for doing his utmost to defeat the Government and yet upon his single voice decline to carry on the business of the country which he had deliberately taken out of Mr. Gladstone's hands. Colonel Ponsonby gave no answer, but called Mr. Gladstone's attention to the leading article in *The Times*, which he thought justified Mr. Disraeli, if he held the same opinions, in declining office.

Mr. Gladstone considered Mr. Disraeli responsible for the crisis, and therefore bound in justice to Your Majesty to consult his friends before positively refusing.

Colonel Ponsonby, having yesterday said something to Mr. Gladstone which made him think Mr. Disraeli's refusal was not final, corrected that misapprehension to-day by telling him he had asked Mr. Disraeli if he had intended his refusal of Your Majesty's offer of office to be final and Mr. Disraeli said it was to be so for the present.

In spite of an eager search for precedents, Gladstone could find nothing that would lighten his perplexity, and at "1.30 P.M." he wrote to Colonel Ponsonby (March 14):

MY DEAR COLONEL PONSONBY—Close consideration of Mr. Disraeli's memorandum has thrown me backwards. I do not quite clearly understand it: and I have written to the Queen accordingly as a first step.— Yours sincerely, W. E. GLADSTONE.

Colonel Ponsonby now went to see Sir George Grey[1] and Lord Grey[2]: and his note on these interviews runs:

---

[1] An old Liberal Minister who had retired from politics. He had been Colonial Secretary and Home Secretary in former administrations.

[2] Lord Grey had been in Lord John Russell's Cabinet.

THE IRISH UNIVERSITY BILL, 1873

Undated.

I went to consult Sir G. Grey. Many asked me why I did not speak to Sir G. Grey, so I determined to do so. Sir G. Grey thought Disraeli right in refusing to accept office, and saw no other course than that the present Government should return to office and that Gladstone should continue to be Prime Minister. It would never do for him alone to retire.

I saw Lord Grey next morning (Friday). He thought Gladstone was making a mistake in hesitating to accept Disraeli's refusal of office, though he saw that the Conservatives had so managed it that they put the Government in a very awkward position. It was Gladstone's fault originally in making the existence of the Government depend on the Bill.

He afterwards advised me to be careful that the Queen should not herself implicate her name in the matter.

Gladstone was determined to call on Disraeli for an explanation, but the Queen could not be asked to do so. He said that Gladstone had told his colleagues nothing of what was going on.

The danger of relying on conversations, which could possibly be twisted into meaning almost anything, seems to have occurred to both Queen Victoria and her private secretary. In answer to Mr. Gladstone's suggestions through Colonel Ponsonby that the Queen should write to Mr. Disraeli pointing out the error of his ways, she wrote on March 14:

The Queen will write the letter and would certainly

wish Colonel Ponsonby to go to Mr. Gladstone and read to him the version of what passed. Ought the Queen not to add to the letter that she said to Mr. Disraeli she *might* have to call upon him again, as she did not know if Mr. Gladstone was content to go on, and also that he had said to her that if there was no one to go on with the Government he would be ready to serve her. Should she state either of these things or both or none?

Colonel Ponsonby's reply was a brief negative. It ran:

Colonel Ponsonby humbly thinks not. There is no written record of it. In 1851 Mr. Disraeli called Lord Russell to account for quoting a statement he received from Your Majesty. It would therefore be desirable that nothing should be said which is not substantiated in writing. If necessary Mr. Disraeli might be asked to write on the point.

To this the Queen replied:

Better do nothing more at present. The Queen can herself, if necessary, later write to ask Mr. Disraeli the question. It is most important that all should be written.

Later on that afternoon Colonel Ponsonby again saw Mr. Disraeli, who evidently was not to be budged from his attitude. That evening Colonel Ponsonby made the following notes:

THE IRISH UNIVERSITY BILL, 1873

I took the Queen's letter in which she said she had no doubt that Mr. Disraeli's refusal was absolute. Mr. Gladstone got rather angry and said that if Mr. Disraeli chose to upset his Government he was bound to make an attempt to carry on one for himself. Government would be impossible if the Opposition persisted in throwing out important measures and refusing to take the responsibility of their acts. He thought the Queen might support her Ministers by insisting that the Opposition should use every means in their power to form a Government, or at least to give reasons for not doing so. Indeed it was only fair to Mr. Disraeli to let him know what Mr. Gladstone thought.

I replied it would be impossible for the Queen to write or communicate in this way with Disraeli. All this was fair enough for a debate in Parliament, but the Queen could take no part for or against either party. If she were to accuse Disraeli of bad conduct in beating the Government without being prepared to come in she would be taking the part of the Liberals. Gladstone thought she might fairly support her own Government, but he would not press the matter. But he would not accept Disraeli's incomprehensible answer. What then, I asked. Well then, he said, I shall write to the Queen and leave it to her to do what she likes about the matter. He told me he would have no objection to her forwarding the question.

We therefore agreed he should write and that the

Queen would be at liberty to follow her own wishes as to sending his letter to Disraeli.

I saw Lord Grey, who said he did not think the Queen could do otherwise than forward Mr. Gladstone's letter, but he cautioned me against allowing the Queen's name to be used on one side or the other.

Queen Victoria was well pleased with her secretary's tact, but all the tact in the world could not alter the fact that Gladstone had resigned, that the Queen had accepted his resignation, that Disraeli would not take office without a dissolution, and that neither Gladstone nor Disraeli would or could advise a dissolution. It was equally clear that there was no one else who could form a Cabinet.

That evening Queen Victoria replied to Colonel Ponsonby (March 14):

The Queen thanks Colonel Ponsonby for his letter and she must express her high sense of the very judicious manner in which he answered Mr. Gladstone. The course proposed to be pursued she thinks decidedly the best. But she cannot think how it will end. Is Mr. Gladstone waiting to hear if he is to write to the Queen, or will he write without hearing again? If so, she hopes he will write soon. Possibly some middle course might be pursued and someone else be consulted, but that cannot be done till after the Queen hears from Mr. Gladstone and again from Mr. Disraeli.

The Queen thanks Colonel Ponsonby for the great

assistance he has rendered her, which has relieved her from much extra fatigue.

The next day (March 15) Colonel Ponsonby received the following letter from Mr. Gladstone:

MY DEAR COLONEL PONSONBY—(1) I have prepared a statement which I am just going to copy out fair for the Queen. It will not, I hope, cause Her Majesty any embarrassment.

(2) We are going to Cliveden at five. Should the Queen have occasion to see me at Windsor to-morrow afternoon, or Monday morning, I am at Her Majesty's command. This rather assumes that Her Majesty may see it fit to take some step in the interval.

(3) Pray read *Standard* and *Daily Telegraph* of to-day. Neither paper knows anything, it is plain; but both are moved to say Disraeli has taken time from the evident naturalness and propriety of such a course. The *Post* is just the same; and the *Daily News* thinks as much or more. *The Times* alone has another doctrine and plainly has intelligence.—Yours sincerely,

W. E. GLADSTONE.

Note by Colonel Ponsonby

The unusual course followed by Mr. Gladstone of asking the Queen for further explanations before he could call the Cabinet together made it necessary for Her Majesty to consider how she could meet his request.

(1) To have refused would have retarded affairs.

Besides which the Queen wished there should be no misunderstanding.

(2) If she assured him Disraeli's refusal was complete she would be responsible for answering for him.

(3) If she called for more explanations, that would have supported Gladstone's view.

So with Gladstone's consent she sent the letter to Mr. Disraeli.[1]

On the following day (March 15) there is this note by Colonel Ponsonby:

The Queen sent Mr. Gladstone's letter to Mr. Disraeli, saying she thought it the best mode of preventing a misunderstanding. I took it to him. He read it and said, "It is a State paper! I will answer it to-morrow unless you desire an immediate reply, which I could easily give." His answer came on Sunday and was sent that night to Cliveden.

Mr. Disraeli's answer[2] controverted or denied almost all Mr. Gladstone's assertions; in their place he said:

Before Mr. Disraeli, with due deference, offered his decision to Your Majesty he had enjoyed the opportunity of consulting further those with whom he acts in public life and they were unanimously of the opinion that it would be prejudicial to the public interest for a Conservative Ministry to attempt to conduct

---

[1] A fuller and slightly different version of this memorandum is given in Buckle's *Life of Disraeli*, vol. ii. p. 213.

[2] For full text see Buckle's *Life of Disraeli*, vol. ii. p. 214.

Your Majesty's affairs in the present House of Commons.

Queen Victoria promptly sent this to Colonel Ponsonby with the following note:

Pray read this carefully and then let me see you. It gives no further answer beyond what the Queen had said and is calculated, if shown to Mr. Gladstone, to lead to a most interminable controversy.

It was, however, sent to Mr. Gladstone, the Queen concluding by saying that as it was evident the Opposition had positively refused office, she now called on Mr. Gladstone to resume the Government.[1]

Mr. Gladstone could not have been very sorry to receive the Queen's request to resume office—at any rate it was the only apparent way out of the awkward position in which he had placed himself.

The press now leapt to the conclusion that the Queen had refused to grant Mr. Disraeli a dissolution and that consequently he had declined to form a Government. Mr. Delane, the editor of *The Times*, was, of course, anxious to get the truth, and Colonel Ponsonby's note dated March 17 throws light on what the inner circle thought of affairs:

I saw Mr. Gladstone on Monday, the 17th, by the Queen's desire. He said he would have much to arrange with the Cabinet. He thought they would all resume office, but they must decide on the conduct of public business.

At the House of Commons that evening I sat next

---

[1] Colonel Ponsonby's notes.

Delane while a statement for the Press was being made, and not feeling satisfied I asked him what he thought. He said it seemed as if the Queen had refused to grant a dissolution for Mr. Disraeli. On passing through the Lobby, Harcourt told me that all who sat near him were convinced it meant this. I went on to the House of Lords and asked Lord Granville what should be done to correct the error. He did not see that anything could be done. Lord Sydney and Bessborough were indignant with Mr. Gladstone, and Sir G. Glynn told me it was some deep game of his. I thought of asking the Duke of Richmond to correct it. But he had never been consulted. So I merely told the Queen, who did not think the words bore any such meaning and I left the subject alone. But the impression on the public mind remained that the Queen had refused a dissolution. Delane told me later he had seen Disraeli, who said he could not explain all in one sentence—that he never meant it and that he would explain all on Thursday. Delane added that I should see it put straight in *The Times* next day.

Mr. Disraeli's statement in the House of Commons that evening was a skilful attempt not to bring the Queen into politics, but the impression produced may be gathered from the following letter to Colonel Ponsonby from Sir G. Grey (March 17):

Dear Colonel Ponsonby—I think I ought to write you a line as to what happened in the House of Commons this evening. From the short statement made by Mr. D. a general impression was produced, at least among the members who were in my part of the House, that he had merely declined to form a Government during the present Parliament without a word having been said as to a dissolution. Now it is obvious that he could not be expected to form a Government with a view to carry on the affairs of the country in a House of Commons like the present, in which there is a large majority against him, and it was fully expected that if he formed a Government he would have advised a dissolution. As the matter now stands, it looks as if he had been refused a dissolution, or that it had never been mentioned. I have no doubt this will be set right on Thursday, as it ought to be on Her Majesty's account. I write this for *yourself only*, as in the conversation I had with you on Thursday evening last I fully understood from you what I have no doubt was the fact, that the offer to Mr. Disraeli to form a Government was made unfettered by any condition which would have obliged him to go on with the present House, beyond winding up the necessary business of the session.—Yours truly, G. GREY.

Two days later (March 19) Sir G. Grey wrote again:

DEAR H. PONSONBY—I am very sorry I missed you when you called here. It is a pity that Disraeli's language should have created the false impression which it certainly did, and not unnaturally, but it is quite clear he could not have intended this, and the matter will be cleared up to-morrow. I shall be curious to hear how Gladstone explains his having kept the result doubtful so long; it seems to me he treated both his colleagues and Parliament somewhat cavalierly.— Yours very truly, G. GREY.

Note by Colonel Ponsonby

Mr. Gladstone told the Queen that the impression still existed that she had refused to grant a dissolution to Mr. Disraeli. He could dispel this at once by reading Disraeli's memorandum, but thought it would come better from him. The Queen sent me to see Disraeli, who said he saw no reason for reading it. Mr. Gladstone might do so, but he himself certainly would not. He thought Gladstone had behaved in an extraordinary way about the letter he wrote the Queen and this memorandum.

Mr. Gladstone said to me that Disraeli was behaving in an extraordinary way about keeping up the mistaken notion respecting the refusal to dissolve. But he would do whatever the Queen wished. I proposed that Mr. Disraeli should take steps to remove any misconception that might exist, though he denied there was any, and that the memorandum should not be read at all.

That same day Colonel Ponsonby wrote the following letters to Mr. Gladstone and Mr. Disraeli:

WINDSOR CASTLE,
March 19th, 1873.

DEAR MR. GLADSTONE—The Queen hopes that Mr. Disraeli will explain any doubt which may have arisen in consequence of his speech of Monday, and thinks that it will be as well that the memorandum should not be read.   HENRY PONSONBY.

19th March 1873.

DEAR MR. DISRAELI—As some questions may arise to-morrow which may require that an allusion be made to the memorandum you gave me for the Queen on the 13th, it is possible that Mr. Gladstone may have to refer to it. Would it be better that you should first read it?—Yours very truly,   HENRY F. PONSONBY.

Note by Colonel Ponsonby

Mr. D. told me he saw no reason to read his letter. I then saw Mr. Gladstone, who said if the Queen wished it he would.

But it seemed to me better that no one should read it. With the Queen's permission I wrote:

WINDSOR CASTLE,
March 19th, 1873.

DEAR MR. DISRAELI—I told the Queen you offered no objection to the memorandum being read, though you would not read it yourself, seeing no object to be gained thereby, and feeling a dislike to making public your communication with the Queen unless it were absolutely necessary to do so.

That you did not think a false impression had been generally created by your statement but that at any rate you would explain away any doubt with respect

I   113

to this on Thursday and make it clear that although you did not ask for a dissolution the Queen was quite ready to grant it.

As the only object of reading your memorandum would be to remove mistaken notions that may exist, Her Majesty thinks it would be better if the memo. were left unread, trusting to you to correct any misconception that may have caused some persons to think she had refused you a dissolution of Parliament. —Yours very truly,   HENRY F. PONSONBY.

P.S.—You are, of course, at perfect liberty to read the memo. should you think it necessary.

The following day (March 20) Mr. Disraeli made his promised statement to the Commons defending his refusal to form a Government. He was in brilliant form and almost seemed to be playing with Mr. Gladstone:

I know well [he averred] what will occur when a ministry takes office and endeavours to carry on government with a minority during the session, with the view ultimately of appealing to the people. A right honourable gentleman will come down here, he will arrange his thumbscrews and other instruments of torture (*laughter*), and we shall never ask for a vote without a lecture; we shall never perform the most ordinary routine office of Government without there being annexed to it some pedantic and ignominious condition. (*No! no! and cheers.*) I wish to express nothing but what I know from painful personal experience (*Laughter.*)[1]

[1] *Annual Register*, 1873.

114

He went on with brilliant raillery, giving facetious examples of what might happen to a minority Government—the slights and humiliations that might be imposed upon it. He would lead a majority Government or none at all.

The result was that Mr. Gladstone had no alternative but to resume office, and so the crisis terminated.

Two days later Mr. Disraeli wrote to Colonel Ponsonby:

GEORGE STREET,
March 22nd, 1873.

DEAR COLONEL PONSONBY—You observed that I put the matter right which we talked about. I did not speak of Her Majesty's "judicious impartiality" but the Queen's "judicial impartiality".

I will send you in a day or two a copy of the speech corrected, for there are many errors of that kind and some nonsense.—Yours faithfully,   D.

This narrative may perhaps fittingly end with an exchange of bouquets—not between Mr. Gladstone and Mr. Disraeli, who if anything disliked one another even more as the result of the manœuvres and counter manœuvres, but between the Queen and Colonel Ponsonby. While this threatened crisis was no more than a trifling incident in Queen Victoria's experience, it meant much more to Colonel Ponsonby, who had just succeeded General Grey and who was therefore more or less on trial. A false step or an imperfect grasp of the situation might have had serious consequences, and either of the antagonists might have suggested his being replaced by someone with more experience. Possibly had he failed to be strictly impartial it might have been suggested that in future the post of private secretary to the Queen should change with the Government. Colonel Ponsonby's letter ran (March 20):

Colonel Ponsonby, in humbly congratulating Your Majesty upon the termination of the crisis, begs leave most respectfully to thank Your Majesty for the clear directions Your Majesty has throughout given to him, which has made his duty of conveying Your Majesty's wishes an easy one, and though Your Majesty has been most graciously pleased to approve of Colonel Ponsonby's exertions, he cannot but feel that all he did was facilitated by the manner in which Your Majesty carefully considered each difficulty, promptly decided upon it, and with accurate knowledge of precedents skilfully avoided taking any step that might be misconstrued.

Colonel Ponsonby most humbly takes the liberty of saying that he can scarcely regret the recent crisis since it has so well brought out Your Majesty's characteristic love of fairness and justice to both parties and clear judgement which enabled Your Majesty to deal impartially with the unusual and difficult position which arose.[1]

To this Queen Victoria replied (March 21):

It is for the Queen much more to thank Colonel Ponsonby for the great help he afforded her and for the great judgement, tact and zeal he showed during those trying days—and she was especially touched by the anxiety he showed that she should in no way be misrepresented.

[1] Published in *Letters of Queen Victoria*, vol. ii. p. 249.

The Queen would wish to have the papers back when Colonel Ponsonby has numbered them.[1]

Perhaps the best epitaph written on the whole affair is that written by Dean Wellesley [2] to Colonel Ponsonby on March 18:

The Queen wishes me to write to Gladstone about the Canonry—myself. In the course of her letter there is this paragraph speaking of the late crisis. "She is anxious to tell the Dean how admirably Colonel Ponsonby has done, such temper, tact, impartiality and judgement." It is pleasant to be appreciated even for a while, although our gracious Mistress is something like Horace, *Fortuna nunc mihi nunc alii benigna.* Still you may say *"laudo Manentem"*, but be not too much elated but be prepared also for *"Resigno quae dedit"*.

[1] *Letters of Queen Victoria*, vol. ii. pp. 249-50.
[2] Dean of Windsor.

CHAPTER V

THE VISIT OF THE SHAH OF PERSIA, 1873

To the majority of the inhabitants of London at this period, the East was a closed book, and when it was announced that Nasr-ed-din, the Shah of Persia, was coming to London it conveyed fantastic notions to the man in the street. Those who in their childhood had read the *Arabian Nights* were able to conjure up some idea of what an Eastern potentate was like, and a few scholars who had grappled with the *Rubáiyát of Omar Khayyám* knew a certain amount of the trend of Persian thought, but the majority of Londoners had to rely on their imagination.

Had the Shah arrived in Western dress and worn a frock-coat and tall hat, nobody would have been vastly interested, but he fulfilled their highest expectations by being dressed in an astrakhan cap and a long coat embroidered with gold, while he wore as many diamonds and precious stones as his apparel would bear. His total inability to make himself understood and his undisguised admiration for childish pleasures all fitted in with the preconceived notions people had formed of an Eastern potentate.

One of the peculiarities of the late Victorian era was the prevalence of catchwords. Phrases taken from topical events or music-hall songs and often with no intelligible origin were repeated *ad nauseam*, and were

118

greeted with loud laughter as worthy indications of exceptional wit. Possibly the first of these catchwords was "Have you seen the Shah?" However little reason or sense there may have been behind some catchwords, this catch-phrase at least would appear to have some justification, for rarely in history had London had so much cause for surprise or wonder as that occasioned by the visit of this Oriental monarch.

Early in 1873 he had decided to visit Europe. His first country of call was Russia, where he appeared with three wives, three uncles and a whole retinue of officials. The three wives proved too much even for Russian morals, and before the Shah had been there many days he was compelled to send the ladies back to Persia.

From Russia the Shah proceeded to Germany and Belgium and finally on June 24 arrived at Dover. In addition to his three uncles, he was accompanied by His Highness Hajee Meerza Hussein Khan; the Grand Vizier, whose Persian title was Sadr Azam; and His Excellency Yahya Khan, Minister of the Palace, who was the Grand Vizier's brother and had married the King's sister. This gentleman was principally remarkable for a seam across his face that had cost the man who gave it his life. One other member of the suite deserves to be noticed and that is His Excellency Meerza Malcolm Khan, Minister Plenipotentiary and Envoy Extraordinary in England.

At Dover the Shah was met by the Duke of Edinburgh, Prince Arthur, Major-General the Hon. Arthur Hardinge representing Queen Victoria, and Colonel Ellis representing the Prince of Wales. The party proceeded to Charing Cross, where the Prince of Wales and the Czarevitch, who was on a visit to England, welcomed them, and one of the first things the reporters noticed was that among the Shah's attendants was an official who carried a silver stove, which hung from his hands by chains. The duties of this gorgeous official were to heat the golden teapot when required, and to light the mixture used by the Shah when he smoked his pipe.

Perhaps no better sidelight on the visit can be given than that expressed in the following letters from Major-General the Hon. Arthur Hardinge to Colonel Ponsonby. The first (dated June 18) runs as follows:

MY DEAR PONSONBY—We, Cowell [1] and I, being still only in the primary oscillations of the Persian King, have scarcely yet touched the sublime, though we may be said to be patiently progressing towards its attainment. I took up my quarters here last night, to be prepared for the unforeseen, which, if rumour may be depended upon, is but the probable accident of this interesting conjunction! Notes from the Lord Chamberlain, interviews with Master of the Horse, and confidential communications with Hekeem El Mema'lik (whose office seems analogous to that of Spencer Ponsonby [2]) proved the reward of my solicitude.

The latter was sent forward to prepare the way for the King of Kings, and having graduated at Paris, and taken his degree in an English mission, presents a cosmopolitan development at once plastic and intelligent. He has actively supervised the delicate distinc-

---

[1] The Master of the Household.
[2] Comptroller, Lord Chamberlain's Office.

tions of Persian precedence, and has ticketed the doors of this now Royal labyrinth, previously to the arrival of the Queen's bewildered guests.

The Duke of Edinburgh and Prince Arthur started at eleven from Charing Cross, to find the arrangements at the Lord Warden, complete in themselves, further set off by an advantageous framework of sudden sunshine. Nothing could have been more favourable to the desired impression upon the barbaric mind than the multitudinous gaieties of harbour and of pier, bunting and gauze floating wantonly, in contrast with the ordered regularity of a very creditable guard of honour furnished by the 38th Regiment. The atmosphere was just so hazy that the fleet, accompanying the three steamers, loomed the larger from indistinctness, whilst the *Vigilant* came alongside with tranquil grace, undisturbed by too much alacrity on the part of the bluejackets in lowering the scarlet gangway upon the paddle for the descent of our princes to the deck, where the Shah stood conspicuous by a blaze of diamonds.

This important ceremonial having been effected under the auspices of the Viscount, H.M.'s gentlemen were next presented, after which commenced my earnest task of forcing the lethargic suite into the train.

Persian domestics, with miscellaneous properties of rugs, pipes and cases of jewels, of stupendous dimensions, swarmed with desultory apathy into happy-go-lucky compartments, each wedded to some bulky object of responsibility, from which he would not be

put asunder. This embarrassment was at length over-
come, and the brilliant potentate landed into a *bosquet*
of exotics, overarching the entrance to the Lord
Warden, thence he was conducted to a retiring-room,
where he might collect his thoughts for the crucial
ordeal of petticoated deputation headed by the Mayor
of Dover. The address, delivered by the Recorder, was
rendered into more mellifluous Persian, and the Shah,
with dignity and self-possession, made an animated
reply, retranslated with tremulous English by Sir H.
Rawlinson, its salient point, in political importance,
being the avowal that English and Persian interests
became identified by this visit of the Shah.

Twenty-one sat down to luncheon with the Royalties in a separate room. In an adjoining apartment a
good collation was served to the satellites, as to whom
belonging I am unable to record positively any incident of the high feast, though I hear that His Majesty
only transgressed western decorum by the sly disposal
of the thigh bone, "d'une toute petite caille", under the
table. I was better employed, *energising* my functions
to wean the children of the sun from the flesh-pots of
our Court, and after this had been accomplished, the
first contretemps that befell us was the warning odour
of an axle-tree fired by the friction of rapidity. This
obliged us to put back into the last station for water
and grease, a mischance the Persian envoy happily connected with an allegory, "Nous brûlons de l'impatience
de Sa Majesté d'arriver à Londres!"—an impatience
that just sufficiently retarded our arrival at Charing
Cross, that just as we had marshalled the host

into their gilded coaches, the heavens played us the trick of baptizing the infidels, a universal downpour that served only to exemplify the good nature of our English crowd, and the immobility of our military discipline.

Reaching the Palace, the Prince of Wales did many presentations. The Czarevitch added his respects, and at last the Shah was allowed to resume that Eastern isolation in an English palace most congenial to his tastes.

Damped though it was by the rain, H.M.'s entrée into London was far more impressive than anything yet prepared by foreign Powers. The garden here, accessible from his windows, has for him a special charm; thither he sallied forth as soon as left to himself, and became so jealous of its pleasures that he desired that the windows from which his movements might be watched should be closed. In harmony with these readopted habits, his dinner was served on the floor. The amalgamated households dined together amidst the glitter of gold plate.

This is what I learn of the chief personages.

Grand Vizier, though next in rank to the Shah, grandson of a journeyman, pedigree being held of small account.

The Shah's first wife is also of the humblest origin, but the sediment of respectability sinks (they say) to the bottom of the social system without impairing the power of religious sovereignty. The half-brother of the Shah is poor in purse and mind. His uncle, militarily distinguished, has dipped his fingers into the Royal coffers, but the coin has again slipped through his spendthrift hands.

The Vizier's brother, unlike himself, has Russian proclivities.

On the whole Persian envoy seems the coming man, though but just recovering from paternal disgrace. His father joined the Freemasons and for a time tickled the Shah with that mysterious straw, but, popelike, he became alarmed at the dark brotherhood, and exiled his favourite, who turned Russian tool at Constantinople so that his son, though he affects English sympathies, may be suspected of insincerity.—Yours very truly,   ·   A. E. HARDINGE.

A Homeric programme had been arranged for the Shah, and wherever he went he was met by an enthusiasm and a curiosity that it would be as impossible to describe as to account for. On June 19, he received the Diplomatic Corps, dined with the Prince and Princess of Wales at Marlborough House, and finally went on to a ball given by the Duke and Duchess of Sutherland at Stafford House. The next day (June 20) he paid his first visit to Windsor, where he was received by the Queen in full state. Her own account, written in her Journal, of this meeting is worth repeating:

Felt nervous and agitated at the great event of the day, the Shah's visit. All great bustle and excitement. The guns were fired and bells ringing for my Accession Day, and the latter also for the Shah. The Beefeaters were taking up their places, pages walking about in full dress, etc. Arthur arrived, crowds appeared near the gates, the guard of honour and band marched into the quadrangle, and then I dressed in a smart morning dress, with my large pearls, and the Star and Ribbon of the Garter, the Victoria and Albert Order, etc. Was much surprised at seeing no troops lining the hill, as was done when the Sultan came here. Sent for Colonel Ponsonby, who could not understand it, as he knew the order had been given. He ran down to give some directions, in hopes of getting them still, and some makeshift was arrived at just as we heard the Shah had arrived at the station. Arthur and Leopold had gone down to meet him, and Lenchen, Louise, Beatrice and Christian were with me in my room, watching the gradual approach, heralded by cheering.

The carriage was quite near, followed by eleven others! and we hastened down. The great officers of state, the ladies and gentlemen, Lord Granville, etc., had all preceded us below. The band struck up the new Persian March, and in another moment the carriage drove up to the door. The Grand Vizier, who, with my sons, was in the same carriage as the Shah, got out first, and then the Shah. I stepped forward and gave him my hand, which he shook, expressing to the Grand Vizier my great satisfaction at making the Shah's acquaintance. Then took his arm and walked slowly upstairs, and along the corridor, the Grand Vizier close behind, and the princes and princesses, including all the Persian ones, the ladies, etc., following, to the white drawing-room. The Shah is fairly tall, and not fat, has a fine countenance and is very animated. He wore a plain coat (a tunic) full in the skirt and covered with very fine jewels, enormous rubies as buttons, and diamond ornaments, the sword-belt and epaulettes made entirely of diamonds, with an enormous emerald in the centre of each. The sword-hilt and scabbard were richly adorned with jewels, and in the high black astrakhan cap was an aigrette of diamonds. I asked various questions through the Grand Vizier, but the Shah understands French perfectly and speaks short, detached sentences.

When we entered the white drawing-room, into which only the princes and princesses, the Grand Vizier, Lord Sydney, Lord Granville and Malcolm Khan came, I asked the Shah to present the princes, and he presented them. The Shah presented the Grand Vizier as "Mon premier Ministre". He is very agreeable and pleasing and speaks French perfectly. I presented my three daughters to the Shah, before his presentations. Then I asked him to sit down, which we did on two chairs in the middle of the room (very absurd it must have looked, and I felt very shy), my daughters sitting on the sofa. Lord Granville handed me the Garter and diamond star and badge, and helped by Arthur and Leopold I put it over the Shah's shoulder. He then took my hand and put it to his lips, and I saluted him. The Sadr Azam pinned on the star. After this the Shah gave me his two Orders (Malcolm Khan carrying them in a box), the one being his miniature set in magnificent diamonds, the "Sovereign's" Order, which has never been given to a woman before. It is worn round the neck. The other is a new one, instituted before the Shah left Persia, for ladies, and is a very pretty star and small badge, also in diamonds, the latter hanging from a pink-watered silk ribbon bordered with green, which is worn across the shoulder. He put this over my shoulder, and my cap was rather in danger, but the Grand Vizier came to the rescue, as well as Lenchen and Louise.

The doors were then opened into the green drawing-room, where everyone was assembled, and we proceeded slowly to luncheon, the Shah giving me his arm. We lunched in the oak room and sat down twenty. The Shah sat on my right, and the Grand Vizier on my left, Lenchen next the Shah, Louise next the Grand Vizier, Prince Abdul between Lenchen and Beatrice, and one of the old uncles on her other side. The band played during luncheon, and the pipers at dessert, walking round the table, which seemed to delight the Shah. I talked a good deal to the Grand Vizier, and through him to the Shah, but also directly to the latter, in French. He takes great interest in everything, spoke of Vicky and her children, and said she was well; that he should so much like to see Scotland, had had my book translated into Persian, and had read it.

The Sadr Azam said the Shah had reigned twenty-six years, and was forty-three, his eldest son, the heir, being nineteen. The succession in Persia is direct, not as in Turkey. The Shah ate fruit all through luncheon, helping himself from the dish in front of him, and drank quantities of iced water. After luncheon we walked down the corridor to the tapestry room, where I took leave of him, and left him to rest, and where his servants, pipe-bearer, cup-bearer, etc., went to attend on him. He is naturally much tired and is accustomed to rest after meals.

I remained a little while in the corridor, talking to the Persian Princes and to Sir Henry Rawlinson (who speaks Persian perfectly), and the following were presented to me: two of the second class of gentlemen, some of whom (especially chamberlains and a master of ceremonies) are tall and very good-looking, his doctor, Dr. Tholozan, a Frenchman, and Dr. Dickson, for twenty-five years attached to the British Legation, who saved the Shah's life two years ago. Went to my room to rest a little, and at about half-past three saw the Shah (who had taken off his aigrette and put on his spectacles) go downstairs and drive off with his whole suite. They went without an escort to take a drive round Virginia Water, and to stop at the Fishing Temple. Felt so thankful all had gone off so well.[1]

When the Shah left Windsor, he showed the crowd a miniature of the Queen set in diamonds, which she had given him, and kissed it with reverence.

The Windsor festivities were followed by a reception at the Guildhall, where the revelry of quadrilles amused the Shah, "who never dances".

The following day included a visit to the Royal Covent Garden Italian Opera, and Hardinge's next letter (dated Sunday, June 22) notes that the Grand Vizier was relegated for the first time to a second place.

[1] For full text see *Letters of Queen Victoria*, vol. ii. pp. 258-61.

THE VISIT OF THE SHAH OF PERSIA, 1873

MY DEAR PONSONBY—My friend Hekeem el Mema'-lik was still between the sheets when I had my message of matutinal inroad upon him this morning. I told him to bestir himself in getting the autographs His Majesty had been pleased to call for, and to number his equestrians for Windsor Review.

In going to the opera last night, the Shah took Lords Ailesbury and Sydney with him in the carriage, for the first time breaking the indivisibility of himself and his Sadr Azam. The latter's position of favourite provokes the combined enmity of the princes, who never agree amongst themselves except upon such occasions when they hope to upset the arrangements of the Vizier. For instance, they tried to send back the grooms with the Shah's horses yesterday as they passed them on the road to Woolwich. This puerile obstructiveness demands that urbane tutelage of which our *Indian* officials are the perfect masters.

In haste, yours,   A. E. HARDINGE.

The Sunday was devoted to a naval review at Spithead, and during the following week the Shah visited various provincial centres. On Saturday, June 28, he left Trentham for London. That afternoon he again exercised one of his hobbies—that of walking round the Palace gardens. On this occasion it was raining, so the Shah borrowed an umbrella. Presently, perceiving the rain to have stopped, he pitched the umbrella over his head by way of getting rid of it without even looking behind.

There was some trouble when the Shah insisted on seeing the professional prize-fighters spar in Buckingham Palace gardens. Queen Victoria took a broad point of view of the incident, and said that she did not object to his seeing an exhibition of boxing but it should not have taken place in her garden.

The next day General Hardinge wrote to Colonel Ponsonby:

MY DEAR PONSONBY—There is a lull. The Shah keeps to the garden till four, and confines himself to receiving Persians, and a new French Minister accredited to Teheran; at four he dines out.

I shall probably take him by the park to Kew and so thence by Richmond. He has a Persian bill of fare for to-night's dinner, and many lambs have been handed over to the "butchering" knife of Persian cooks. His Majesty intends sending the household the compliment of some of these dishes, which makes Cowell serious.

I find the French Minister has gained his point about Cherbourg. I heard him persistently at that work, at Chiswick, with no counter influence to fortify what, as I told you before, was H.M.'s real wish to return by Dover. The Grand Vizier tells me the Shah was much pleased with Chiswick and the Persians still further impressed with the dignity and affability of the Queen.

I have asked for a list of the suite who accompany the Shah to take leave at Windsor. The numbers will be *kept down*, but I cannot yet furnish the Windsor equerry with their names.

I hear the Russians are amazed at the improvement effected in the ways of the King of Kings. He kept their Emperor waiting (with intention they declare)

for more than an hour. Is Persian regeneration to be
attributed to American bowls?

Yours very sincerely,   A. E. HARDINGE.

The time for the Shah's departure was now approaching, but he did not leave without paying a second
visit to the Crystal Palace "without his diamonds", and
a visit to Madame Tussaud's. Hardinge's account of
these visits (dated July 3) is very vivid:

MY DEAR PONSONBY—The Royal adieux were the
climax of the honours from Throne and people that
have been heaped upon the Shah.

H.M. returned here at seven. Half an hour being
given for change of raiment, H.M. joyously started for
Madame Tussaud's.

Some mounted police accompanied H.M.'s carriage
as the popular fervour to howl "There he is—Shah,
Shah" has (wonderful to relate) not one cry abated,
and when Shah drives without a military escort, which
of course cannot be furnished with a stamp of the
foot, Persian progress is sometimes clamorously ob-
structed. The precaution was not unnecessary: the
park was refreshing stillness, Baker Street seethed with
populace and enthusiasm.

The report in *The Times* gives a most accurate
account of the interest that riveted the Shah, in his
spontaneous recognition of a creamy Emperor of
Germany, or a waxen Bismarck, with an undisguised
doubting whether they were not endowed with life.

Sharper still the scrutiny of those personages, in whose
vacant features he tried to forecast the future—his

131

European receptions. Madame Tussaud's son rather vulgarly did the honours of his stiff potentates, but the Shah was so pleased that he sat down amidst press reporters, who with a few ladies were alone admitted, and they collectedly wrote evidently some impression of his inspection, for he read it very carefully over. In a short time we shall have the Persian effigy in this attitude of composition.

The troubles of these non-official days are likely to be the greatest. The Shah had decided to go by train to the Crystal Palace at 1 o'clock to-day. Last night a chamberlain rushes in to announce that the Czarevitch takes leave at one, and that an hour can be given for the train. I expostulate meekly, and as I find that all the Marlborough House Royalties are at Apsley House, I contrived, by the Prince of Wales' mediation, to obtain a somewhat earlier visit of the Russian Grand Duke and so save the arrangements already fixed.

How they will get their luggage off is a riddle. Some of them have gigantic cases. *Boule de neige* in short that will overburden any foreign locomotive. I am just going to see the Grand Vizier on this subject.

Then there are *mille cancans* about the payment of their purchases. Treasurers pay in roubles and deduct *douceurs* for themselves upon the already shortened cash.

Yours very sincerely,   A. E. HARDINGE.

The final letter of the series refers to the Shah's naïve enjoyment of the treats that the Crystal Palace could then afford:

THE VISIT OF THE SHAH OF PERSIA, 1873

Thursday, 3rd July.

MY DEAR PONSONBY—I have just telegraphed by the Shah's desire personally to the Queen, to offer his thanks for the enjoyment of a very successful day at the Crystal Palace.

The Czarevitch's earlier visit enabled us to keep punctual time, a remark that does not extend to the princes, who have been throughout a stumbling-block to these observances.

Picture to yourself this scene. One is telling Frederica to take him to Hanwell. Some Persians (not princes) went there this morning, and wrote in the Visitors' Book that they have only found there agreeable hosts; another must go to the British Museum, and a third desires to be driven to siege operations at Chatham.

We are obliged, of course, to moderate these eccentricities as the Royal stables, which have *wonderfully* stood *great* pressure, could not sustain unlimited dispersion, but T.R.H.'s, even when ordered to accompany their King, refuse to get into their carriages till the Shah has been seated in his own, and to-day kept us ten minutes waiting before the train could start.

The building, large as it is, was crammed when we entered, but perfect order kept. The Shah lingered at the shop-stalls, comparing *naïvement* the photos of himself, that were in abundance, with his own looks in many mirrors. At one time he took up an opera glass and turned it upon a galaxy of ladies—a manœuvre that "brought down the House". At another time he

133

asked an old lady what her name was (Mrs. Baillie) and where she lived. He was charmed with the Alhambra and much interested with seeing the composition for one of its cornices, requiring repair, actually in the mould. The struggle between the stuffed tiger and lion he could hardly be induced to leave, and near this spot the directors had supplied a small table with refreshments including sweetmeats from Teheran, in the hope that the British public might see him eat, which he did most unconcernedly. He saw the fountains play from the gallery, but was again soon in motion to get to the outskirts of the garden, to examine the balloons that were to touch the skies with real men in them. The first was soon buoyant, but the second, named Prince Arthur, had got so damped on the fireworks night that it required a tedious amount of inflation before it would leave its anchorage. It was a long walk for him, in that almost monotonous avenue of curious gazers, but the activity of the police expanded space, and when we reached the wide stairs leading down to the middle basins, the Shah signified his wish, as a candidate of liberal principles, to descend without even the protection of our Civil force. I warned His Majesty of the risk of too much popularity, but he had become a desperate democrat, and pshawed my conservative advice. I, therefore, could only form line to protect his rear, and the centre of the position was held safe, but the flanks of the populace wheeled round and after a time he was in the midst of a somewhat irrepressible mob, but complacently condoned the crowding of his choice, till a carriage rescued him from too reiterated recognition. I was therefore glad to get him back into his pavilion, and though he had been on his legs all day, it required management to dissuade him from again running the gauntlet of the ground-floor galleries. "Pas du tout, pas du tout", was his answer to my fears that British welcome had touched upon "the divinity that doth hedge in a king". As he went back through the shop-stalls, a young lady of the commercial society presented him with an embroidered smoking-cap, an example fervently followed in other forms by her *accroche-cœur* compeers. He rested only fifty minutes here before he again started to take another look at the Albert Hall and the picture galleries.

Yahya Khan, who accompanied him during the day's doings, is completely exhausted, but the Shah all the more delighted with his own energy. Mine is on the wane, so I close my epic, if not my eyelids.

Yours very sincerely,   A. E. HARDINGE.

The Shah afterwards admitted to an official, in passable French, that the visit to the Crystal Palace "C'était la plus heureuse soirée que j'ai goûtée en Europe".

Two days later he left via Portsmouth for Cherbourg and Paris, leaving as his greatest gift to the people of England the catch-question "Have you seen the Shah?"

CHAPTER VI

THE QUEEN'S SPEECH, 1881

ACCORDING to the Constitution, the King's (or Queen's) Speech or "the gracious Speech from the Throne" as it is alluded to in both Houses of Parliament, is the announcement of the policy of the Government of the day and is drafted by the Prime Minister in consultation with the Cabinet. Although there have been innumerable instances of slight verbal alterations being made by the Sovereign, it is generally acknowledged that a constitutional Sovereign cannot alter the actual policy adumbrated in the Speech, and must in fact read it out aloud even if he or she disagree with every word of it.

This does not, however, imply that the Lord President of the Council can present it like a pistol at the head of the Sovereign a few hours before it is read in the House of Lords. The usual procedure is for the Speech to be sent to the Sovereign some days before it is submitted officially in Council, and it was perhaps more the clumsy way in which the Speech from the Throne in 1881 was sent down to Osborne at the last moment in the January of that year that annoyed Queen Victoria than the actual contents of the Speech.

At this time Mr. Gladstone, then seventy-two years of age, was Prime Minister, and as such extremely punctilious, so that it could not have been through any fault of his that Queen Victoria was treated with cynical discourtesy and asked to assent to the Speech at a few hours' notice.

Queen Victoria had moreover been so accustomed to have her finger in every Government pie that she saw no reason why she should not prevent her Ministers from making what she considered a tactical blunder, and of course there was a large number of people who agreed that the promised evacuation of Kandahar would be a great mistake. Afghanistan had always presented a most perplexing problem to Victorian statesmen, and while many thought that the policy which had hitherto been pursued of active interference in Afghan affairs followed by complete evacuation of the country was quite wrong and invariably led to massacres and civil war, others were convinced that there was nothing to be gained by keeping a foothold in this turbulent country. It will be remembered that the Afghan war of 1878–1880 had resulted in the temporary occupation of Kandahar by British troops, and the intention of the Liberal Government was to evacuate the country.

"The war in Afghanistan", ran the Queen's Speech, "has been brought to a close, and, with the exception of the Kandahar force, my troops have been recalled within the Indian frontier. It is not my intention that the occupation of Kandahar shall be permanently maintained; but the still unsettled condition of the country, and the consequent difficulty of establishing a native government, have delayed for a time the withdrawal of the army from that position."

When the Queen's Speech was first drafted by the Cabinet, Lord Spencer, then Lord President of the Council, was under the impression that he had a comparatively simple task in summoning a Council at Osborne in order that the Queen might officially give her approval to the Speech. He therefore proceeded simply to fix the date without submitting the draft Speech, and wrote to Sir Henry Ponsonby[1] on December 27, 1880:

MY DEAR PONSONBY—I was anxious to revert first to good intentions and give Her Majesty as much notice as possible about the Council next week and wrote to W. E. G. I got his reply this morning, but to my horror I found that I had no letter paper here, so if the untidiness of my letter is noticed, please explain. I did not want to delay a post.

We hope that the 5th of January will be chosen.

As you may suppose every day is important just now with a Land Bill's principles yet to be settled. I wish you could stand in my shoes in the House of Lords if I am to fight the Irish Peers. The only person less pleasurably situated will be Forster in the House of Commons, for he will be under double fire of Tories and Parnellites.

I begin to think it would be even pleasanter to be ruling at the Viceregal Lodge.

Wishing you the best of luck, and believe me, yours very truly,   SPENCER.

Queen Victoria, however, selected the 4th, and two days later Lord Spencer again wrote to Sir Henry Ponsonby:

---

[1] General Ponsonby had been made a K.C.B. in 1879.

MY DEAR PONSONBY—Her Majesty graciously answered my letter about the Council.

As you know she fixed the 4th, and the Cabinet are ready to obey her commands, but it is very inconvenient to have the Speech settled a day earlier than is absolutely necessary under present circumstances.

I shall not suggest a change to Her Majesty and we wish to meet her wishes, but it is possible that you may know or find that a change could be made to the 5th, and I write to ask you to use your discretion to find this out. If it mattered little to the Queen, possibly she might be willing to alter the day; but do not say anything about it if it is inconvenient.

Yours very truly,   SPENCER.

P.S.—Please if possible telegraph to me before the Cabinet is up to-morrow. We meet at two o'clock.

The Queen gave way to Lord Spencer's pleading, and the 5th was finally decided upon. The Queen, however, was not anxious to meet Mr. Gladstone at Osborne, and Lord Spencer tactfully suggested to him that he would be more comfortable at Hawarden. That day (December 31) Lord Spencer wrote to Sir Henry Ponsonby:

MY DEAR PONSONBY—Your telegram and the gracious change of the Queen's pleasure about the Council was most acceptable and convenient.

I have pressed Mr. Gladstone not to go as I understand I was authorised to do in the Queen's kind allusion to Prince Leopold and you being available for attendance. He seemed quite ready to go, but as he had a touch of lumbago, I think I was right.

To judge by the replies I get to my appeals for another colleague to go down you would suppose that the Cabinet were either decrepit from old age or going to die off from sickness. I am sure that the Lord Steward [Lord Sydney] will be anxious for the trip.

We presume, unless we hear to the contrary by telegraph, that the Council will be held at one o'clock.

Yours truly, SPENCER.

Lord Spencer had no doubt told the two other Privy Councillors that it would be a purely formal business that would not last long, and that therefore they would be back in London between five and six o'clock in the evening, but he of course knew nothing of the explosive material he was handling nor did he even imagine that it would be nearer nine or ten o'clock before they would be home again.

A week later (on January 5) the Privy Council meeting was held, and the following account of what preceded it that morning and afternoon was written by Sir Henry Ponsonby on January 5:

The Council was fixed for the 4th, but postponed on the request of Spencer. On Tuesday the Queen complained she had heard nothing of the Speech. On Wednesday morning Prince Leopold showed me the Speech, which the Queen had just received, and objected to two paragraphs—about Kandahar and flogging. I observed to him that the Queen had agreed with Childers on the second point. With regard to the first, she had allowed the despatch to go last November, declaring the policy of retiring from Kandahar, but on condition that no announcement was then to be made. Prince Leopold said that was what she complained of and that I must tell the ministers who were coming that this paragraph must be omitted. I said they could not do so, but I would telegraph to Gladstone. I wrote this all to the Queen and telegraphed in cypher at 11.10. The words objected to were—"It is not my intention that the occupation of Kandahar shall be permanently maintained". When the ministers came (Harcourt highly indignant because they had by some mistake sent the small bathing-carriage [1] to bring up four big men) I told Spencer the Queen objected to one paragraph. He said, "That must be Kandahar. I knew the previous controversies, but hoped it was settled now. We can not change anything." I told him I had telegraphed and he hoped the reply would come before the Council at one. The Queen, who had come to the drawing-room, sent for me and asked whether they would omit or modify the words. I replied that the two ministers, Spencer and Harcourt (Lord Sydney, the third, was not a Cabinet minister), said they could not. The Queen said, "Then I will not approve. It was

[1] The bathing-carriage alluded to was a one-horse wagonette open at the sides but enclosed on the top. Cabinet Ministers were accustomed to a landau drawn by a pair of horses, which made nothing of the long hill from East Cowes to Osborne. On the other hand, the one-horsed bathing-carriage, designed probably for at most two bathers, was clearly the wrong conveyance for three Privy Councillors and the Clerk of the Council, more especially as Sir William Harcourt alone weighed over fifteen stone. In all probability the horse must have walked all the way uphill from Cowes, and therefore it is not to be wondered at that Sir William Harcourt was peeved when he reached Osborne.

distinctly understood when I assented to the despatch being sent in November that no announcement should be made till the time came—and now, without telling me anything about it, they put the words into my mouth in my Speech. I will not approve. If they omit it I will approve of the rest—with this exception." I told this to Spencer and Harcourt, who regretted they had no power whatever to make any alteration. The Queen said then she would wait till Gladstone answered the telegram, and went up to her room again. She then spoke to me still more warmly, saying she was treated as a child by being kept in ignorance and then forced at the last moment to assent.

I returned, and the minister, Harcourt, said it should be explained that this was really the Cabinet's speech. It was their policy, and any change was an interference with their policy. I said that both in Lord Beaconsfield's and Mr. Gladstone's former administration alterations had been made. Harcourt observed that probably these were mere verbal alterations, and that they were made on the responsibility of the Prime Minister who was present. Then he regretted Mr. Gladstone was not here. The Cabinet deliberated on this paragraph, which had been brought forward at the last moment on Tuesday by Hartington, and it was their policy to announce the retirement.

This I reported, and the Queen said she did not want to omit the paragraph but to modify it for holding Kandahar in the future if necessary. Harcourt's contention was that he and Spencer, being junior members of the Cabinet, had no authority to modify anything. Spencer observed that if this were not in the Speech, questions would be asked and it must be announced in a day or two. . . . As the question had come to a deadlock, I proposed to Harcourt the following memorandum:

"If the Queen should be graciously pleased to give permission to Her Minister to make the proposed Speech, the Ministers in attendance at Osborne will convey to Mr. Gladstone Her Majesty's earnest hope that should circumstances arise which make the retention of Kandahar necessary, the Government will not hesitate to hold that position." Harcourt objected that the Queen did not give permission, but must approve. If she did not approve, of course, the ministers must resign. So he changed the first part to "The Queen, in approving the Speech, commanded the Ministers in attendance to convey to the Cabinet Her Majesty's earnest hope, etc.". I sent this in to the Queen as a proposal. Her Majesty thought it weak and wrote a counter-proposal but kept it till the answer had been received from Mr. Gladstone. He had been consulting Lord Granville and replied at 3.45 that the question had been settled in November, this being a refusal to alter the Speech, which, as Harcourt said, must be sent to the leader of the Opposition by 7 o'clock, so there was no time to assemble a Cabinet thereon. The Queen now sent the following memorandum to the Ministers: "The Queen, in approving the Speech *generally*, commands the Ministers in attendance to convey to the Cabinet her disapproval of *that* part of the Speech *referring* to Kandahar, and the Queen *only*

143

gives her assent to the Speech under the *express under-standing* that the *Cabinet will give her an assurance* that, should circumstances *arise rendering* the *retention* of Kandahar desirable, the Government will not hesi-tate to continue to hold that position". I took this to the Ministers and Spencer said that it disapproved of the speech whereas they asked for an approval!

I returned to the Queen. Prince Leopold was there. She said nothing would induce her to approve of the sentence, but she would change "disapproval" to "re-gret".

When I went back with this alteration, Harcourt said it made no difference. It would be impossible for them to make conditions on behalf of the Cabinet of any sort. They could not possibly agree to what was inserted on the paper, but if the Queen approved of the Speech they would afterwards take any commands from her to London. Harcourt went on that to dis-approve was to eject the Ministry and that, on the eve of the opening of Parliament, was revolution. He could not help privately observing that the Queen by this claimed the right to control the policy of Ministers, which could not be. I told the Queen the Ministers could not agree. She was very angry, called in the Council, approved the Speech and then sent me to see Mr. Gladstone on the subject in London.

The Queen's letter, written late that night, runs as follows:

January 5th, 1881.

The Queen thanks Sir H. Ponsonby for his letter. She had a bad headache when she got up as she has been very anxious and worried about Ireland and this incredible behaviour of Ministers did *not* make it better. The Queen has never before been treated with such want of respect and consideration in the forty-three and a half years she has worn her thorny crown, and there are no longer men like Lord Halifax who would stand by her as he did in '59 when Lord Norfolk and Lord Palmerston behaved so shamefully about their Italian policy and Lord Halifax helped us out of it. But to tell the Queen nothing—Lord Hartington knowing the Queen's views—and to put this into the Speech when she expected nothing of the kind and when since that correspondence in November about the despatch she never had heard a single word, is monstrous. Mr. Gladstone never enables the Queen to judge of anything he speaks of in the Cabinet and never (as he ought and as she has always been accustomed to) of the different opinions held elsewhere.

She is kept (purposely) in the dark and then expected simply to agree. And when she does have an opinion, she is treated as she was to-day, her Ministers, after keeping her waiting for three hours, refusing to take her letter!

Sir Henry must tell Mr. Gladstone, Lord Granville and Lord Hartington that she will not *stand* such treatment. The disrespect and contempt of her position shown her, she will *not* tolerate.

After *all*, the only objection to a positive declaration about Kandahar was—it will encourage the Afghans, it may lead to another war, so many more precious lives be sacrificed.

Sir Henry cannot overrate the Queen's indignation. Mr. Gladstone tries to be a Bismarck, but the Queen will not be an Emperor William to do anything *he orders*. When does Sir Henry go? He must cypher a telegraph to her and write when he can.

In reply Sir Henry Ponsonby wrote to the Queen a letter of which the following is his rough note:

I regret Your Majesty has a headache. Spencer and Harcourt admitted that the question should have been submitted in time for discussion. It was supposed that in allowing despatch in November you had sanctioned the plan. The Ministers would not change the Speech — but would resign, and there would be a revolution. Harcourt was in a great state of anxiety. The letter contained conditions—they would be deceiving her if they implied they would pledge themselves.

They asked only for Your Majesty's approval to your Ministers' suggestion. He will tell Gladstone that it is want of respect to ask for such sudden approval of a whole line of policy.

The following two days Sir Henry Ponsonby saw, not only Mr. Gladstone and Lord Hartington, but also the Prince of Wales and Lord Granville, and his memorandum runs as follows:

January 7. Gladstone was disappointed at hearing of the event at Osborne as he had believed the Speech was in accordance with the Queen's views, and Hartington in bringing the paragraphs to the Cabinet had not told them there was any doubt.

I saw Hartington, who regretted the incident. The despatch had been sent last November, and the announcement must be made. He had thought of writing beforehand to the Queen but had not done so. I asked why not as he knew she had strong feelings. He confided to me, not to go further, that this was precisely the reason he had not written. I advised him to write to the Queen, and he promised to do so.

Next day I was sent for by the Prince of Wales, who had heard the story from Prince Leopold. I explained some misapprehension he had and told him, as I afterwards wrote to Prince Leopold, that "The Ministers did not refuse to take a letter up from the Queen as he had said, but refused to undertake conditions on behalf of the Cabinet. The Queen suggested modifications in a paragraph of her Speech. The Ministers in attendance expressed deep regret that their powers did not permit them to make any alteration in that document and said that should the Queen not think fit to approve, all they could do would be to report the matter to their colleagues. Lord Spencer and Sir W. Harcourt were not enabled to pledge the Cabinet to any conditions, but would convey any amendments the Queen might think fit to honour them with to the Prime Minister."

I saw Lord Granville, who thought that some mode of coming to an agreement might have been found. But he believed Harcourt had been right on the whole. I saw Gladstone again and told him the three points of complaint were that the Cabinet had been fixed for the last moment to please the Government, and that then the Queen was told it was too late to alter anything, that she was badly informed on all matters, and that on this especially she had been entirely misled. I asked him whether it would not be better to write to the Queen and he said he would do so when returning to her the above-mentioned memorandum.

The Government now made every effort to appease the Queen's wrath. Lord Hartington confessed that it was his fault in not keeping the Queen better informed, and Mr. Gladstone pointed out that the troops could remain at Kandahar as long as it was thought necessary, but the Queen still resented the conduct of the Privy Councillors, as will be gathered from the following letter which she wrote to Sir Henry Ponsonby on January 7:

The Queen thanks Sir H. Ponsonby for his letter and telegraphs. She has had a letter from Lord Hartington in a very proper tone, but he has not much to say for himself. The Queen has written him an answer (to go tonight) which she has asked him to show to Mr. Gladstone. The Queen does not quite understand why Sir Henry quotes Sir Wm. Harcourt's opinion so often? His opinion has no weight whatsoever with *her*, for he has never been in office before and she thinks her experience of forty-three years more likely to enable her to know *what* is *her position* and *standing* than he does. It is very condescending of him to allow her forty-eight hours' notice of the Speech, twenty-four hours would be nearer the mark! But "a distinct policy" ought to be brought before her a week at least before it has to be promulgated. In this case it is no doubt known in

India by this time and the Afghans will receive great encouragement by it.

Our "patriots" intend to take the side of the Basutos and Boers. That fearful sentimentality for our enemies is simply disgraceful.

There are two notices of very bad motions about the House of Lords and the Consolidated Fund.

Mr. Gladstone and others ought to take a very firm, strong tone. Can Messrs. Bright and Co. do so after their speeches? If not, they should keep away.

The Queen was much pleased to hear the Prince of Wales also sent a message. It is for him as well as for herself that the Queen must insist on being treated with proper consideration and respect.

To this letter Sir Henry Ponsonby replied (January 8):

Lieut.-General Sir Henry Ponsonby presents his humble duty to Your Majesty.

He only quoted Sir William Harcourt's words because he was one of the Ministers in attendance—the other, Lord Spencer, being too ill to see anyone after the unfortunate affair here. He only left his room to go to the House of Lords in the evening of Thursday.

Sir Henry Ponsonby, however, saw him yesterday, when he repeated his deep regret at what had occurred. Knowing Your Majesty's opinion on Kandahar he had hoped that all had been settled before the Speech was agreed upon, and he was surprised and distressed to find this had not been the case. He also repeated what he said here, that the Ministers in attendance would take any letter or message from Your Majesty to the Cabinet, but that they could not pledge the Cabinet to any proceeding as they were not empowered to do so. He was extremely annoyed to hear that Your Majesty considered that he had been wanting in consideration, for he would have done anything that he himself was able to do, but that if he had promised anything on behalf of the Cabinet he would have deceived Your Majesty, as he had no power to do so.

The two motions referred to by Your Majesty are not expected to come on for a long while. That referring to the House of Lords is probably only put on paper for the purpose of raising a debate and then being withdrawn. The Irish party intend to prevent the passing of the Address for three or four days if they can. The prospect is most unsatisfactory. But their conduct has united all parties against them. Sir Henry Ponsonby sincerely trusts that Your Majesty has not suffered from all this trouble, which he can well understand has so much annoyed Your Majesty.

Later on that day (January 8) Sir Henry again wrote to Queen Victoria:

Mr. Gladstone's entire acceptance of Your Majesty's views on Kandahar is in accordance with what he said to Sir H., that the announcement did not prevent Your Majesty's troops from holding that position so long as it was necessary to do so.

Lord Hartington wrote that it was originally said that the announcement was not to be made till time arrived for actual withdrawal of troops. True, the despatch (November) was for the guidance of the Viceroy, but it was intended always that the announcement should be made in the speech. He can only express deep regret that he did not earlier tell Your Majesty. Mr. Gladstone also wrote — returning the memo.—that the Cabinet entirely accepted the views of Your Majesty, and should circumstances arise rendering retention of Kandahar desirable, the Government will not hesitate to continue to hold that position; and he regretted the annoyance caused. Had he himself any doubt he would have arranged business so as to have communicated sooner with Your Majesty.

Mr. Gladstone had in fact eaten humble pie, and his complete admission of error pleased the Queen. At her request, Sir Henry Ponsonby wrote from Osborne to Mr. Gladstone on January 9:

DEAR MR. GLADSTONE—I think it may be worth telling you that your letter to the Queen gave great satisfaction, and that from what H.M. said to me last night she is evidently much pleased by it. She thinks the misunderstanding arose from Hartington's omission to tell her of the proposed announcement, but he has himself written so well to her that I hope the matter may be considered at an end.

The Queen is much disturbed at the Irish obstruction in Parliament.

Yours very truly, HENRY PONSONBY.

To this, Mr. Gladstone replied (January 10):

151

SIDELIGHTS ON QUEEN VICTORIA

My dear Sir H. Ponsonby—Many thanks. I am glad that the business has ended well. Hartington's frank and straightforward ways are sure in such a case to please a person of corresponding character.

I hope the Queen did not hear of an absurd misreport which made me say that if that was a complaint of [a certain matter] it was owing to an inadvertence on the part of the Queen. For Queen was to be read "complainant".

Yours sincerely,   W. E. Gladstone.

Meanwhile, stories about the Council began to be whispered in the drawing-rooms in London. At first the press knew nothing beyond the bare fact that the train conveying the Privy Councillors back to London had been three hours late.

Truth, edited by Mr. Labouchere, nosed out the story, but obviously the information supplied was from no authoritative source, as the following extract will show:

WHAT THE WORLD SAYS

"I am in a position to state on indubitable authority that the Queen did not consent to the original draught of her most gracious Speech, and thus it was that the train which was to take Lord Spencer and his colleagues back to town was delayed more than three hours. The telegraph wires were working during the whole of that time between the noble lord and the Premier, the ultimate result being the modified and almost Conservative Speech which the Chancellor, in the absence of Her Majesty, read to both Houses of Parliament."

152

The Lord Steward, Lord Sydney, who was the third Privy Councillor, was, of course, silent about what happened at the Council, but he was shocked to find, as the following letter will show, that stories were being told about the Council and that these stories were supposed to emanate from Prince Leopold. On January 9 he wrote to Sir Henry Ponsonby:

My dear Ponsonby—I met Gladstone at dinner last evening at Spencer House and he seemed well pleased by a letter from Osborne that came that afternoon. It seems to be all serene and he is sorry that there should have been any misunderstanding in the matter of Kandahar, which appears to have arisen from the last conversation with Hartington. However, the despatch of November was submitted.

I had a letter from Victor Montagu last evening which said he had "been put behind the scenes" of what one may call "the Memorable Day". It is very wrong in Prince Leo telling such matters to indifferent people, especially to a Tory sailor—not famous for discretion. . . .

The Rector of Cowes, Barker, preached an Irish sermon this evening at Chapel Royal, which I think Gladstone liked very much.

Yours sincerely.　　　　　　　　　Sydney.

The following day Lord Sydney wrote again (January 10):

My dear Ponsonby—I telegraphed to Prince Leopold. As a rule the House meets at five, and the public business begins at 5.15, at which hour Lord Lytton will make his speech.

153

The episodes respecting Wednesday have been droll. Her Majesty inquired how we all looked at luncheon; the answer given was: Lord Spencer, Lord Sydney and Sir Wm. Harcourt in usual spirits—then she observed next day to Evelyn Paget,[1] "I suppose your Uncle S. has not got over yesterday as he has not written to me".

Victor Montagu lunched here and I gather that Lady E. told all sorts of stories to the ladies at tea of what was alleged to have passed, and not facts. If Lady E. was told these things in the drive, she is not justified in telling them out, especially with visitors present.

V. Montagu is like telling the Town Crier, and then Prince Leopold told all sorts of things afterwards. A letter was written for the Cabinet subsequently, which I believe was laid before them on Saturday, otherwise it was not intended to have mentioned the matter to anyone, excepting Gladstone and Granville, but of course a little is told to Alec Yorke[2] in allusion to the "events of the day", and the lords-in-waiting proclaim these stories. Whether correct or not it is impossible that these should both be gossip. However, I do not think it is much known here as yet. Amongst other statements made were:

No. 1. "That the Speech only came down with us."

Secondly. "That Kandahar had never been mentioned before."

Thirdly. "That the Speech was sent (to the Queen) five or six days before the meeting."

---

[1] Maid-of-honour.   [2] Groom-in-waiting.

154

And various other small matters; facts or not which ought never to have been spoken about to the public.

Prince Leopold laid down the doctrine that it was the *Sovereign's* Speech and *not the Ministers'*. I should have thought he knew the Constitution better.

Torrington has been here about his toilette at Vienna and Berlin, which the Prince of Wales is much occupied about, and invents white trousers with gold lace, which is not *our* uniform.

Yours sincerely,   SYDNEY.

Considering the number of people who knew something of what happened at Osborne, it is astonishing that all London was not ringing with the story.

Queen Victoria was now anxious to be sure that she had not in any way violated the Constitution by challenging any part of the Speech from the Throne. She, therefore, wrote to Lord Beaconsfield, having learnt from long experience that he could always be safely relied upon to give advice diametrically opposed to any Mr. Gladstone might give.

The following reply (dated January 11) full of Delphic platitudes, but omitting all mention of Gladstone, was intended to convey the impression that Lord Beaconsfield entirely agreed with her views, but it is significant that he does not touch the actual point at issue. This letter is of particular interest as it is one of the last that the great Conservative statesman ever wrote to Queen Victoria:

MADAM AND MOST BELOVED SOVEREIGN—The principle of Sir W. Harcourt, that the speech of the Sovereign is only the speech of the Ministers, is a principle not known to the British Constitution. It is only a piece of Parliamentary gossip.

The Speech from the Throne must be approved in Council by the Sovereign, but to be so approved, it should be previously considered by the Sovereign. Ample time ought to be secured to the Sovereign for this purpose, so that suggestions may be made and explanations required and given.

The degree of resistance which the Crown may choose to make against any expressions which the Crown disapproves must depend upon circumstances. If, for example, there was a proposal to surrender Malta under an alleged engagement of the Treaty of Amiens, the Sovereign would in all probability be supported by the nation in resisting such a counsel. The unfortunate state of parties at this moment limits the power of the Throne, but that is no reason why the constitutional prerogative of the Crown should be treated as non-existing. Even under the present circumstances Your Majesty has a right which it would be wise always to exercise, to express your Majesty's opinion on every point of the policy of your Ministers and to require and receive explanations.

Last night Lord Lytton [ex-Viceroy of India] made his debut in the House of Lords, and at once mounted to the first rank of present Parliamentary orators. This is a most important adhesion to our debating bench. The Duke of Argyll had expected from the new Peer, who had never addressed either House of Parliament, a personal and egotistical address, and of a florid character. His Grace was much disappointed. He had to reply to an admirably practical address on the surrender of Kandahar (which never must be surrendered), and this in a tone severely chaste, and in the best style of Parliamentary debating. The Ministers had so depreciated and underrated Lord Lytton that this success was to me proportionately gratifying. They have found their master, and the moment we are in possession of the Afghan papers we shall return to the great controversy.

I think it right to state that there are instances in which the Speech from the Throne has been altered after it was approved in Council, but so far as my experience can guide me, they were always instances in which news from abroad or the Colonies had affected the statements of fact. Then no change was made without obtaining the previous sanction of the Sovereign, and if the Cabinet could not be assembled, the Prime Minister took the responsibility of the change.

I did receive, Madam, the New Year's card and wished to have responded to it in a vein not unworthy of its merry picture.

Your Majesty's devoted servant,

BEACONSFIELD.[1]

The final letter to conclude this chapter is from Lord Spencer to Sir Henry Ponsonby (dated January 12, 1881), from which it will be seen that Queen Victoria had won her point that the Sovereign must always be consulted in advance as to what should be read in the Speech from the Throne.

[1] *Letters of Queen Victoria*, vol. iii. pp. 181-2.

SIDELIGHTS ON QUEEN VICTORIA

MY DEAR PONSONBY—It is a great relief to me to hear that the Queen was satisfied with Mr. Gladstone's and Lord Hartington's explanations.

Both Sir W. Harcourt and I readily concurred in the assurance which the Queen asked for, but that was quite a different thing to giving it at Osborne for our colleagues.

I hope that Prince Leopold understands the position now you have explained it to H.R. Highness very clearly.

Yours very truly,   SPENCER.

CHAPTER VII

THE FRANCHISE BILL, JANUARY TO JULY 1884

OF all the vexatious questions that periodically arise to perplex the British democracy, the question as to how that democracy shall elect its representatives is one that arises in every decade.

In 1884 the thorny problem of an extension of the franchise threatened to bring about a deadlock between the two Houses of Parliament. The Liberals under Gladstone were then supreme in the Commons, with a majority of 115, and were determined to pass the Bill extending the franchise to country householders. The Conservatives were equally determined not to let it pass, but realising their helpless state in the Commons, looked to their overwhelming majority in the Lords to resist and to defeat the Liberal proposals.

The Liberal Party, tired of having lesser Bills rejected or mutilated by the House of Lords, welcomed the prospect of a fight on a major issue, but curiously enough Gladstone, while determined to carry through his Franchise Bill, disliked the idea of an attack on the House of Lords. In those days there was, of course, no Labour Party and therefore the Liberal Party consisted of all the extremists as well as the moderate men, and the extremists were crying out for the reform and even the abolition of the Second Chamber.

The question developed into a real struggle between

the House of Lords and the House of Commons—
possibly only the third serious clash of its kind, but by
no means destined to be the last. Only a decade earlier
Republicanism had raised its head in England, and
the Gladstonian ministry now contained men like Sir
Charles Dilke and Mr. Joseph Chamberlain who saw
many virtues in a Republican form of government. It
is interesting to speculate what might have happened
in this 1884 clash had there not been some moderating
influence in the State such as was then exercised by
Queen Victoria.

As early as January 4, 1884, Mr. Gladstone had
written to Queen Victoria reporting that the Cabinet
had decided that "the first great measure of the year
should be a Bill for extending to the counties the
occupation franchise and also the lodger franchise now
enjoyed in boroughs". It was evident that he meant
the Bill to go forward alone, and not to be followed
until a year later by any schemes for the adjustment
of electoral areas.

The Bill for the extension of the franchise was introduced in the House of Commons on February 29, 1884,
and the Second Reading was carried on April 8. In
the debates on the Third Reading, Colonel Stanley
moved on May 23 a provision which was intended to
secure that the Franchise Bill should only come into
operation after a Redistribution Bill should have been
passed. On the motion the Conservatives were divided:
Lord R. Churchill, Mr. Gorst and Mr. Raikes, "one of
the closest adherents of the leaders", opposed Stanley's
amendment, which Mr. Stanhope and Sir S. Northcote defended. The result of the division was:

> For Stanley's motion . . 182
> Against 276

"It is now therefore pretty clear", wrote Gladstone to Queen Victoria,[1] "that a section of the Opposition" wanted the Bill, with Redistribution later so as to avoid "the very perilous contingency" of a conflict with the Lords, while the other and much larger section objected "either to an extension of the suffrage or to dealing with that subject alone".

The Third Reading was carried on June 26 and the Bill sent up to the House of Lords. On that occasion Mr. Gladstone, as he wrote to Queen Victoria, felt compelled to refer to the threats which had been uttered by important personages "that the Bill was doomed on its arrival in the House of Lords". He believed that a collision between the two Houses on this subject would be "fraught with danger to our institutions, and sure not to end in the defeat of the House of Commons".[2]

To this letter the Queen replied to Mr. Gladstone on June 28, 1884:

No one [she wrote] can more deeply regret any great divergence of opinion between the two Houses of Parliament and especially anything approaching to a collision than she does. But on the other hand she does think that the House of Lords *cannot* be expected merely to acquiesce in and pass a Bill of vital importance to the balance and well-being of the British Constitution, which has been carried through the House of Commons. The House of Lords must give its opinion and could not be respected if it *did not* do so.

It is for this reason that the Queen cannot but regret the strong language used by the Prime Minister

[1] *Letters of Queen Victoria*, vol. iii. p. 504.
[2] *Ibid.* vol. iii. p. 510.

on Thursday night, and trusts that he will adopt a more conciliatory tone, which would be far more likely to conduce to an impartial and peaceful solution of the many difficulties which are so threatening at present.[1]

Mr. Gladstone (on June 30) acknowledged the Queen's "condescending frankness", in which she expressed her regret that he had used "strong language", "but", he observed, "your Majesty has not pointed out any language of this character as employed by him". The language of the Opposition, Mr. Gladstone continued, was "violent and boastful" and "long before the Bill was approaching the House of Lords, Lord Salisbury (the leader of the Conservatives) had, at one or more public meetings, threatened its rejection", and "his nephew and private secretary [2] had made bold to indicate, in the House of Commons, the same result".

Twice, in his recollection [Mr. Gladstone continued], the House of Lords has gone into a distinct conflict with the House of Commons; and both times it has suffered severely. When in 1831 it had (not in Mr. Gladstone's judgement without much excuse) rejected a Reform Bill, it had to undergo the humiliation of passing a like measure after a few months under threat of a creation of peers which would have wholly overborne its independence. When in 1860 it rejected (again not without some excuse) the Paper Duties Bill, it virtually lost all power of dealing with taxing Bills, and since that epoch financial debates in that House have all but ceased.

[1] *Letters of Queen Victoria*, iii. 509-10.
[2] Mr. A. J. Balfour, later Lord Balfour.

When conduct much more rash is openly and repeatedly threatened, without the smallest check or protest from any Tory quarter, Mr. Gladstone cannot by persistent silence appear to think lightly of these or other such crises, and is compelled by his duty to the Crown to make some effort to avert them, always, however, subject to the condition that it is done in proper and respectful language.[1]

The Queen was considerably perturbed by this uncompromising epistle, and her note to Sir Henry Ponsonby on it ran:

The Queen thinks that this letter is very serious and that she *must*, before leaving Windsor, see Lord Salisbury herself—and perhaps others—to ascertain what can be done. Alas, she feels so forlorn and helpless now and has no one to turn to. She received this letter from the Duke of Argyll, which also alarms her. Mr. Gladstone's language is very alarming. She must also see Mr. Goschen or else get Sir Henry to see him. The Throne itself may be in danger if Mr. Gladstone proceeds as he intends and we must try to work upon him.

Gladstone's minatory language evidently had its effect on the Queen, even as his speeches had effect on the Opposition, and before a week was over, it was clear, as the Queen noted in her Journal on July 3, that Lord Salisbury was

much more moderate and prudent, as regards the Franchise Bill. The idea was to speak in favour of the lowering of the Franchise, but to insist on its being

---

[1] *Letters of Queen Victoria*, iii. 510-11.

coupled with Redistribution, and therefore to reject it in its present form. It was believed this would result in an autumn session, when the Lords would do the same and bring on a dissolution. I urged most strongly (to Lord Rowton[1]) that Lord Salisbury, etc., should make it clear they were not against a lowering of the Franchise. Lord Rowton entirely agreed and said he would speak in this sense to Lord Salisbury. Lord Cairns and the Duke of Richmond were acting cordially with him.[2]

When the Bill came up to the House of Lords, Lord Cairns, who had been Lord Chancellor in the preceding Conservative administration, however, moved on July 7 an amendment to the effect that the House, "while concurring in the extension of the franchise, could not consent to a measure which was not accompanied by provisions for so apportioning the right to return members as to ensure a true and fair representation of the people, or by any adequate security that the Franchise Bill should not come into operation except as part of an entire scheme". This amendment was carried on July 9 by 205 votes to 146, and certainly suspended even if it did not destroy the Bill. In the division lobby, however, Gladstone found that he was supported by Archbishop Benson, and in the debate surprised to find the Duke of Argyll and Lord Wemyss, both Conservatives, championing the Bill. Gladstone almost immediately announced that the Franchise Bill would be reintroduced in the autumn session, and threatened the House of Lords with drastic reconstruc-

---

[1] Who had been the secretary and confidant of Lord Beaconsfield.
[2] *Letters of Queen Victoria*, vol. iii. pp. 511-12.

"COME A CROPPER."

Reproduced by kind permission of the Proprietors of "Punch."

tion if it remained obdurate. The Conservatives joined battle eagerly.

Queen Victoria had been converted by Lord Beaconsfield to the theory that the broader the basis of the Constitution the more secure the Crown, and therefore there was nothing in the new Franchise Bill to which she could object, but when it came to a dispute between the two Houses of Parliament she determined to intervene—and there was a good and recent precedent for this intervention by the Sovereign. In 1869, when the Bill for the disestablishment of the Irish Church produced a collision between the two Houses, she had successfully prevented a deadlock and induced them to arrive at a compromise.

The Queen now determined to intervene again, and on July 9, the date of the rejection of the Bill by the Lords, sent her private secretary, Sir Henry Ponsonby, to see Mr. Gladstone, but hardly had he gone when she became nervous lest some letter or telegram should be sprung on her from one of the conflicting parties, and she told Major Bigge,[1] her assistant private secretary, to recall Sir Henry by telegraph. The telegram, however, apparently missed him, and he did not receive it until his return to Windsor Castle the next day. Meanwhile, the Queen impatiently waited up till 1 A.M. for the return of her secretary, who, however, did not come. Finally, she left the following note for Sir Henry:

Waited till near one for you. Must see you at Frogmore [2] at half-past ten.

---

[1] Afterwards Lord Stamfordham.

[2] Frogmore is the name of the house in the grounds of Windsor Castle. At one time it was occupied by the Duchess of Kent, but except when Prince and Princess Christian lived there temporarily when Cumberland

Meanwhile, she had written the following in her private Journal:

9th July—The Government has been beaten by 59 in the House of Lords yesterday, about the second reading of the Franchise Bill. Received a letter from Lord Granville reporting that he had made "a very confidential communication to Lord Cairns and the Duke of Richmond,[1] to the effect that the Government were ready to pass identical resolutions saying that they had passed the Bill, in the full hopes of introducing one of Redistribution next Session". After consideration, Lord Cairns had said he and Lord Salisbury could not accept this, and could only propose that the date of the operation of the Franchise Bill should be delayed till after the Redistribution had passed. This the Cabinet would not accept, a similar proposal having been defeated in the House of Commons.

Heard soon after from Mr. Gladstone, who said it would not do to dissolve after an adverse vote of the House of Lords, and that they would advise me to bring the Session to *as rapid* a close as possible, and have an autumn one. He then hinted at the agitation this might produce, but which the Government would try to prevent. After dinner, Lord Granville spoke to me for some time, much distressed and very anxious,

Lodge was being rebuilt, no one has actually occupied the house permanently. There being no privacy near the Castle, Queen Victoria was accustomed to do her work in the Frogmore garden under the shade of the trees, or if the weather was threatening, in an open summer-house. Messengers brought down her official boxes and letters and telegrams from the Castle and returned with the answer.

[1] Lord President of the Council in the preceding Conservative Ministry.

fearing nothing could be done, but greatly regretting Mr. Gladstone's threatening language about the House of Lords, which had no doubt done great harm; that he himself wished for a dissolution now, as likely to prevent the three months' agitation for an imaginary evil. Felt tired and worried. Sent for Sir H. Ponsonby to speak about Mr. Gladstone's proposal.[1]

The next morning, a blazing hot day, the Queen sat in the summer-house awaiting still the return of her private secretary. Finally, about noon, abandoning hope, she left the following note for him:

The Queen waited and waited to see Sir Henry, but she is so tired and overpowered by the heat she cannot wait longer. She was terribly put out at having no one to consult about the affair. The answer must be given to her by one o'clock. The Queen must see Sir Henry at Frogmore at half-past ten to-morrow morning.

That morning (July 10) the Queen had received Mr. Gladstone's usual Cabinet letter, and had replied:

The Queen has to acknowledge Mr. Gladstone's letter of yesterday. She will not withhold her assent to his proposal for an autumn Session in order to reconsider the Franchise Bill; but in doing so she must express her opinion that it would have been a more fair and judicious course to have dissolved Parliament so

---

[1] These were the facts which Lord Salisbury blurted out in the House of Lords on July 8, and both Lord Granville (the Leader of the House) and Lord Cairns expressed the greatest surprise at the publicity thus given to secret negotiations.

as to have obtained the opinion of the country on the questions raised in the House of Lords.

This would have prevented any agitation which the Queen fears may be raised by the postponement of the measure. The opinion of the people constitutionally given at the polling booths is far more valuable than the excitement forced on by noisy demagogues.

The Queen is glad to observe Mr. Gladstone's assurance that the members of the Government will not promote any such agitation.[1]

The Queen, however, was too late to prevent Sir Charles Dilke, one of the most promising of the younger Liberal Ministers, from pouring scorn upon the House of Lords in a speech to his constituents, and the Queen hurriedly wrote to Sir Henry Ponsonby (July 11, 1884):

Pray cypher to Mr. Gladstone.

Sir C. Dilke has already begun to attack the Peers. You told me this winter that he and Mr. Chamberlain must be told to be prudent in their language for the future. If you wish for future conciliation, threats and abuse of the House of Lords must not proceed from members of the Government.

Gladstone's reply was gall, wormwood and vinegar all mixed in judicious proportions. He had had "no time to read the speech" so would "Your Majesty graciously point out" the offending phrases, when Mr. Gladstone would "expostulate" with the erring Dilke. It was, however, he continued, the House of Lords who had "committed a gross and deplorable error",

[1] *Letters of Queen Victoria*, vol. iii. pp. 512-13.

and it was his duty and that of his colleagues to expose all such heresies by "what they deem to be just reasoning".[1]

Sir Henry Ponsonby's comment to the Queen on July 11 was certainly judicious:

General Sir Henry Ponsonby with his humble duty is sorry that Sir Charles Dilke made so strong a speech. Your Majesty's reminder to Mr. Gladstone may prevent any other Ministers from touching on what will soon become a burning question.

Mr. Goschen's[2] moderate speech at the Liberal meeting yesterday did not receive much encouragement.

The Queen's note, indicating the answer to be sent by Sir Henry to Mr. Gladstone, ran as follows:

Sir C. Dilke's tone violated decency, but explanation enough. I want, and hope the Government want, the question to be discussed, which is impossible if leaders on each side assume that opposite party is moved by dishonest, selfish and dishonourable motives. The utterances of Ministers carry weight of authority, but the leaders of the Opposition are not free from responsibility. The Queen laments strong language but can't think as much as Government of irresponsible Balfour. She would have preferred to have heard the opinion of people expressed at a General Election. But since Ministers think that the opinion of country better be learnt at meetings and speeches

[1] *Letters of Queen Victoria*, vol. iii. pp. 513-14.
[2] The Rt. Hon. G. J. Goschen, M.P. for Ripon.

during the recess, it is the duty of the Government to prevent movement from degenerating into a senseless and turbulent agitation.

This note was tactfully elaborated by Sir Henry Ponsonby as follows, and sent to Mr. Gladstone:

The Queen certainly considers that the tone of Sir Charles Dilke's speech did not accord with the meaning of what she had understood Mr. Gladstone to convey to her as regards the addresses of the Ministers. But after the explanation given it is unnecessary to refer again to this point.

The wish of the Queen, which she hopes is also that entertained by Mr. Gladstone, is that the question of the extension of the Franchise should be discussed in a fair and calm spirit.

If the leaders of the two great parties in the State assume that the opposite party is only moved by dishonest, selfish and dishonourable motives, it is useless to anticipate good results from a reconsideration of the case.

The utterances of the Ministers naturally carry with them the weight of authority, and the words of the leaders of the Opposition are not free from responsibility.

The Queen laments the use of strong language or unwise threats from anyone, but can scarcely think it necessary to be as much concerned as Mr. Gladstone is by the irresponsible observations of an independent and uninfluential member of the Conservative party, such as Mr. Balfour. As she has already said, the Queen would have preferred to have heard the opinion of the people on the question legally expressed at a General Election, but since her Ministers think that the views of the country may better be learnt from the meetings and speeches of the recess, it is the duty of the Government to prevent the movement from degenerating into a senseless and turbulent agitation.[1]

Mr. Gladstone replied at length on July 14, once again putting the blame on the Lords, and strongly opposing dissolution.[2] To this letter Queen Victoria drafted a reply on July 15. It runs as follows:

Would Sir Henry prepare a letter for the Queen in answer to this; the following words should be embodied in it. The Lords are *not* in disharmony with the people, but unfortunately Mr. Gladstone's Government leans so much to the extreme Radical side, instead of to the sound and moderate portion of his following, that measures are presented to the House of Lords which the Conservatives and moderate Liberals do not feel they can with safety agree to. No one is more truly Liberal in her heart than the Queen, but she has always strongly deprecated the great tendency of the present Government to encourage instead of checking the stream of destructive democracy which has become so alarming. This it is that, she must say justly, alarms the House of Lords and all moderate people. And to threaten the House of Lords that they will bring destruction on themselves is, in fact, to

[1] For text, as still further revised, see *Letters of Queen Victoria*, vol. iii. pp. 515-16.
[2] See *Letters of Queen Victoria*, vol. iii. pp. 516-18, for full text.

threaten the Monarchy itself. Another Sovereign but herself must acquiesce in any alteration of the House of Lords. She will not be the Sovereign of a Democratic Monarchy.

Fortunately, Sir Henry Ponsonby toned this frank epistle down to a diplomatic note, which was a cautious appeal to Mr. Gladstone not to allow the situation to get out of hand. Regarding this the Queen wrote to Sir Henry:

The proposed letter to Mr. Gladstone is very good, but might still be strengthened. Could Sir Henry not see someone of the other members of the Government and make them feel the responsibility of *not* bringing on a dangerous agitation? The Queen wishes them to be well warned.

The letter, amended still further, was finally sent to Mr. Gladstone on July 15. Needless to add, Queen Victoria's sturdy declaration that "She will not be the Sovereign of a Democratic Monarchy" was omitted.

Meanwhile, Sir Henry Ponsonby, having missed the two messages of recall, had seen Mr. Gladstone, and he now telegraphed to the Queen:

Mr. Gladstone was rather taken with the suggestion of the Queen's intervention, but there are many difficulties. He will consult his colleagues, and I am to see him at six. In case he asks what amount of assurance short of an actual clause will satisfy, may I consult Rowton or the Duke of Richmond?

The Queen replied that he was only to see Lord

Rowton besides Mr. Gladstone, and Sir Henry Ponsonby's account of these two interviews runs as follows:

When the Queen sent me to Gladstone last Wednesday, she was beginning to be alarmed, and I think had hardly expected the Lords would have voted as they did. Gladstone saw me at luncheon — with Mrs. Gladstone and Horace Seymour [1]—eating rapidly as he was due at the Cabinet. He began to talk of the communication made to the Opposition. Mrs. Gladstone ordered the servants out of the room and helped us all herself.

I asked if Her Majesty could intervene. He said he thought not, but afterwards said she might see the Government proposal to the Opposition, and perhaps she might press it also—as the Bill was not yet lost, but he must ask the Cabinet.

I came again at five. He said that the Cabinet were grateful to the Queen, though they did not think it much use, but there would be no objection in asking the Opposition why they would not accept the proposal, which was that a joint resolution approved by the Queen should promise introduction of Redistribution Bill next year. Cairns replied that this was not binding more than an assurance.

The history of this affair was that the Duke of Richmond, not liking the turn things were taking, asked Peel [2] if he could privately ascertain whether there was any middle course the Government could propose.

---

[1] Assistant Private Secretary to Mr. Gladstone.
[2] Clerk of the Privy Council.

They proposed this, which the Duke took to Cairns. But they had not consulted Salisbury at first. Hence the fury of Cairns at Gladstone blurting out the whole affair.

When Gladstone told me that the Queen might sound Opposition I telegraphed to her and got reply that I was to do it through Rowton. I rejoiced, as this prevented it being an official message from the Queen. But Rowton hesitated, saying the Conservative leaders would be hurt. I told him he was only a messenger (he did not quite like this), and I took him to Arlington Street [Lord Salisbury's residence] and waited for him. He told me that Salisbury would not listen to Granville's offer. He wanted a legal clause forbidding the new Franchise Bill from coming into effect till Redistribution was passed. Anything less than a law is only a promise which would be waste paper if Gladstone and Granville ceased to be Ministers. Lord Salisbury asked why Granville did not accept his proposal of putting in the date.

N.B.—I did not see Salisbury, only Rowton. I wired this to Windsor and went off to dine with Dilke. On getting home I found the telegram ordering me back to Windsor.

Sir Henry, of course, returned immediately to Frogmore, and saw the Queen early on the morning of the 12th. Meanwhile, Lord Granville (the Liberal leader of the House of Lords) had asked the Queen for immediate approval of prorogation, which, as Sir Henry's narrative continues, "the Queen did not much like, and said it should be dissolution. She asked me if I saw any hope of agreement between the two parties. I did not and she agreed to prorogation, though she considers that this plan will make Government responsible for all the agitation, whereas an election would have been the calm and proper expression of the people's opinion. She also told me that personally Granville agreed with her, but he could not maintain his opinion for a dissolution against the combined opinion of the rest of the Cabinet."

It was about this time (July 11) that Lord Wemyss, who, in spite of known Conservatism, had voted against Lord Cairns's amendment, gave notice in the House of Lords that he intended to move a resolution to the effect that since the Lords were now in possession of "full knowledge", the Bill "should be proceeded with and considered with a view to its being passed in the present session", and that the Queen should summon Parliament for an autumn session "for the purpose of reconsidering the Redistribution Bill" which the Cabinet "have undertaken to use their best endeavour to pass so soon as the Franchise Bill has received the Royal assent".

Three days later (July 14) Lord Salisbury promptly condemned the motion as "informal and disorderly" and threatened his uncompromising resistance, while Lord Granville announced that the Government supported the resolution. If the Franchise Bill were passed, he said, the Government would enter upon the great task of redistribution early in November. So far, all the offers for a *rapprochement* had come from the Liberals.

Meanwhile matters had grown considerably worse. Nevertheless, Sir Henry Ponsonby, at the Queen's request, again went up to London on July 12 to see

Lord Granville, and Sir Henry's notes on his visit, written two days later, run as follows:

Granville did not think there was any chance of reconsidering the matter. Nor did Rowton, whom I saw, as he told me that Salisbury was most determined. But Hartington [the Liberal Secretary of State for War] was more encouraging. He did not see much hope, and, —if it depended on Salisbury, none—but he believed that many Conservatives still hesitated. The Government could not give way at all. He would not certainly. But he deplored agitation. If the Tories tacked Redistribution on to Franchise they could stop both for ever. It was impossible to accept such a proposal. The Government plan was to pass the Franchise Bill now. They would have a lever to press on Redistribution next year. His (Hartington's) Redistribution scheme was a fair and moderate one. Of course, it would not please the Tories. But if they were wise they would accept it. And if the Franchise were passed, they would. Also, he expected the Radicals would not like his scheme. But if Franchise were passed they would also accept it. Thus a fair and moderate scheme would become law. But if not, then wild schemes would be proposed and the settlement of the whole matter as far off as ever. He quite understood the Tory view of getting things settled their own way, but he did not see why a strong Government was to give in to a weak and disorganised Opposition. Dissolution was out of the question for the reasons given by Mr. Gladstone.[1]

[1] These are given fully in a letter to Queen Victoria quoted in Buckle's *Life of Disraeli*, p. 518.

Everyone seems sure that Salisbury won't give in. If, therefore, the Conservatives vote with the Government, it will be a revolt against him. Clearly the Queen cannot enter into this. Granville said she ought only to communicate with Lord Salisbury or Northcote—and this she agrees to. The Prince of Wales is working through Rosebery. He wanted to vote with the Government, but his friends dissuaded him from taking a part in the discussion.

I see the Tory papers this morning are fierce against any compromise. Gladstone telegraphed to the Queen in the middle of dinner, "Am more hopeful than when I wrote yesterday".

Sir Henry's letter to Queen Victoria on these interviews runs as follows (July 12):

Lord Rowton feared that there was no room for any further reconsideration of the matter, and maintained that Lord Salisbury would not change from the position he held. Lord Cairns and the rest would certainly agree. Lord Rowton considered the situation serious, but they had not created the difficulty.

After seeing Lord Rowton, Sir Henry Ponsonby heard of Lord Wemyss' motion, which it was said would receive the support of a large number of moderate Peers. He was told that many felt bound by their allegiance to Lord Salisbury to vote for him last Tuesday, but also think they are free to vote for Lord Wemyss.

Lord Hartington spoke seriously about the situation, which might become grave. He had not much hope in Lord Wemyss' resolution, but it showed that the door was not shut, and that there was still a hope left—a small one. Lord Granville, after explaining the regrettable incident of his private communication with Lord Cairns, observed that he doubted whether at the present moment the excitement was very great, but it must become so rapidly. He scarcely thought Lord Wemyss could succeed, but he believed there are many who would support him.

Sir H. Ponsonby now, at the Queen's request, went to see Lord Salisbury, and Sir Henry's note of the conversation which took place runs as follows:

In reply to the Queen's inquiry he [Lord Salisbury] said that he never had any doubt that his communication with Cairns was private. But it was clear that Gladstone equally thought there was nothing private about it.

He doubted Wemyss' motion coming to much, but still there was hope. He thought the Queen could only communicate with *Chiefs* of Opposition.

Queen Victoria now did a very surprising thing. She sent for Lord Rowton, the living voice of the dead Lord Beaconsfield, to come to Windsor. To those who might have thought that it was an unconstitutional step for a monarch to ignore her constitutional ministers and to consult the private secretary of the defunct leader of the Conservative Opposition, answer could be made that she was not seeking advice, but information. The net result of the conversation was that Lord Rowton went to Lord Salisbury to ask if he could make any proposals for an arrangement.

FRANCHISE BILL, JANUARY–JULY 1884

Sir Henry Ponsonby's note of Lord Rowton's visit (July 14) is as follows:

Rowton came this afternoon by summons. He went over all the arguments and said that Salisbury and the leaders could not possibly accept the compromise offered. In the meanwhile Gladstone wrote that Rosebery proposed that Franchise Bill should be passed and new Session to begin before Christmas for Redistribution. The Queen told this to Rowton, who came into my room impressed by it. As I had read it I did not see how it met his demands at all. But I said I was glad he thought it might be considered. He paused and then said "I am not sure". I went to station with him—by the time he got there he said, "I am sure it will not be accepted". However, he does nothing. He awaits the meeting of the Conservatives (at the Carlton Club) to-morrow. Harcourt writes to me that he was at Combe Wood [Lord Wolverton's residence] yesterday "where Gladstone breathed nothing but peace on earth and goodwill towards all men—even the Tories", and says that if Salisbury refuses, the blame will be his. Granville's letter to me is sour. I gave him a brevity from the Queen's letter, saying the Government would be responsible for rows, which he did not quite admit. He ends with "The Queen will know best how to manage the same pressure towards this end (peace) on the Conservative leaders as Her Majesty has upon the Government", which, as Bigge observes, is a nasty one for us here.

On that same day (July 14) Sir Henry Ponsonby

received a very frank letter from Sir William Harcourt, an aristocratic Liberal of a vanishing type, who was the Home Secretary and was destined two years later to become Chancellor of the Exchequer under Gladstone. His letter ran:

. . . If the Queen wants (as we all do) to smooth down affairs and keep the peace she should use her influence with the Tories to behave reasonably and accept the conciliatory terms we have offered. It is no use laying the blame on the wrong shoulders. The House of Lords have no right by the Constitution to demand or force a dissolution, and this is a demand to which we ought not and never shall yield. If they get a dissolution it will be in six months' time—when perhaps they will wish they had never provoked it.

In the meanwhile Mr. Gladstone (with whom I spent Sunday at Lord Wolverton's) breathes nothing but peace on earth and goodwill to all men—even the Tories. They will never succeed in making out the lamb to be the wolf. If Salisbury succeeds in persuading his party to reject Wemyss' motion the consequences will be on his own head.

The next day (July 15) an important meeting of the Conservative party was held at the Carlton Club which was to decide the attitude of the party to Lord Wemyss' motion. Lord Salisbury promptly led an attack on this motion, and his followers endorsed his decision to oppose it. That day Sir Henry Ponsonby received the two following letters. The first was from Sir Edward Hamilton, principal private secretary to Mr. Gladstone, which ran:

Will you please let Her Majesty know that Mr. Gladstone does not require to have back the enclosure [copy of letter to Lord Granville] to his letter written on Sunday?

As I am writing, I have not yet heard what the result of the Carlton meeting has been. But I shall be much surprised if there is any inclination shown to accept a compromise. I believe many Peers would like to support Lord Wemyss, but I doubt their having the strength of their opinions, as they will have to elect between risking the leadership of Lord Salisbury and voting according to the dictates of prudence; and I expect loyalty towards their leader will prevail.

The second was from Sir Francis Knollys, private secretary to the Prince of Wales, enclosing a letter which the Prince had received from Lord Randolph Churchill, who had suggested that Sir Michael Hicks Beach, who was destined for high rank in the next Conservative Ministry, should be consulted. The letter (dated July 15) ran:

The Prince of Wales would be very glad if you would call at Marlborough House at a little before six this afternoon as he is anxious to see you.

In the meanwhile please read the enclosed. I hear that at the meeting of the Conservatives to-day there was rather a difference of opinion as to the course to be adopted and that nothing was actually settled. Sir M. H. Beach did not speak.

At six o'clock that same day, as requested, Sir Henry Ponsonby called at Marlborough House and saw the

Prince of Wales, and his letter to the Queen, reporting the conversation, runs as follows (July 16):

On arriving here in the evening, the Prince of Wales desired to see him and asked him to show the enclosed to the Queen. It is from Lord Randolph Churchill and it shows how strongly he feels, as this is the first time he has written to His Royal Highness for some years.

Sir Henry Ponsonby told His Royal Highness that Your Majesty had communicated with Lord Salisbury, but he thought it doubtful whether it would be right to send messages to anyone else.

The Prince of Wales said the crisis was so serious as to justify interference where any chance of success existed. His Royal Highness had heard that several Peers and more Commoners were dissatisfied with Lord Salisbury's decision, and had said so privately at the meeting. In fact, that the rule of Lord Salisbury would destroy the Conservative Party altogether and imperil the Constitution.

Sir Henry Ponsonby therefore sends this to Your Majesty.

Note

(R. Churchill's letter—wants me to see Beach.) Advised not—R. C. not wise adviser. The Queen cannot stoop to minor party views. Prince of Wales advised to consult Shaftesbury — too old. Lord Derby tender to Salisbury, but says he is wrong and responsible for row, which will be serious. Harcourt does not think so serious as he believes

Lords will pass it in October, but Opposition entirely responsible.

The Queen's reply to Sir Henry's letter runs as follows (July 16):

The Queen does not wish to do anything that might lead to a split in the Conservative party, but still thinks Sir M. Hicks Beach might be consulted. Perhaps the Prince of Wales could do something.

Meanwhile the Queen was bringing all the pressure she could to bear upon Mr. Gladstone and Lord Salisbury. Her mediator with the former was the Duke of Argyll, with the latter the Duke of Richmond. Unceasingly insistent, flexible yet determined, she finally won through. First she begged the Duke of Argyll (July 17) as "a personal friend of mine, as a great statesman, and as a friend of Mr. Gladstone, to go to him and speak to him very strongly", urging the Government to bring in both Bills at the autumn session. The Duke of Argyll (July 18) found Mr. Gladstone "not indisposed to concession".

There seemed, however, little hope of agreement behind the scenes, and Lord Wemyss was determined to introduce his resolution so that the whole matter could be thrashed out in the Lords. He therefore moved on July 17 that the Franchise Bill should be passed strictly on the understanding that the autumn session would be devoted to redistribution. To this Lord Granville, as leader of the Liberals in the Lords, readily agreed on behalf of Mr. Gladstone. But Lord Salisbury was adamant, opposing the resolution strenuously, and pointing out that either the Lords would then be forced to pass *any* Redistribution Bill that the

Government cared to advance, or the Commons would be faced with the prospect of an appeal to the new constituents without any redistribution. In the result, Lord Wemyss' motion was defeated by 182 votes to 132, and Lord Cadogan's amendment, that the Franchise Bill and the Redistribution Bill should be considered together in the autumn session, was passed without a division. All other offers made by Gladstone, through Lord Granville and Lord Cairns, to Lord Salisbury had been met with the same uncompromising spirit, the same lack of success.

The Queen now asked Sir Henry Ponsonby to write for her to Mr. Gladstone urging that still further efforts should be made to secure a compromise, and to his suggested draft she appended the following letter (July 18):

The Queen thinks the letter for Mr. Gladstone will do very well. The points the Queen wishes to impress on both sides, but most on that of the Government, are:

(1) The necessity of saving the country and Constitution from any *serious damage*, which was *far before party*. Party will become a scourge and ruin this *Government's position* and name of this great Empire if it puts itself —as it seems to the Queen to do—*before* the safety of the institutions of this country of which we are always boasting. Mr. Gladstone loses all the landmarks it seems to her and may be sweeping away, in his wild vindictive passion, without noticing it, *all* that keeps the State together.

(2) Both parties *must* give way a little and it will never do to *dictate to the House of Lords*, or to threaten. Mr. Gladstone speaks of the growing danger of a con-

flict, but only *thinks* it is the Conservative Party who do the mischief, whereas the violence and dangerous destructive principles of his *Radical* adherents and even colleagues are just as much to blame as the House of Lords, or rather the Conservative leaders.

(3) Mr. Gladstone must be prepared for the Queen to hold him responsible for the agitation and danger which may be got up by the extreme Liberals and for her calling on him and insisting on a dissolution as the only safe means of putting a stop to it.

(4) The Queen wishes Mr. Gladstone, if he finds he cannot get on and will not yield, to be brought to resign, to save the country, and Lord Hartington take the lead.

(5) Lord Salisbury and others should be asked what they mean to do to avoid this strife.

The Queen is quite determined to do *anything to save the country*. It is wicked to willingly try and ruin the country.

These minutes are to guide Sir Henry.

When will he be back?

She writes in desperate haste and has a dreadful headache.

Queen Victoria was under the impression that she was holding the scales evenly between the two parties, but it is evident from this letter that she thought all concessions should come from Mr. Gladstone.

Tempers were now rising high in both parties and Members of Parliament stumped the country with violent speeches. Mr. Chamberlain, whose views at that time were still very crude, made a particularly ferocious speech in which he alluded to the Queen's unconstitutional action in sending for Lord Rowton. Queen Victoria wrote a letter of protest to Mr. Gladstone and implied that he should restrain some of his wild colleagues, but Mr. Gladstone began by pointing out he really could not read all the speeches of his Ministers, and in a second letter added that only one isolated expression in the speech could be regarded as exceptional.[1]

The following letter from his private secretary, Sir E. Hamilton (dated August 7), gives a fuller indication of his views:

Mr. Gladstone has himself written to you about Chamberlain's speech. I don't think it contained anything very reprehensible, but it would no doubt be greatly advantageous were he to be a little more moderate and not sail so near the wind.

I dread to think of the language which will be in prospect if the Lords are foolish enough to throw out the Bill a second time. There will then be no power of restraining it. If it were constitutional for the Queen to interfere, she could not render a greater assistance to the defence of the Constitution than by counselling Lord Salisbury to be prudent. The real trump card for Lord Salisbury to play would be to introduce a scheme of reform of the Upper House himself.

The Rowton paragraph is unfortunate, but contradictions often do more harm than reports, however unfounded they may be.

The Queen passed both her letter to Mr. Gladstone

---

[1] *Letters of Queen Victoria*, vol. iii. p. 524.

and his reply on to Sir Henry Ponsonby with the note:

The Queen wishes Sir Henry to read these letters. She feels it necessary to keep Mr. Gladstone up to the mark. He is very shifty about Mr. Chamberlain.

The Queen was now very angry with Mr. Gladstone, and not only regretted (August 10) that "he was not inclined to carry out his promise to the Queen to keep his unruly colleagues in hand", but also refused to invite him to attend a Privy Council at Osborne.

On August 9 Sir E. Hamilton wrote to Sir Henry Ponsonby:

I am very sorry that Mr. Gladstone is not to attend the Council on Monday. In spite of his pressure of work he had quite intended to present himself at Osborne; and I think he ought to have seen the Queen before he and she went their respective ways. He was, however, annoyed by the receipt of her letter this morning; and this consideration (especially as I could not say you had encouraged him to come) determined him not to put himself out gratuitously and embark on a tiring journey to Osborne when he might not be welcome.

He previously told me to telegraph as I did, in order that if on second thoughts Her Majesty wished him to come he would still put in an appearance at the Council. The answer being very decisive, he will, of course, not come. I much regret it, because I think occasional audiences do great public and personal good.

I am afraid she may be still further annoyed by his

187

reply, which, however, I think the tone of her letter fully warranted.

Of course, there may be a misunderstanding and the Queen may have dispensed with his attendance from considerate feelings; but even this will not in my judgement justify the terms of her letter to him, considering what ample explanations he has already afforded her.

On August 14 Parliament was prorogued, and the only hint of any further effort for a few weeks to heal the breach is contained in the following note from Queen Victoria to Sir Henry Ponsonby:

Would Sir Henry copy this:

Why could not both parties give way and come to some agreement about the Franchise Bill? The Queen has abstained from mentioning the Franchise Bill, but if Sir Henry thinks she had better, he might suggest something.

The Government ought to delay the Bill and bring in the Redistribution at the same time, but Mr. Gladstone is so obstinate and self-willed.

CHAPTER VIII

THE FRANCHISE BILL, AUGUST TO OCTOBER 1884

WHEN Queen Victoria had originally offered to intervene she imagined that it would be quite a simple
matter, but she soon found that the amazing obstinacy
of these two great personalities made it difficult for
her to exercise any interference on constitutional lines.
The moderate men on both sides seemed quite willing
to come to some arrangement, but the leaders had got
into such a position that they were unable to give way
at all without loss of dignity.

With the prorogation, public interest shifted from
Westminster to the provinces, and politicians strained
their uvulas and lacerated their larynxes. Throughout
the recess the flood of oratory roared forth. The
Liberals denounced the Peers as traitors, while the
Conservatives, in their new-found love of democracy,
demanded that the will of the people should be consulted before the franchise should be extended. Both
demanded unconditional surrender. The nation, after
a few weeks, grew weary of both their houses, and the
most bellicose Taper or the most tenacious Tadpole
had to admit that the only hope of settlement lay in
mutual concessions.

Lord Cowper led the way. On August 14, this Liberal
ex-Viceroy of Ireland wrote a letter to *The Times*
in which he begged the Government to present a

189

Redistribution Bill in the autumn session, but for the moment his letter passed almost unnoticed.

In mid-August, Mr. Gladstone submitted to the Queen a long and masterly memorandum on the political situation, which was much more elaborate than the usual official submissions. Lord Granville was the only colleague who had seen it. Starting from the assumption that the Tories were right and the Liberals wrong, he proceeded on the basis of a strongly expressed desire to hold in check a movement for a great constitutional change, but he pointed out that such a movement would go forward with irresistible force if the Bill were again rejected. He concluded by affirming that there was nothing he "would not gladly do for the purpose of helping to close the present controversy, and in closing it to prevent the growth of one probably more complex and more formidable".[1]

The Queen did not read the paper, but sent it to Sir Henry Ponsonby so that he could tell her what it was all about, and her next letter to him (dated August 22) runs as follows:

Sir Henry has not returned Mr. Gladstone's long paper, nor told her what the drift of it is. Please do so.

The Queen hopes Sir Henry had some conversation with Sir Redvers Buller, who is called, as he himself said, "a Radical", but who is so utterly disgusted at the lamentable policy of Mr. Gladstone's Radical Government as regards foreign and Colonial policy, that he says *if* he stands for Parliament he could not support Mr. Gladstone's fatal policy. We shall lose Natal to a

[1] Morley's *Life of Gladstone*, vol. iii. p. 99.

certainty, he says—all our prestige and power in South Africa is gone.

This expedition in Egypt [1] is hurried on with enormous expense and no preparation, and probably many valuable lives will be lost! ! !

It is all the Queen can do to bear the dreadful state of things! The Government, after ruining everything, may be turned out and not suffer a bit for all the mischief and misery they have caused (principally Mr. Gladstone), but the poor Queen *must remain* and look on at it in silent, helpless despair! The Queen knows Sir Henry *never will* blame Mr. Gladstone and the Government for their conduct, but she thinks he has too much intelligence, sense of justice and impartiality not to advise that dreadful mistakes *have been and are being* made.

Meanwhile Lord Cowper's letter to *The Times*, in which he had proposed another compromise on the Franchise Bill, was being seriously regarded in many quarters, and Sir Henry in his reply to the Queen on August 23 drew attention to it. His own private account of the situation at that date runs:

Gladstone has sent the Queen a most important private Memo. on the situation. He says the House of Lords has always been the fortress of the Tories, but he himself strongly objects to its being abolished, if it will use its power with moderation, as such a proceeding would lead to serious consequences. He believes

[1] The expedition to rescue General Gordon was decided upon about this date, and Lord Wolseley sent out to command it.

that if Franchise passes, the cry against the Lords will die away, but if Franchise is again thrown out it will increase. Even if the Tory view is correct and that they come in with a powerful Government, the Liberal minority will damn against the Lords and the abolition will become a part of the Liberal creed. If so, it will eventually come to pass. Therefore, he hopes Franchise will be passed.

I believe that the Government are trying to negotiate with the Opposition on Cowper's proposal. But I believe Radicals and ultra-Tories object.

The Queen now considered Mr. Gladstone's long memorandum of mid-August, and according to Lord Morley, was "deeply struck both by the force of his arguments and the earnest tone in which they were pressed", and although doubting whether there was any strong desire for a change in the House of Lords, still she "did not shut her eyes to the gravity of the situation".[1] The result was that she decided to ascertain the views of one or two of the Conservative leaders, with a view to inducing them to modify their attitude.

On August 24, Sir Henry returned to Mr. Gladstone the elaborate memorandum with a series of queries based upon the Queen's misgivings. Mr. Gladstone again wrote at length in answer urging that "the further stoppage of the Franchise Bill involves a great Constitutional hazard. .... To your question, why not join Franchise with Redistribution, my reply will be best given in Midlothian."[2] And off he stumped to make his second Midlothian campaign.

---

[1] *Letters of Queen Victoria*, vol. iii. p. 531.
[2] Lord Morley's *Life of Gladstone*, vol. iii. p. 99.

The following day (August 26) the Queen returned the memorandum to Sir Henry, and wrote that she was "greatly struck by the fairness and impartiality of it", and urged that Sir Henry should read it in strictest confidence to Mr. Goschen. Among the Conservative leaders whose views the Queen was eager to ascertain was the Duke of Richmond, who had been the leader of the House of Lords in 1868 and Lord President of the Council under Lord Beaconsfield from 1874 to 1884, and was noted for his conciliatory views. The Queen was now at Balmoral, and to her Sir Henry Ponsonby wrote from Osborne on August 31:

May he tell Mr. Gladstone that, should an opportunity offer, Your Majesty may perhaps speak to some leading member of the Opposition and ask him if he sees any prospect of coming to an agreement on the Franchise and Distribution Bills?

Of course it would be better to mention no names.

Sir Henry Ponsonby hopes Your Majesty will be able to see the Duke of Richmond.

He suspects from what he has heard that the leaders are a little jealous about receiving communications through Lord Rowton. Indeed Lord Rowton himself was a little shy of speaking to them.

Lord Cowper's proposal has been adopted by Lord Randolph Churchill.

Note by the Queen

Yes, but Mr. Gladstone must also be prepared to give way a little.

Should the Queen ask Mr. D. Milward after Mr. Gladstone's visit to Balmoral?

In the result, Sir Henry wrote to Mr. Gladstone on August 31, saying how much the Queen appreciated his abbreviated memorandum, but asking what concessions the Government would make if the Queen was to open negotiations with Conservative leaders with a view to avoiding the possible serious crisis that Mr. Gladstone feared.

Mr. Gladstone replied from Dalmeny on September 2, stressing the fact that a second rejection of the Franchise Bill would mean that an organic change would have to be made in the House of Lords. Upon the question of further concessions he answered bluntly that "after so many bids we can bid no more without encouragement".[1]

All through this period the much-maligned Peers kept their own counsel—save for Lord Salisbury, who frankly admitted that the Conservative Party had "very cogent reasons" for objection to the omission of a Redistribution Bill. These "very cogent reasons" were that new enfranchisement without redistribution would mean a loss to the Conservatives of 47 seats to 94 on a division. That was where the enfranchisement shoe pinched!

It was now very evident that for any compromise to be successful it must be of such a kind as to save the face of both parties. Sir Henry Ponsonby, acting of course for the Queen, was indefatigable and infinitely ingenious in suggestions. Mr. Gladstone, meanwhile, was endeavouring to secure a majority in the Lords. He had "garnered in a rich harvest" of bishops in July, and was urging his colleagues to make every effort to bring more peers into the Liberal fold so that the Franchise Bill might be passed when it reappeared in

---

[1] *Letters of Queen Victoria*, vol. iii. p. 534-5.

the autumn. Mr. Gladstone, in fact, was stiff, uncompromising and almost arrogant. A week earlier (August 28), the *Pall Mall Gazette* had published a leading article commenting upon Gladstone's visit to Midlothian that month. "The Prime Minister", it began, "has arrived at Midlothian after a triumphal procession which recalls the glories of his great campaign . . . popular enthusiasm appeared to have mounted as high yesterday as at any time in 1879 or 1880. . . . Midlothian welcomes him with open arms." The article went on to emphasise Mr. Gladstone's "position of peculiar difficulty".

For some reason best known to himself, Mr. Gladstone sent this article to Sir Henry Ponsonby for the Queen. The Queen's reply to Sir Henry, by the hand of Lady Ely, was curt. It ran (September 1):

The Queen desires me to return you the enclosed. Her Majesty says she has not read it, as she did not like the commencement. JANE ELY.

The following week found the Queen, Sir Henry Ponsonby and Mr. Gladstone in Scotland, the Queen, of course, at Balmoral, and Mr. Gladstone staying with Lord Fife at Mar Lodge; and the following letter from Sir Henry Ponsonby to Lady Ponsonby (dated September 6) sheds a very interesting light on what people thought of Balmoral:

Gladstone, with Mrs. Gladstone, came to write his name down yesterday and asked me to show Mrs. Gladstone the Minister's room and the house. "There", he said, "is the room where I have been very comfortable; it is not such a hole as Harcourt describes it" —from which I gathered that the Home Secretary had not been complimentary, when at Invercauld, about Balmoral. With them was Lady Dalhousie—looking lovely. I said I hoped she thought the house pretty. She replied, "A frank question requires a frank answer, and I will tell you I never saw anything more uncomfortable and that I coveted less". Lady Mandeville, who called later, blue with cold, was equally sour in her remarks on our Highland Palace.

We took the Gladstones later to Invercauld—raining all the way. Miss Helen Gladstone was at tea—nicely and quietly dressed, and a good face. Miss Stonor was there and her brother, who had been to the hill and had returned in pride after shooting a stag and a hind.

Mr. Gladstone said at Mar he did not know which was the best, Rossini, Bellini or Donizetti. Napier Sturt [1] from the further end of the room called out: "For once in your life, Mr. Gladstone, you are wrong. In racing parlance they would be handicapped by Rossini giving Bellini and Donizetti 21 lbs." But Mr. Gladstone considered he was right, and great argument ensued.   H. P.

Three days later the Queen, who had received a letter from the Duke of Richmond in which he suggested that the Franchise Bill should not become law until the Redistribution Bill was passed, scribbled the following note for her private secretary:

BALMORAL CASTLE.

Would Sir Henry show this to Mr. Gladstone and would he also speak to Lord Fife, who says if the

[1] The Hon. Napier Sturt, brother of Lord Alington.

Government would *consent to delay* the action of the Bill, or rather its coming into operation, till '87, he believes the Opposition would pass it, and that Sir H. James,[1] who is at Mar Lodge, is of the opinion that Mr. Gladstone should yield this, and that he would tell Mr. Gladstone so.

Would it be of any use if Mr. Gladstone, after seeing him, drove over here to luncheon again on Friday or Saturday so that the Queen could again speak to him? She thinks that would be the most useful. She fears she could not see him to-morrow, Thursday, as she has an engagement, unless he and Lord Fife would stay till after luncheon. But then he would not have seen Sir H. James, and that is important. Lord Fife is very anxious and uneasy about it, and says *there must be a compromise*, or the consequences may be very serious.

The next day (September 10) Mr. Gladstone came to stay at Balmoral, leaving Mrs. Gladstone at Mar Lodge, and as the Queen could not see him, he went for a walk with Sir Henry Ponsonby and discussed the situation. Sir Henry's notes run as follows:

Gladstone walked with me yesterday morning and talked very openly on the situation. He thinks that, apart from the agitators, there is no actual desire for what he calls organic change in the House of Lords if they will only act moderately, but that if they again reject the Bill there will be a row. At any rate, if the Tories are right they will come into office, but the Liberals will not rest quiet then till they effect this

---

[1] The Right Hon. Sir H. James, Q.C., the Liberal member for Taunton. Later, Lord James of Hereford.

organic change. He is against the change. He can't defend the present anomalies—but it works fairly if used with wisdom, and a change would be far more than he could undertake to guide. Besides which he likes the hereditary principle, and fears that if wiped away we shall have a powerful plutocracy which he detests. The House of Lords, it is true, are always opposed to a Liberal Government, but we must suffer a little to avoid worse evils. Therefore he earnestly hopes the Tories will see a way out of the difficulty. I asked what concessions the Government would make. He said they had made enough already, at any rate they could offer nothing more. If the Opposition made any suggestion he would consider it.

I asked about Lord Cowper's letter. He said there was nothing impossible in that, if the Tories would adopt it, though he did not much like it. He thought there was some reason in Lord R. Churchill's suggestion that they should at once go on with the Distribution Bill in the Autumn Session, but that must be after the passing of the Franchise Bill. These were only his own ideas and therefore liable to modification after consulting the Cabinet. But one thing was clear, the proposal must come from the Tories.

The Queen is going to see the Duke of Richmond. I told Charles Peel, who conducted the intercourse when the last rejection took place. He says the Duke of Richmond is more amenable than any other of the Tory Peers and sees the danger ahead, which many of them do not. But of course he must act under Salisbury. However, no one need know of his being consulted, as if he comes here he comes naturally as an Aberdeenshire neighbour. I asked Peel what the Tories would propose—of course he did not know, but his idea is that they would suggest that the Franchise Bill should not come into operation till the Distribution Bill was passed—or, if this were blocked, till 1887. I later asked Gladstone about this. He replied that Albert Grey [1] had made a similar proposal, but Northcote would not adopt it. Therefore he did not expect the Tories would take it. I think Gladstone would take any course that would lead out of the difficulty, but, of course, the extremists will not let him have his own way entirely. John Morley [2] made a good and moderate speech yesterday. Gladstone wants the Queen to see Morley. Of course, impossible. The Queen asked Gladstone to stay on till to-day and invited Fife to stay here also. This will leave Mrs. Gladstone nearly alone with Lady Lonsdale, whom she hates.

The weather here for the last three days has been lovely. We all went out for a drive in Glenbeg, which was beautiful. Mr. Gladstone enthusiastic, and so also was Fife, who, strange to say, had never seen it before.

On September 14 the Queen saw the Duke of Richmond, who in turn saw Lord Cairns. Later, the Duke sent the Queen a memorandum in which he asked if it would not be possible to insert a clause in the Franchise Bill by which it would come into operation at the same time as the Redistribution Bill. The Queen sent this to

---

[1] The Liberal member for South Northumberland, son of General the Hon. Charles Grey, later Earl Grey and Governor-General of Canada.
[2] Later Secretary of State for India and Viscount Morley of Blackburn.

Sir Henry Ponsonby, who sent it on to Mr. Gladstone. Gladstone's reply was brief. It ran:

It may be right to mention that nearly the same proposal as that which you name was made and rejected on both sides, supported by no one, and withdrawn.

Consequently, Sir Henry wrote to the Queen on September 14:

General Sir Henry Ponsonby humbly begs leave to return the Duke of Richmond's letter and proposal, as what he suggests is what the Government have repeatedly said it was impossible for them to agree to, viz. that the Franchise Bill should not become law till the Distribution Bill had passed.

The next day (September 15) Mr. Gladstone, who had returned to Mar Lodge, Lord Fife's residence, drove with Mrs. Gladstone and their daughter Helen to have luncheon with the Princess of Wales at Abergeldie Castle, which is about three miles from Balmoral. It was arranged that as they passed Balmoral, Sir Henry Ponsonby should meet them at Crathie Bridge, but there was much to discuss and brevity was not the strong point of Mr. Gladstone. Sir Henry had therefore to get up into the four-wheeled dog-cart and drive on with them. He stood 6 feet 2 inches and Nature had never intended him for a bodkin, but he must have managed to get up alongside of Mr. Gladstone and the coachman while Mrs. and Miss Gladstone sat behind. It must have been very difficult to discuss serious politics in so cramped a position, and as there was time to spare, Mr. Gladstone and Sir Henry Ponsonby de-

cided to get down and walk, while Mrs. and Miss
Gladstone, still sitting on the back seat, drove on to
Abergeldie.

Sir Henry Ponsonby's own account of the conversation (dated September 16) runs as follows:

I met Gladstone on the Crathie Bridge and gave him
my letter to read which contained the Duke of Richmond's proposal, but I avoided the Duke's name,
though, of course, Gladstone knew at once it was not
mine, and without circumvention called it his "waste
of breath"! and added "did he really make such a proposal". He said it was unnecessary to discuss it as I must
see myself that he simply asked for the point which was
under contention. He then argued at some length (I
drove on with him—Mrs. and Miss Gladstone sitting
behind) upon the proposal I had written before, suggested to me by Mr. Charles Peel, that the Franchise
Bill should not operate till 1887, or until the Redistribution Bill was passed. He said this would not do as
it would force on Parliament to sit for seven years and
would leave Government till then at the mercy of the
Opposition—besides which the Opposition would not
take it—which was true.

As we passed under the Merchant's house at Crathie,
or rather, as they call it, East Balmoral, at least twenty
men, women and children appeared on the bank—I
did not know there were so many grown inhabitants—
and gave him three ringing hearty cheers—a Balmoral
demonstration! He was highly pleased. He then told
his womenkind to go on in the carriage while he walked
with me. Helen Gladstone objected particularly to

201

having to go and sit and wait with the Princess of Wales at Abergeldie for him, but Mrs. Gladstone rather liked it.

He then told me he was terribly taken aback by my letter showing that even the most liberal-minded of the Tories did not budge one inch from his demands, and this of course made compromise impossible. He was a little relieved by my saying the Duke of Richmond spoke only for himself, but he had no longer hopes of Lord Salisbury. He believed Lord Salisbury would not care if the House of Lords were abolished to-morrow. He would still be the Tory leader, and of course, in whatever House existed, a far more powerful man than he was at present. Who could advise the Queen now as an independent? Argyll—he was too much united to the Liberals; Lord Hampden—well, yes, but he doubted the Tories listening to a very un-doubted Liberal; Malmesbury—he thought that a good idea. Winmarleigh too weak (the Duke of Richmond had already told me that Winmarleigh and others had approached Lord Salisbury, who asked if they wanted to move him by octogenarians in their second childhood); Northcote—mere slave to Salisbury; Beach—yes, he believed he had power and intelligence. But it was getting short of time—in six weeks Parliament meets and then it will be too late, and he had to consider what he should do if the Bill were again rejected. Of course, if rejected by a much smaller majority, there would be hope for sending it up again, but there was no reason to expect this. Dissolution? but on what—the cry would be the abolition of the House of Lords before anything else. His own re-signation? This he would like best, but he did not think he could, and it might possibly merely have the effect of leaving power in the hands of those who would be forced to proceed to most ulterior measures. Resignation of the Government? This would not be fair to the Queen, who could not find another; or even if they did form another Ministry would dissolve and he felt sure would be beaten, and he would have to return to office, after a period of confusion, pledged to measures which he hated, but which he could not then deny the necessity of, for the good of the country. The creation of peers? He did not know what the Queen would say, and he did not like the expedient. He was much perplexed. All could be avoided if the Tories would meet him half-way. Although he objected strongly to Lord R. Churchill's proposal that the Government should at once in the autumn proceed with Distribution, yet there was sense in it; or the Tories might very fairly claim the right to be informed on the provisions of the Distribution Bill—but they would concede nothing. I told him that they disbelieved in the heartiness of the agitation. He answered that if the Liberal meetings had taken place in Chatsworth, Knowsley, and other Liberal parts, as the Tory picnics had done, he should also doubt it. But as they were got up by the people themselves, he could not doubt it. Seventy thousand men at Glasgow last week could not all have been paid to walk through the streets and pass resolutions. But he would say nothing himself on this as he only heard of these meetings from the newspaper or the addresses sent to him. His Whips, however, told him that the cry was increasing, and that the question would be put at the hustings now, not only about Franchise, but about the House of Lords.

It was a most interesting conversation, and he was most earnest. I walked back here, and after luncheon repeated it all to Her Majesty, who was naturally disturbed, and the postponement of my leave till we have time for consideration is one of the first consequences.

The afternoon post brought me a letter from Albert Grey, to whom I had written, pressing his amendment as the best compromise. I think there is much in what he says, but if neither Party accepts it one cannot proceed with it.

The Gladstones were in full delight of their expedition up Ben Macdhui. He and Helen Gladstone walked up and down a mile each way. Mrs. Gladstone rode up, and Lady Ely tells me that sitting has been very uncomfortable to her ever since. On Sunday, Albani, who is at Old Mar Lodge, came to Fife's private church and sang the anthem "Angels ever bright". Gladstone delighted. She also sang the Psalms, etc.

One thing for certain did emerge from this conversation, and that was that Gladstone would not as yet consider any proposal by which the passing of the Franchise Bill depended upon the passing of a Redistribution Bill, and Sir Henry Ponsonby wrote that day to Mr. Gladstone:

I have told the Queen that I think it would be useless to make any proposal to the Government which causes the operation of the Franchise Bill to depend on the passing of the Distribution Bill. If I am wrong you can correct me.

Suggestions still poured in. To those who suggested a dissolution as a means of solving the complicated issue, Mr. Gladstone said that he would only dissolve on the question of organic changes in the House of Lords, and not on the merits of the Franchise Bill. As neither he nor the Conservatives wanted this, a dissolution seemed to be out of the question.

Mr. Albert Grey, M.P., the son of General the Hon. Charles Grey, who had preceded Sir H. Ponsonby as private secretary to the Queen, now embodied in a letter to Sir Henry Ponsonby (dated September 14) his former proposal that the Franchise Bill should not come into operation until 1887, or until the Redistribution Bill was passed, whichever was the earlier. His letter ran:

MY DEAR GENERAL—My proposal was not that the Franchise Bill should not come into operation till 1886, but that no elections should be held on the new electorate created by the Bill before the 1st January 1887, unless Parliament should otherwise determine.

The arguments for the particular form of this proposal were:

(1) There is a good precedent for this course. The Act of 1867 contained a clause which suspended the operation of that Act, as far as the holding of elections was concerned, till January 1, 1869. . . .

This date was subsequently altered to November 1, 1868, by a clause in the Boundaries Act, which completed Mr. Disraeli's measures of reform and which was passed in the Session of 1868.

The Government admit that it would be desirable to pass both Extension and Redistribution in one session, but they maintain that the difficulty of doing this would be so great that they have reluctantly been obliged to separate two measures which they would have preferred to have dealt with together. They accordingly propose to pass Extension one session and Redistribution the next.

Supposing that the Extension Bill had been carried with my amendment incorporated in it and the Government were to succeed in carrying out their intention of carrying a Redistribution Bill next year, the date mentioned in my amendment would be changed by a clause in the Redistribution Bill, in the same way that the date in the suspension clause of the Act of 1867 was changed by the Boundaries Act of 1868.

(2) The acceptance of my amendment would afford the Government ample security that they would have full opportunity of carrying into effect the very policy they themselves professed and avowed.

(3) The course suggested by my amendment would not be open to the objection, which you point out, to the proposal that the Franchise Bill should not come into operation till 1886, viz. that the new electors would not be competent to vote till 1887. At the same time I must say that this objection does not seem to me to be fatal to the proposal you refer to, as it would be quite open to Parliament to insert in the Redistribution Bill provisions altering the registration dates.

The objections to this proposal of mine were not serious.

Mr. Gladstone said Parliament was most likely to pass a Redistribution Bill if it knew it only had one session in which to do the work instead of two. Sir Henry James backed up his leader by remarking that a sportsman with a one-barrelled gun took greater pains over his shot than the man with a double-barrelled gun. (Sir Henry, however, who is a very good shot, always uses a double-barrelled gun.)

The most fatal objections to my amendment were that it went too far for the Radicals and not far enough for the Tories. Hicks Beach and George Hamilton denounced it as soon as I brought it forward, and as I saw that I could not possibly get a good division, as the Tory leaders gave my proposal a curse instead of a blessing, I got Mr. Goschen to appeal to me to withdraw, which accordingly I did, no division being, in his opinion, and in mine, much better than a very bad division—several of the Liberals, too, who had promised me their support, having learnt that the Opposition Front Bench would not support me, were at Ascot instead of in the House. If all the Liberals who had promised me had been there, I should have divided—as a demonstration of Liberal opinion— as, however, half of them were not there, this was impossible.

Now, you remark that Ministers say it is not likely that any compromise can be arranged on some such basis as that supplied by my amendment, because Northcote and the Front Opposition Bench expressed their intention to vote against it and the Radicals don't like it—and I will admit that what I have said up to now tends to confirm Ministerial impressions.

You will, however, recollect that in the observations which took place in the House of Lords with reference to the private negotiations between Lord Cairns and Lord Granville, it was stated that Lord Cairns had said that if the Government would accept some such amendment as mine, they would go on with the Bill; and it was only on Lord Granville's intimation to Lord Cairns that the Government could not undertake to accept such an amendment, on the very inadequate plea that the House of Commons had already rejected it, that the Bill was sentenced to its doom of suspended animation.

This offer of Lord Cairns shows that at that time at any rate the Conservatives were not unwilling by way of compromise to agree to the passage of the Bill with some such security as that offered by my amendment.

This as to the Radicals. I have not personally the very smallest doubt that had the Lords sent back the Bill thus amended to the Commons, the House of Commons would have gladly accepted it.

Baxter told me that if the Lords did amend the Bill in this way, he would actually go down to his constituency and speak in favour of the Bill as amended.

Henry Fowler, the Member for Wolverhampton, the most rising and influential of Radicals outside the Cabinet, told me he would speak in favour of the Government accepting the Lords' amendment; so did Sir George Campbell, a man of no weight but a fair type of the extreme and impracticable Radical. I do not believe a dozen Radicals would have voted last July against the acceptance of the Lords' amendment. I have asked extreme men among my constituents who are very savage against the Lords—would you have rather had the Franchise Bill with my amendment safe on the pages of the Statute Book and a fair prospect of a dissolution on the new electorate, or no Franchise Bill at all and the probability of a General Election on its present electorate? In every case the answer has been: The Franchise Bill with your amendment.

I am afraid I have been unduly long, but I have not hesitated to tell you all I know, for I think you will be glad to know it. May I now suggest to you the course which I have for long thought the Lords might, without any loss of honour or dignity, follow?

Let them amend the Bill and not suspend it, and let them plead as justification of the change in their tactics, that they know now what they were ignorant of before, viz. that had they amended the Bill in July, the House of Commons, in spite of the refusal of Lord Granville and the Government to the terms offered by Lord Cairns, would have accepted it. This course it seems to me could be taken without the loss of one jot or tittle of their pride, and then if the Commons refused to accept their amendment, should it be a reasonable one, the blame and onus of throwing out this Bill would be transferred from the Lords to the Commons.

By adopting the course they have, the Lords have,

in the opinion of nearly everyone I meet with in this part of the world, placed themselves in an indefensible position, and the feeling against them is growing very strong. I do trust with all my heart that you may be successful in your effort to bring about a compromise, and believe me, yours very sincerely,

ALBERT GREY.

Sir Henry Ponsonby now replied to Albert Grey (September 16):

Your letter was a solace to my thoughts and was not a whit too long as it argues out the points which occupy my mind. The position is this. The Government decline to listen to any proposal which causes the operation of the Franchise Bill to depend on passing the Distribution Bill, because that places their Bill at the mercy of the Opposition. The Opposition decline to consider any proposal which would alter the Franchise Bill so that it would come into force without Distribution, because this places them at the mercy of the Government. If these two determinations are inflexible, compromise is impossible, but as the reason given in each case gives room for further discussion your amendment comes into prominence as a possible mode of satisfying to some extent the two requirements.

The proposal I mentioned to you was suggested as having strong support on both sides, and it seemed to me similar to yours, though yours is couched in precise language. According to both parties the new Franchise could be claimed as soon as the Distribution Bill passes, and if it does not pass the obstructives will gain nothing as far as the Franchise Bill goes, and that would come into operation on a certain date and the new electors could vote on the 1st January 1887. The Tory Chiefs, as I understand, positively refuse to listen to this as it destroys their demand, and Ministers dislike it as interfering with the convenience of dissolution. As far as I can make out, the Liberals would, as you also tell me, accept it, and therefore possibly the Ministerial objection (which is not an absolute refusal) must be modified. But since the Tories won't listen to it, it is not probable that the Chief will propose it as an amendment and the independent motion of men like Lord Wemyss finds no favour at all.

To this letter Mr. Grey replied (September 18):

My DEAR GENERAL—You ask, is it possible to induce or coerce the two opposing forces to meet? I answer, that depends on the Moderates and on the Tory Moderates. If they can organise sufficient pressure to coerce their Leaders to accept a good *practical* compromise like the one you suggest, open though it be to formidable objections, I feel certain that there is sufficient independence on our side to coerce our Leaders, if they want coercing, to do ditto, but the Tory Moderates must make the first move. It is necessary if there is to be a compromise that the Lords should amend and not suspend the Bill. Could not the Tory Moderates secure this? Might they not come forward and say, "We have reason to believe that had the Lords amended the Bill last July in the way suggested by Lord Cairns the Commons would have agreed to pass the Bill as they amended it. We must therefore *insist upon* the Commons having a chance of considering next November the Lords' amendments, notwithstanding anything the Government may say in debate."

There are many men on the Tory side as well as on the Liberal side who dislike being sacrificed to the pugnacity of Chamberlain and Salisbury. Randolph Churchill has declared himself to be in favour of compromise, but then he cannot be relied on, for he never holds the same views on any question for more than one and a half hours.

The men who occur to me as men who are likely to have the wish and the power (if they will only use it) to organise a pressure on their own Leaders in favour of compromise, are Sir Henry Holland (Conservative M.P. for Midhurst), Albert Peel (Liberal M.P. for Warwick), Lord Emlyn (Liberal M.P. for Carmarthenshire), in the House of Commons, and Pembroke and Brownlow in the Lords.

Pembroke told me in a very decided tone at the time of the crisis, that if the Government would accept as a compromise the suspension of the Bill till 1886, and Lord Salisbury prove unwilling to agree, the Lords would not follow him.

I may also tell you that Sir Michael Hicks Beach said to me last Easter (we were staying at the same house), "If your amendment should be accepted I would have no objection to the Bill".

I will write to Loyd-Lindsay, my wife's uncle, and ask him if he cannot do something.

You are quite right in thinking Lord Grey would

not prove a good mediator, and for an additional reason to the one you give, viz. that he sticks to principle and kicks at compromise. He objects strongly to any amendment which has no favour in his eyes, maintaining that no security short of making the Franchise Bill depend upon the passing of the Redistribution Bill is worth consideration.

With a heavy shipload of good wishes to your efforts to put an end to this most unhappy position, believe me, yours very sincerely,   ALBERT GREY.

Mr. A. Grey's proposal was the most feasible compromise yet suggested, but as events were to prove, it was not the final solution.

Another suggestion was made by Sir E. Hamilton, Mr. Gladstone's private secretary, who wrote to Sir H. Ponsonby on September 15:

MY DEAR SIR HENRY PONSONBY—I presume all hopes of a compromise are not absolutely at an end; and I think it behoves every individual, however insignificant he may be, who is desirous of peace, to contribute his mite of suggestion. I have a humble contribution to make; and I wish to make it to you, as you will best know the "lie of the land" on both sides after the recent visits to Balmoral of Mr. Gladstone and the Duke of Richmond. Of course, my suggestion is made entirely on my own responsibility; and I should not think it worth putting forward, had it not been favourably viewed by the few with whom I have broached it.

I assume that the Franchise Bill will be passed in the House of Commons in the autumn session, practically identical in terms to those of the Bill of last session; and as such it will be sent up to the House of Lords again. They will, I take it, either deal with it as they did in the summer, or (which is more probable) read it a second time and postpone the further consideration of it indefinitely, in order, as they would urge, that the Government should proceed to introduce the Redistribution measure.

It is too much to expect the Government to lay on the table a complicated Bill of that kind without any guarantee that the Lords would accept the other (Franchise) Bill. It is too much to expect the Lords to swallow the Franchise Bill without some further guarantee as to the Redistribution scheme.

My proposal, then, is this: that as soon as the Franchise Bill leaves the Commons and is sent up to the Lords, the Government should move resolutions in the House of Commons, explaining fully the terms of their proposed Redistribution measure. These resolutions would no doubt give rise to a lengthened debate; but with a little patience it ought to be perfectly feasible to get an expression of opinion upon them in the House of Commons. If they were favourably entertained, the House of Lords might fairly count upon the acceptance of the Bill giving legal effect to these resolutions. The House of Lords would have a distinct guarantee of the Government as to the Redistribution measure and therefore might fairly pass the Franchise Bill, as their main contention now is that they can't pass one part of Reform (Franchise) without knowing the contents of the other part of Reform (Redistribution). It would be a give-and-take on both sides, which is essential to a compromise. Both the Lords and the Government would, however, avoid eating their own words.

You will kindly understand that I put this forward wholly and entirely on my own responsibility. I have no notion whether Mr. Gladstone would accept such a compromise; but of this I feel tolerably sure, that he would wish to give a favourable consideration to a proposal of this kind, if it came from the other side, sooner than keep up the conflict, which he desires to avoid.

I may add that there are precedents for proceeding in the way I suggest, *e.g.* the Irish Church resolutions in 1868, but, of course, to be of any material use, the Redistribution resolutions would have to be fuller and lay down the lines of the Bill more in detail.

Such a procedure would have this further advantage—that, while it is not easy for the general public to follow a complicated measure in Bill form (and a Redistribution Bill must be more or less complicated), they would be able to understand the contents of a series of resolutions. Another advantage of proceeding by resolutions is that in connection with them there is only one stage in the House of Commons. . . .

That Sir Henry preferred Mr. Albert Grey's proposals to Sir E. Hamilton's is evident from the following draft of a letter which he wrote to Sir E. Hamilton on September 20:

MY DEAR HAMILTON—I am scarcely in a position to make both sides listen. Mr. Gladstone explains his views clearly. But other side naturally suspicious of my views, and I have only seen the Duke of Richmond. I think Tories disbelieve feeling among the people and say that what the Queen should do would be to stop the Ministers from agitating against institutions of the State they are bound to support. They believe Mr. Gladstone, etc., as individuals, but these have no power to make it certain that Distribution will follow Franchise. If he does not, Tories will be entirely swamped. I say nonsense. Parliament would not pass unfair Bill. They say it will be conceding to agitation, and then, of course, Tories will be laughed at and destroyed.

Present conflict is a struggle for existence on Tories' part. With this basis compromise is difficult. Still we can try. I prefer Albert Grey's amendment. I hear Tories accept it now and I am told the Liberals would (D. of R. won't). Your proposal more like Cowper's. How can you resolve the intricacies of Redistribution, boundaries for instance? Still, I will see if it can be listened to.   H. P.

To this letter Sir E. Hamilton replied on September 21:

MY DEAR SIR HENRY PONSONBY—Many thanks for your interesting letter. There are none so blind as those who won't see; and the tactics of the Tories entirely surpass my comprehension. I believe myself they are cutting their own throats, but I suppose they would say, "Thank you, we know our own business best".

I readily admit that Franchise by resolution would

216

not be free from difficulty; but then with every alternative difficulties present themselves. The Government showed last Session that with determination they would carry a measure practically intact. Therefore, there is a fair guarantee that they could stick to their Redistribution without going into local particulars. If they failed to carry the House of Commons with them, they would be bound to dissolve; and a dissolution could only take place, whether the Franchise Bill were passed or not, on the present electoral basis. [Why? H. P.]

In reply, Sir Henry Ponsonby mentioned the "1886" proposal, which, he said, was supported "by many Liberals (one a Minister, but not Cabinet) and by many Tories". No one, he added, liked a compromise, but this seemed to be the best as it would secure the ultimate safety of the Franchise Bill and would prevent obstruction.

Sir E. Hamilton's reply (dated September 24) runs as follows:

MY DEAR SIR HENRY PONSONBY—When I say that if the Government fail to carry their measure of Redistribution they would be bound to dissolve on the present electoral basis, I assume that the Redistribution Bill must be fought out next year, which is the sixth Session of the present Parliament, and which for working purposes and for other reasons I regard as practically its last. If then the Government failed to carry their Redistribution Bill, or in other words were beaten upon it (because they could not drop it for mere want of time—they would have to sit on for nine months if necessary), they would be obliged in honour and in deference to constitutional usage to resign or dissolve almost immediately, and both courses would entail prompt dissolution. Such a dissolution must necessarily take place before the 1st January 1886, which is the date already in the Franchise Bill of last Session, anterior to which the new electors will be unable to vote. That is my security.

I presume that the proposal to which you refer, and which you say has met with some favour on both sides, is intended practically to defer the operation of the Franchise Bill for yet another year—up to 1st January 1887, unless a Redistribution Bill is previously passed.

If this were to satisfy the Tories I should say, "Let the time be extended by all means". But I don't believe it will be any *real* additional safeguard to them; because (as I have said) I believe a Redistribution Bill must be passed next Session or never in this Parliament. A Parliament in its seventh Session (in 1886) would be practically an expiring Parliament, and no expiring Parliament would ever be able to tackle such a question.

I notice that Northcote, in his Newcastle speech, says that the question is whether "We (the Tories) are to be allowed to know what the whole measure of the Government is". He says nothing about additional guarantees against the passage and operation of the Franchise Bill without Redistribution. Now my suggestion, in the main, would supply him with what he wants. This autumn the Tories would know the effect of "the whole measure". They would have the Franchise proposals of the Government "cut and dry" in a Bill, they could have the Redistribution proposals in a less detailed form, but practically explained to them in a series of resolutions. The chief objection to such a course would be that it would lead to considerable waste of time. You would have immense debating on the resolutions; and you would probably have a *réchauffé* of the debate when the contents of the resolutions were embodied in a Bill. But waste of time is better than a war between the two Houses, and the resolutions would distinctly test the feeling of the House and country on the Redistribution scheme of the Government. If they were carried, the main *raison d'être* for stopping the Franchise Bill would vanish. If the Commons disapproved the resolutions the Government would be bound to resign or dissolve. The Lords might fairly be expected to wait till the result of the resolution was known before taking definite action on the Franchise Bill.

But I will spare you any further airing of my own ideas, especially as my writing is necessarily (in an express train) not of the best.

Yours sincerely,   E. HAMILTON.

Meanwhile (on September 20) the Duke of Richmond had written to Queen Victoria summarising the events of last week in which he had taken part:

The Duke of Richmond and Gordon with his humble duty to your Majesty. The Duke communicated to Lord Cairns the substance of the conversation the Duke had the honour of having with Your Majesty, and also the memorandum the Duke received from Sir Henry Ponsonby.

The Duke entirely concurs in all that Lord Cairns says in his letter.[1]

The Duke would venture to remind Your Majesty that the one thing the Conservative Party contend for is that a General Election should not take place under the new Franchise without a Redistribution Bill having been passed.

The pledge of the Government to endeavour to pass such a measure would not be sufficient.[2]

Sir Henry Ponsonby's comment to the Queen on this letter was as follows:

BALMORAL,
Sept. 21st, 1884.

General Sir Henry Ponsonby begs leave to return the Duke of Richmond's letter.

Lord Cairns desires a compromise and discusses the situation very fairly. He makes three suggestions:

---

[1] Lord Cairns, in his letter dated September 19, wrote that, when the two branches of the legislature disagreed, he would always be very glad to see a compromise. The only modes of compromise which seemed to him to be open were: (1) to provide in the Franchise Bill that it should come into effect on a day to be named in the Redistribution Bill; (2) to provide in the Franchise Bill that it should come into effect on the 1st January 1886, unless the Redistribution was passed sooner. But the Government could hardly, after what they had said and done, accept either of these proposals. He therefore suggested (3) that the House of Lords should read the Franchise Bill a second time and then pass a resolution "that H.M. Government having undertaken to introduce and use their best endeavours to pass a Redistribution Bill, this House will go into Committee on this (Franchise) Bill as soon as the Redistribution Bill shall have come up to this House".

[2] *Letters of Queen Victoria,* vol. iii. pp. 539-40.

(1) Is similar to that proposed by the Duke of Richmond which Mr. Gladstone could not accept.

(2) Is what Your Majesty suggested; but the Duke of Richmond and Mr. Gladstone did not like it, but did not reject it; and

(3) Is a new proposal altogether, but it places both Franchise Bill and Distribution Bill entirely at the mercy of the House of Lords. And he feels convinced that Mr. Gladstone would not accept it.

Lord Cairns thinks that the Opposition would accept No. 2 but that the Government could not.

There may be, and no doubt are, objections to it, but Sir Henry James thought that many Liberals would listen to it. At any rate it is the proposal which meets with least resistance on both sides.

Perhaps, without mentioning names, he might ask Mr. Gladstone's opinion on the two latter proposals— and he might thank the Duke of Richmond and tell him that Your Majesty will see whether the suggestions are such as it is probable the Government will accept, or at any rate acquiesce in.

On September 24, Sir Henry Ponsonby sent on to Mr. Gladstone Lord Cairns's suggestions, without mentioning whence they came, adding that the Queen was cognisant of the correspondence and that she hoped Mr. Gladstone would see some means of accepting one of the proposals.

Gladstone, now in the height of his Midlothian campaign, at last poured out his heart to Sir Henry Ponsonby. He vowed (September 25) he would "cheerfully summon the Cabinet for the consideration of any proposal on which the Queen may have the desire that they should be consulted". He objected to Sir Henry Ponsonby's proposals, however, and went the length to ask that the Opposition should ask the Government for "clearer specifications and more binding pledges in regard to the *principles* of Redistribution. *What in this respect do they want?*" was his cry. "I have honestly tried to learn and have totally failed."

With this letter he sent the following covering letter to Sir Henry Ponsonby (September 25):

MY DEAR SIR H. PONSONBY—I send you a letter approaching the dimensions of a pamphlet. I have little time to write, but wish to say two things.

Right and left I have been declining addresses, except where my train stops, and I have chosen a train that stops at exceedingly few places. I believe that if I took a train in England stopping like the Scotch trains, exactly the same scenes would be exhibited.

Secondly, I have to report with great regret that on Tuesday evening Lord Rosebery's horse got his leg into a hole and threw him violently. He has been heavily bruised and has much pain, besides the fracture of the collar bone, which in itself is no great matter.[1]

Sir Henry Ponsonby submitted Mr. Gladstone's letter to the Queen with the following covering note (September 26):

General Sir Henry Ponsonby humbly begs leave to submit a letter he has received from Mr. Gladstone.

In this he declines at once the first proposal as Sir Henry Ponsonby felt sure he must do. But he enters at

[1] Quoted in *Letters of Queen Victoria*, vol. iii. pp. 542-4.

length into the objections to the second proposal without actually refusing it.

Some of these can be answered while others naturally are such as may be made to any compromise.

In the end of the letter Mr. Gladstone also makes suggestions—which may be considered, though Sir Henry Ponsonby doubts their meeting with any favour from the Opposition.

He would humbly suggest that after Your Majesty has finished with the letter, he might answer Mr. Gladstone's objections.

That he should at the same time ask the Duke of Richmond to ascertain the opinion of Lord Salisbury and Sir Stafford Northcote on this proposal (he could mention at the same time the other proposals).

If the Tory leaders think the first proposal worth consideration, or that they do not absolutely object, then Your Majesty might distinctly place it before the Government and the Opposition.

The Queen approved of these suggestions, and accordingly Sir Henry Ponsonby wrote to Mr. Gladstone on October 1st, and kept the following note of what he said.

True, I did not refer to conclusion of your letter of 25th (which referred to the necessity for excluding the reform of the House of Lords from the arena of political conflict).

You know the Queen is quite alive to serious state of affairs if Lords reject, and she shows this by her efforts for compromise.

I can't say what Opposition think—they must consult each other.

Your objection to my proposal is serious.

I sent to Opposition the suggestion made by Hartington.

On Hartington's suggestion I added—as to myself—"if you do really and unconditionally, etc."

Meanwhile Sir E. Hamilton had taken up again the rôle of peacemaker, and on September 26 he wrote to Sir H. Ponsonby:

My dear Sir H. Ponsonby—There was a very plausible argument used by Sir S. Northcote the other day, which I omitted to notice. He said in effect, "If the Radicals get their Franchise Bill what inducement will there be for them to pass the Redistribution measure of the Government, which is not likely to accord with their taste?"

The answer, however, to this is complete if the idea of proceeding by resolutions were adopted. In such resolutions the Government would lay down the principles of their Bill and to these principles they would be bound, not only in honour but by the House of Commons (assuming they passed), to adhere. If, then, the Radicals insisted upon making the Government (as Sir S. N. says) "put their Redistribution on a false principle", the Government would be in effect beaten and be obliged to resign or dissolve. Dissolution, therefore, and dissolution on the present constituency would be the pistol at the heads of the Radicals; and therefore Northcote's argument falls to the ground.

224

I am not, of course, prepared to say that, in the hint Mr. G. threw out in his letter to you of yesterday, he had in his mind my method of procedure, but it must be something very akin to that, and when I broached the idea to him in the summer he only put it aside and did not reject it.

It occurs to me (but I know I am treading on delicate ground) that, if anything of this kind can be hammered out which takes the fancy of some of the Tories and which promises to lead to a solution, the Prince of Wales might do something towards bringing about the desired end.

I may mention that I had a talk with Dilke to-day, and he was rather taken with the idea.

Yours sincerely,   E. HAMILTON.

This letter was preceded by the following telegram from Sir E. Hamilton to Sir Henry Ponsonby:

Might not the latter part of Mr. Gladstone's long letter to you yesterday be worked in with my suggestion? I think it is easy to give complete answer to difficulties which other side might see in it.

Meanwhile, Sir E. Hamilton had written:

10 DOWNING STREET, WHITEHALL,
27th Sept. 1884.

DEAR SIR HENRY PONSONBY—I am circulating, according to Mr. Gladstone's direction, your letter to him of the 22nd and his reply of the 25th. Will you, to save time, show Hartington (who I understand will be at Balmoral to-morrow) the correspondence and ask him to let me have any remarks he may like to make, in order that I may put them into the box while it is being circulated?

If the Tories insist upon an enactment, it is useless to expect that any arrangement can be come to. If there is to be a compromise, both sides must give up something: but if they were to get an enactment they would be giving up nothing. It has, in effect, been what they have been fighting for all along. Anything short of an absolute enactment which gives every reasonable security against the operation of the Franchise Bill by itself, *i.e.* unaccompanied by Redistribution, would, I think, be favourably considered by Mr. Gladstone.

Yours sincerely,　　　　　　　　　E. HAMILTON.

This was followed on September 29 by the following letter from Sir E. Hamilton to Sir Henry Ponsonby:

DEAR SIR HENRY PONSONBY—I would preface the resolutions, detailing the Redistribution measure, with a resolution pledging the Government to proceed with Redistribution the moment the Franchise Bill is *passed*. If the House of Commons adopts this and the principles of the scheme, I hold that the Government is bound to proceed with Redistribution based on those principles next year, and if it fails in the endeavour, by obstruction or by combination of party against the scheme, the Government is practically beaten and bound to resign or dissolve. Both courses would entail dissolution and dissolution on the old constituency. It seems to me that every security is furnished by the course. The Tories, moreover, might well remember that they are dealing with gentlemen who have not the smallest desire to take unfair advantage of the Opposition.

Mr. Gladstone's objections to your proposal No. 1 was (if I recollect rightly) that it kept the Franchise Bill suspended indefinitely. This would not be the case with the other procedure. The moment the resolutions were passed in the House of Commons the Lords would have to make up their mind whether to proceed with or stop the Franchise Bill, and the Redistribution Bill would not be produced until the Lords had passed the Franchise Bill.

Mr. Gladstone is himself not at all averse to resolutions on the basis of an accommodation with the Tory Party, if resolutions promise to secure the passage of the Franchise Bill; but he does not think that the Government could put forward resolutions as a *bid*; or indeed make any other bid after bidding so much without effect. In short, it is for the Opposition now to make a move. I take it that after Lord Salisbury has gone and committed himself at Glasgow this week, the door will then be closed for compromise.

To further explain — the difference between (A) proceeding by resolution, and by (B) enactment providing that the Franchise Bill should not operate until the 1st January 1887 unless the Redistribution were passed at an earlier date, I conceive to be this:

(A) If the Redistribution Bill passed the House of Commons, the Lords would have strong reasons for accepting it; otherwise they would run the risk of a dissolution in January 1886 on the new constituency without Redistribution.

If the Redistribution Bill failed to pass the House of Commons, the Lords would get what they want, viz. a dissolution on the old constituency next year.

(B) The Commons, and (if not the Commons) the Lords would be tempted to defeat the Redistribution Bill.

In short, with (A) the Government would have some leverage behind them; with (B) none.

Yours sincerely,   E. HAMILTON.

In a postscript he added:

Chamberlain, I understand, does not agree with Dilke; nor does Sir J. Lambert, who is an important man, and has had greater reform experiences than anybody.

Sir Henry, in a letter to Sir E. Hamilton (dated September 30), now summarised the possible solutions to the problems as follows:

(1) Suspension of Franchise Bill in House of Lords until they receive the Redistribution Bill.
(2) Clause deferring date of operation.
(3) Resolution explaining Redistribution.

The precise stage that each of these proposals had reached was as follows:

(1) Mr. Gladstone condemns.
(2) Under consideration.
(3) Put forward.

Lord H. and Mr. G. ask what do they want. I have put forward this feeler.

I told the Q., who says not much use as long as Prime Minister makes speeches like Carlisle. You cannot parley with a man who is threatening you.

Meanwhile, the Duke of Richmond had also been active as a peacemaker, and on September 27 he wrote to Queen Victoria from Gordon Castle, Fochabers, telling her that he expected Lord Salisbury to visit him there privately on October 7, and he asked if he might communicate her views to him.

Queen Victoria replied on September 28, urging that "the great object must be to maintain the important position of the House of Lords unimpaired, which might be endangered by exciting a serious conflict".[1]

The next day Sir Henry Ponsonby wrote privately to the Duke of Richmond:

BALMORAL,
Sept. 29th, 1884.

My DEAR DUKE—I am writing this from myself and not by the Queen's command.

I mentioned to you the proposal to affirm by resolutions the principle of the Redistribution measure before the Franchise Bill was finally passed.

It has been pointed out that if the Opposition do really and unconditionally desire the settlement of the whole question in the present Parliament, their course is to demand from the Government clearer specification and more binding pledges in regard to the principles of Redistribution.

[1] For full text see *Letters of Queen Victoria,* vol. iii. p. 546.

I do not think that at present the Government have any idea of what you want in this respect, and it might turn out that both parties were to some extent agreed on the foundation of the Redistribution proposals.

Four days later (October 3) Sir Henry Ponsonby wrote again to the Duke of Richmond:

MY DEAR DUKE—I return Lord Cairns' letter—of which the Queen has kept a copy. Nothing has been or will be said about Lord Salisbury's visit to you. Did Lord Salisbury mean a compromise when he pointed out what the Government might do? They certainly would not do what he suggests, but possibly this might form the basis of negotiations. For instance, if the Lords would pass Franchise as soon as Distribution was brought into the Commons—would that do?

Yours very truly,   HENRY F. PONSONBY.

Meanwhile (on October 1) Lord Salisbury had made a public speech at Glasgow, in which, while he had some scathing things to say about Mr. Gladstone, he indicated that the Conservative party would no longer insist that Franchise and Redistribution should go hand in hand, but that they would be prepared to consider passing the Franchise Bill in the Lords if at the moment it was sent to the Lords the Government introduced a Redistribution Bill. Mr. Gladstone's views of this may be gathered from the following letter from Sir E. Hamilton to Sir Henry Ponsonby (dated October 5):

MY DEAR SIR HENRY PONSONBY—I had no time to write to you yesterday.

As far as I understand Lord Salisbury's speech, the net result of it (so far as the reform question is concerned) was this: that, while he no longer insisted that there should be one Bill dealing simultaneously with Franchise and Redistribution, he implied that if the Government were men of sense what they would do would be:

(*a*) Either to produce both Bills on the opening of Parliament, or

(*b*) To pass the Franchise Bill in the Commons and as soon as it went to the Lords to introduce their Redistribution measure, which would then unfold their whole reform scheme and enable the Lords to decide what to do with the Franchise Bill and what to do with both Bills.

Now this is practically a bid for "all take and no give". It could not be accepted by the Government. The Franchise Bill would be hung up indefinitely. The Government, in return for eating their own words, would have no guarantee whatever that the passage of even the Franchise Bill this Parliament would be secured.

The only sort of way which occurs to me that Lord Salisbury's proposal could be "hammered into an acceptable shape" (and I can't undertake to say what the Cabinet would regard as acceptable) is this, that Lord Salisbury should be induced to give an undertaking to advise his followers in the House of Lords to pass the Franchise Bill if, and as soon as, the Redistribution Bill be read a second time in the House of Commons.

The second reading of the Redistribution Bill by a substantial majority would be a fair proof that the measure was a reasonable one, and one which all parties would do well to accept. Accordingly, the Lords might take this into consideration and pass the Franchise Bill. Its passage would be some kind of safeguard against the wrecking of the Redistribution Bill in its subsequent stages by pure obstruction. If, on the other hand, in those subsequent stages the Bill came to grief, dissolution would have to follow next year on the old constituencies.

But my belief is Lord Salisbury does not want to come to any terms. A Tory peer friend of mine, who professes to know something of Lord Salisbury's inward mind, told me the other day that he believed the bent of that mind to be something as follows:

Whether or not it was wise to try conclusions with the House of Commons on this particular question (Franchise) was too late now to argue. He feels—a feeling strengthened by the occurrences of the last few years, such as the Land Bills, Arrears Bills, etc.—that the last remnants of any real power to assert themselves in the conduct of public affairs are slipping away from the House of Lords. To give way now would be the final *coup de grâce* to such power. Accordingly, sooner than be reduced to effeteness, he prefers to run the risk of being "ended", when he could turn his talents to other account and by other means, or of being "mended", when the Upper Chamber would have some influence—power given to do without exposing itself to the charge that it was always coming in conflict with the representative Chamber.

Yours sincerely,   E. HAMILTON.

Two days later (October 7) Lord Salisbury arrived at Gordon Castle for his private meeting with the Duke of Richmond. Three days later the Duke wrote to Queen Victoria:

Your Majesty will be glad to hear that Lord Salisbury is in no way opposed to some compromise being arranged. In order that Your Majesty may know, he sends the enclosed,[1] which has been seen by Lord Cairns. The Duke has every hope of arrangement if Lord H.'s speech can be taken as a basis for negotiation.[2]

Lord Salisbury agrees with Lord Cairns. The main contention of the House of Lords, to which I believe they will adhere, is that a fair Redistribution Bill is necessary to make the Franchise Bill equitable and safe, and that one of these measures ought not to come into legal operation before the other. If we had to deal with Lord Hartington alone I believe we should obtain a friendly issue.

Sir Henry now wrote to Sir E. Hamilton (October 11):

MY DEAR HAMILTON—I am holding on here as the negotiations are now coming to a point. The leaders

---

[1] A memorandum by Lord Salisbury in which he said he agreed with Lord Cairns's letter of September 19.

[2] On October 4 Lord Hartington delivered a speech at Rawtenstall in which he took up Lord Salisbury's suggestion and lauded it as containing "some of the elements of compromise".

at Gordon Castle think that the language of the recent speeches by Ministers means that the Government don't intend to listen to any accommodation. H.M., however, urged that some agreement might be arrived at. As Hartington's address admits the possibility of agreement, they think they could discuss the question on the basis of his speech. I do not understand them to mean that they like his proposals. Indeed, I gather they won't accept them at all. And this is the difficulty which I see before us. The Queen's views are almost irreconcilable but perhaps not quite. The Queen has got this from the Tory leaders and suggests that Hartington should meet Lord Salisbury. We are now waiting for answers to the proposal.

The way now seemed clear for a solution to the vexatious problem. It was evident that Lord Salisbury, the leader of the Conservative opposition, and Lord Hartington, the Secretary of State for War in the Liberal Cabinet, were in substantial agreement. Queen Victoria cleverly took the opportunity, and on October 10 telegraphed to Lord Hartington, asking him if he would not meet Lord Salisbury. Lord Hartington, however, was not sanguine and on October 11 he wrote to Sir Henry Ponsonby:

MY DEAR PONSONBY—I received your cipher telegram on Thursday night; also one from the Queen this morning, and a repetition from Mr. Gladstone of a similar telegram from Her Majesty, with an intimation that he would be glad if I could gain the desired result, though not sanguine about it.

I assume that what is intended by taking my speech

234

as a basis is that the Government should consent to introduce the Redistribution Bill, if the passing of the Franchise Bill will be thereby assured. From the discussion in the Cabinet the other day, however, I gathered that there would be a good deal of objection to the introduction of the Redistribution Bill, under any circumstance, and it would require further authority from the Cabinet before any communications on that basis could take place. Rather it was very strongly felt that any fresh move must come from the Opposition, that he had said quite enough, perhaps more than enough, to show that the door is open for an arrangement, if an arrangement is possible, and that it was not for us to make any fresh overture. I do not know at all what has been the result of your communications with the Duke of Richmond, and until I do, or until I have some further means of knowing the disposition of the leaders, I do not see that it would be possible for me to enter into any communication with them.

I need not, however, say that if it should be possible I should be very glad to be of use in this matter.

Yours sincerely,   HARTINGTON.

(Copy Telegram)
October 12th, 1884.

Ponsonby to Marquis of Hartington

We have no positive knowledge yet that he [1] would consent, but we fully believe that he will. If you agree we can, if you wish it, ascertain more particulars.

[1] Lord Salisbury.

Events were now moving fast, even though Mr. Gladstone and Lord Salisbury (who delivered a typical fighting speech at Acton on October 10, in which he appeared to have repudiated Lord Hartington's olive branch) seemed shy of committing themselves. Nor were matters helped by the disclosure in the *Standard* of a scheme of redistribution of seats which had been prepared for the Cabinet months earlier.

On October 12 Sir E. Hamilton wrote to Sir Henry Ponsonby:

MY DEAR SIR HENRY PONSONBY—Many thanks for your letter received this morning. I cyphered to Mr. G. the gist of the Queen's letter of yesterday; and I don't suppose Mr. G. can object to Hartington's trying his hand with Lord Salisbury; but after reading Lord Salisbury's speech yesterday, I can't conceive that there can be any real chance of an arrangement. He does not appear to yield one atom.

I am not sure what will be the effect on the situation generally of the *Standard* disclosure. The paper in question, which evidently came out of the Queen's Printer's Office, was drawn by Lambert, initialled and signed by Dilke as well as Lambert. It purported to give effect to Mr. Gladstone's views and to the views of the Cabinet Committee at the end of last Session. It had never been circulated or considered by the Cabinet, and had, I believe, only been seen by Mr. G. and Hartington. The still more important papers prepared by Dilke were printed at the Foreign Office press and consequently are scarce. The disclosure of the scheme may put up, prematurely, the backs of those places which will have to lose their privileges as separate boroughs. On the other hand, the Government will be able to gauge well the views of the country at large on their inchoate ideas for a Redistribution measure.

Yours sincerely,   E. HAMILTON.

Lord Hartington was now thoroughly pessimistic, as the following letter from him (dated October 13) indicates:

MY DEAR PONSONBY—Your letter is not encouraging, and Lord Salisbury's speech at Acton is still less so.

I don't see any possible advantage in entering upon a discussion, on a basis which has been repudiated. And I do not understand that Lord Salisbury has expressed any wish to enter upon a discussion on any basis whatever. As I said in my last letter, the proposals for an arrangement have come from our side. Whatever you may think of the tone of Chamberlain's and Harcourt's speeches, they have taken care not to shut the door to a reasonable settlement. But any further offer from me without any encouragement whatever from the other side could not fail to be misunderstood.

Yours sincerely,   HARTINGTON.

On that same day (October 13) Mr. Gladstone wrote to Queen Victoria thanking her for "all the well-timed efforts" she had made "to avert a great public mischief and a fierce controversy". He added, however, that he was not sanguine of obtaining concessions from the Conservatives, though he was willing that Lord Hartington should try "as Lord Salisbury seems to be of opinion that the present difficulties would have

237

been avoided had the chief management of affairs been in the hands of Lord Hartington". This letter he sent by Lord Spencer.

The Queen was now thoroughly disgusted with Mr. Gladstone, and her comment on his letter to Sir Henry Ponsonby was as follows (October 14):

The Queen has just received this, Lord Spencer having only just arrived—she will not see him before dinner.

Sir Henry must tell him that the Queen will leave no stone unturned to effect a compromise and that the Cabinet *must give way* to a certain extent. Mr. Gladstone really acts like a Dictator, and Queen and country will *not* stand it. Why will they behave like obstinate children and not bring in the Redistribution Bill, which they have promised and which would satisfy the Opposition?

The Queen sends the bag with all the papers for Sir Henry to check. Any for Lord Spencer and for him, Sir Henry to take notes from.

The prevailing pessimism at Balmoral is well evidenced by the following letter from Sir Henry Ponsonby to Sir E. Hamilton (dated October 14):

MY DEAR HAMILTON—It was Mr. Gladstone who first made the Queen think of intervention since the prorogation and I certainly understood him to say when he was here that he considered the Opposition were justified in asking to be fully informed on the proposals for Redistribution. Hartington has also said the same thing and Chamberlain has also said so. I therefore am very sorry if the Cabinet dislike the expressions of these three leaders. When the Queen attempted to bring two conflicting opinions nearer to each other she imagined there would be mutual concessions, and that both parties would unite with goodwill in coming to a common understanding. If they were only to be dragged towards an unwilling compromise, it would be worth nothing. Such mutual concessions would scarcely bind the two men who agreed to them and would probably be repudiated by the followers on both sides. The hopes of goodwill melted away before the hot speeches from both camps, and the least attempt at any definite proposal is shouted down before it has time to be considered.

I therefore confess I do not clearly see what more the Queen can do.

Meanwhile, Sir Henry's efforts to get into touch with Lord Salisbury had proved abortive. His notes of October 14 give some idea of where the difficulty lay:

After the meeting of Lord Salisbury, Lord Cairns and the Duke of Richmond at Gordon Castle to consider the proposals made to them by the Queen, the Duke of Richmond wrote that he saw no prospect of a compromise, and he enclosed a memo. from Lord Salisbury in which these words occurred:

"The Conservatives and majority of the House of Lords wish for a friendly issue. If we had to deal with Lord Hartington *alone* we should obtain it, for his speech, though it contained no definite announcement, is animated by a conciliatory spirit."

239

I tried to catch Lord Salisbury at Edinburgh, but Lady Hopetoun's sudden death prevented his going there, and I came to London and wrote to him referring to above and asked him from the Queen if he would meet Lord Hartington.

He replied that I had omitted the word "alone", and as therefore he would have to deal with others he saw no object in a meeting. That he thought the best course would be to wait and the conviction will force itself on the Ministry that it *is* possible to pass both Bills in a Session, if the Redistribution Bill be reasonably fair. If so, the question solves itself easily.

On October 17 Sir Henry Ponsonby wrote to Lord Salisbury as follows:

DEAR LORD SALISBURY—I received your telegram on my arrival in London, and in accordance with your suggestion I write the substance of the communication which I was commanded by the Queen to convey to you. Her Majesty observed in your memorandum enclosed by the Duke of Richmond that you thought it possible some agreement might be arrived at if you had to deal with Lord Hartington. The Queen asks if you think this might be facilitated by your meeting Lord Hartington, and if so, whether you could suggest to her any basis on which the discussion might take place.

The Queen is sincerely desirous of doing her utmost to bring about an understanding on the question at issue, which she cannot but believe is capable of being satisfactorily arranged.[1]

[1] *Letters of Queen Victoria*, vol. iii. p. 551.

In reply Lord Salisbury reiterated his opinion of October 14,[1] urging that a conference with Hartington would be useless so long as he was compelled to conform his views to those of Mr. Gladstone and Mr. Chamberlain, and that the best course was to wait.

In this welter of pessimism a ray of hope suddenly shone, for Lord Carnarvon, in a speech on October 20, asked why could not the squabble be settled by three or four independent men. Sir Henry Ponsonby now wrote to him (October 22):

DEAR LORD CARNARVON—In a recent speech you said, "Why should not three or four independent men settle the details of the Redistribution Bill?" or words to that effect.

I agree—why not? The Tories distrust a Liberal Redistribution proposal. The Liberals probably would distrust a Tory proposal. But there must be some middle course nearer the true method of ascertaining the opinion of voters than any party Bill. Is there any mode of promoting this suggestion of yours? I believe that many people would gratefully accept this as leading to a solution of the difficulty. Who would the independent men be?

Would Lord Salisbury and Sir Stafford Northcote assent? If so, I would ascertain the feelings of the Government.

Note

Mr. Gladstone came to see me to call my attention to this speech.

---

[1] For full text see *Letters of Queen Victoria*, vol. iii. pp. 551-3.

Sir Henry Ponsonby now wrote to Queen Victoria (October 22) from Buckingham Palace asking if he might go further with Lord Carnarvon's suggestion. Her reply ran as follows:

The Queen thinks that perhaps it is better so, and that matters will be more easily solved in Parliament. She has written very thoroughly to Mr. Gladstone about Mr. Chamberlain [who had been making fiery speeches] and sends his letter for him to see, asking to have it back.

There are so many different burning questions—Egypt, Army, the Franchise Bill and last, but not least, Brunswick—that, as she finds Major Edwards is leaving on the 28th with the Duchess of Albany, she must ask Sir Henry to return two or three days sooner—and Lord Carlingford to come on the 1st instead of the 3rd. Mr. Sahl is not here and cannot well come, as that strange man, Angeli, who with great difficulty has been persuaded to come when we return to Windsor to paint that long-intended state portrait of the Queen, *will not* come without Mr. Sahl.

The Queen, therefore, would feel very much at sea without some more experienced help. Sir Henry shall have his month made up to him at Christmas and she is very sorry to take him away, but she is much overwhelmed with work and anxiety of all kinds.

The Queen thinks Lord Penzance's letter excellent.

Lord Carnarvon's suggestion had now been communicated by Sir Henry Ponsonby to Sir Stafford Northcote, who replied on October 23:

DEAR SIR HENRY PONSONBY—I do not very well see how the suggestion[1] you make could be worked out in detail. If you think it desirable, I shall be very happy to see you this morning after breakfast, or at a later period when we know what the intentions of the Government with regard to proceeding with Redistribution are.

I remain, yours very faithfully,

STAFFORD NORTHCOTE.

This chapter may perhaps fittingly end with Mr. Chamberlain's opinion of events. At Sir Henry Ponsonby's request, he came to see him on October 23, just before Parliament reassembled, and Sir Henry's note of the conversation is as follows:

Mr. Chamberlain thought the people were getting violent, and if the Lords again rejected it he did not think Government could control them.

He did not love the House of Lords, but he would prefer to see them take an interest in affairs without doing more than the Sovereign did with her power of veto.

But he was loyal to his party and would support them as long as they passed the Franchise Bill.

[1] Carnarvon's suggestion.

CHAPTER IX

THE FRANCHISE BILL, OCTOBER TO DECEMBER
1884

MOST people in Queen Victoria's position would have despaired of all hopes of bringing the two parties together.   The uncompromising attitude of the leaders, the irresponsible utterances of their followers, and the violence of the extremists on both sides were particularly repugnant to her and made her task as peacemaker practically impossible.

But while the public was quite unaware that she was taking any part in this controversy, she continued to employ every means in her power to affect a compromise.

Parliament reassembled on October 23, 1884. A spirit of compromise was in the air, and, except for a few acrimonious souls, members of both parties were seeking to find a bridge over which the Lords could retreat with honour from their position.

The Queen's Speech, remarkable chiefly for its brevity—though that, of course, gave it no title to be regarded as witty—announced curtly that "the Bill for the extension of the Parliamentary Franchise will at once be introduced".

In the Lords, Lord Salisbury skilfully criticised the "notorious infelicity of grammar" that characterised productions from the Royal pen, and vowed he had not altered his attitude to the Franchise since the preceding July.

Sir Henry Ponsonby, in a letter to Queen Victoria, now summarised the opinions of the leaders as follows (October 24):

I saw Lord Carnarvon, who did not wish the interview to be known, as the Tories might dislike it.

Sir S. Northcote would refer the proposal of independent members to Lord Salisbury.

Lord Cowper was all for compromise, while Mr. Goschen scarcely believed that the Government would accept the proposal.

Mr. Chamberlain said that the future would be full of violence if the Bill was rejected. The Birmingham riot, which had been much exaggerated, he deplored, but Dumfries was serious. The middle classes were angry. He did not love the House of Lords, which used its power in bringing about this state of things, but would loyally support Gladstone.

Sir Henry said the Queen disapproved of his recent speech. Chamberlain said he was misunderstood, but the subject was not pressed.

To this letter Queen Victoria replied on October 25:

The Queen dislikes all Mr. Chamberlain says. Sir Henry should have said to him that it was chiefly owing to his speeches and those of some of his colleagues that the bitterness and excitement which he mentions as exciting the country are due. The Queen would take his threats with caution, for she hears from the other side

245

that the Dumfries riot was not nearly so alarming as originally reported.

Mr. Gladstone's speech was far more conciliatory.

It is all very annoying, but really it is far more the Government's fault. Has Sir Henry seen Mr. Fawcett?

The previous day (October 24) Sir Henry Ponsonby had written to Lord Carnarvon:

St. James's Palace,
24th Oct. 1884.

Dear Lord Carnarvon—You say truly that your plan would require the thorough goodwill of the leaders on each side.

I find enough readiness to listen—on the part of the Government—or rather I should say of the chief members of it: but not so on the part of the Opposition. At least I gather that they do not object to the plan of the "righteous men", if such can be found, but they must hold still the Franchise Bill in hand. This the Government will not submit to.

Here again is an impasse. Do you see any peaceable way through it or round it?

Yours very truly,

Henry F. Ponsonby.

To this letter Lord Carnarvon replied on October 26:

Dear Sir Henry Ponsonby—I think there are two practical alternatives—and that the best solution would be a continuation of these two. First, my suggestion in some form (and it admits of several modifications); second, the introduction of a suspending clause with the Franchise Bill. With these two securities, I think, though it is only my personal opinion, we might in the House of Lords dispose of the Franchise Bill before the Redistribution Bill was wholly out of the hands of the House of Commons, and thus meet the Government's view of the case. But there is very little time to lose if any attempt is to be made, as the second reading of the Franchise Bill is fixed for Thursday, and if the debate is hot and envenomed all chance of agreement may be spoilt. I am confirmed in this view by a long and very private conversation which I have had with Sir E. May, who is with us for the Sunday. I have talked over my own notions of the situation and the possibilities of a solution with entire frankness, but I have not mentioned the name of yourself or anyone else with whom I have been in communication. It would be possible for you, if you think there is any advantage in this, to see him *as from yourself*, making my public suggestion the basis of your conversation. He is so much consulted by all parties that there would be nothing extraordinary in your doing this. But I think that our conversation need not be alluded to even to him. I merely throw this out for your consideration.

Believe me, yours truly,   CARNARVON.

P.S.—I have done and am doing all I can to facilitate what we both desire: but I feel that almost everything depends upon a conciliatory disposition on the part of the Government.

No one was more desirous of ending the impasse than Sir Henry Ponsonby; he was infinitely ingenious in inventing devices of possible compromise, and he took full advantage of a letter from the Duke of Richmond to set up a ferment in what had not been at first a promising quarter.

It will be remembered that in September hopes had been raised of some accommodation when Lord Salisbury went to stay privately with the Duke of Richmond at Gordon Castle. Since then the Duke had striven to reach some form of compromise, and on October 24 he wrote to Queen Victoria:

The Duke of Richmond and Gordon with his humble duty to Your Majesty.

Referring to the conversation the Duke had the honour of having with Your Majesty last month at Balmoral, the Duke ventures to inform Your Majesty of what has occurred since he came to London.

The Duke has had an opportunity of discussing the state of matters as regards the Franchise Bill with Lord Salisbury, Lord Cairns and Sir Stafford Northcote. The Duke's opinion is that they are not unwilling to entertain any reasonable compromise which could be brought about. The Duke regrets very much the tone of the Prime Minister's speech last night,[1] which seems to render a settlement extremely difficult. The Duke fancies that in the gracious Speech delivered by command of Your Majesty an intention is hinted at, though it was not put in decided language, that there would be a prorogation of Parliament at the end of the present Session in place of an adjournment. The Duke fervently hopes this may not be so, as the Duke feels sure

[1] In the debate on the Address in the House of Commons.

248

that if Parliament is prorogued there is little chance of a settlement being arrived at. Such a course would prevent a way out of the difficulty which the Duke thinks possible. The Duke must offer an humble apology to Your Majesty for addressing Your Majesty on this subject, but from what Your Majesty said at Balmoral, the Duke thinks Your Majesty may like to know the Duke's view of the present aspect of affairs. The Duke returns to Gordon Castle to-night.

The Queen at once sent this letter on to Sir Henry Ponsonby, and the covering letter, written by Major Edwards,[1] runs as follows (October 26):

MY DEAR SIR HENRY—I now send you a copy of the letter from the Duke of Richmond, about which Her Majesty told me to cypher to you, which I did last night. She again wishes me to remind you how hard it is for her if Mr. Chamberlain makes such speeches when she is trying to arrange a settlement.

She also wishes Lord Granville to know that she thinks it is a pity Mr. Gladstone is not more conciliatory and that the more moderate members of the Tory Party (such as the Duke of Richmond must be allowed to be) think Mr. Gladstone's language on Friday evening will not be any help towards an understanding, but the contrary (as you will see from the enclosed).

On that same day the news was published that Mr. George Trevelyan, the Chief Secretary for Ireland, was to be admitted to the Cabinet as Chancellor of the

---

[1] Assistant Private Secretary, afterwards Sir Fleetwood Edwards.

Duchy of Lancaster. This entailed his visiting the Queen at Balmoral to receive the seals of his new office. That evening Sir Henry Ponsonby noted:

As Mr. Trevelyan was to go to Balmoral, the Queen desired me to tell him she would speak to him on the crisis. I did so and found he knew very little about it as he was not in the Cabinet till now.

I advised him to see Mr. Gladstone, which he did. (At Balmoral Mr. Trevelyan strongly urged the Queen not to dissolve as the great increase of Parnellites would make a renewal of Crimes Act next year impossible.)

At the same time Sir Henry wrote to Sir E. Hamilton expressing the Queen's wish that "Mr. Gladstone will be moderate in his speeches and not menace the House of Lords". To this Sir E. Hamilton replied on October 27:

Mr. Gladstone has had a long talk with Trevelyan, who ought to be well posted up now and be ready to "seize" Her Majesty of the present situation.

As Mr. Gladstone has himself written to you, I need only say that there has been no threat of prorogation— a question which can only arise and be considered if the Franchise Bill is practically rejected a second time.

P.S.—Lord Norton[1] is now trying to pull the strings a bit. With such 'a multitude of counsellors, wisdom ought to prevail.

[1] Previously the Right Hon. Sir C. B. Adderley, Conservative M.P. for N. Staffs, created Lord Norton in 1878. Subsequently he saw Mr. Gladstone, Lord Salisbury and Lord Carnarvon, but his efforts came to nothing.

I should throw cold water on any independent move of the Whigs.

Sir Henry Ponsonby now sounded Lord Salisbury to see if his attitude had altered during the past month. His letter ran (October 27):

DEAR LORD SALISBURY—The Queen telegraphs to me that she has reason to believe the Opposition are not unwilling to entertain any reasonable compromise, but that if Parliament is prorogued as hinted at in her Speech, there is little chance of a settlement being arrived at.

I am not sure what compromise Her Majesty refers to, and I am not aware that prorogation has been hinted at.

I understood your last letter to me to mean that you could not advise the Peers who acted with you to cut off the power of resistance by passing the Franchise Bill now, even if a Moderate Seats Bill were announced.

If I am right in this surmise, I do not see that it is possible to proceed any further in this direction.

But if I have not understood this point, I hope you will correct me and if possible make any suggestion that I may telegraph to the Queen with a view of her consulting her Ministers as to its acceptance.

Yours very truly,   HENRY F. PONSONBY.

Lord Salisbury replied at length.[1] The gist of his letter was that he did not think

"that the mere production of a Redistribution Bill would justify the Lords in disarming themselves by

[1] See *Letters of Queen Victoria*, vol. iii. pp. 559-60.

passing the Franchise Bill into law at once. The task of making a suggestion, to which you invite me, is difficult, because the Prime Minister seems to lay down that any course which does *not* make the Lords pass the Caudine Forks *does* make the Government do so. But for that speech [Mr. Gladstone's] I should have thought that they might well have adopted Lord Cairns' suggestion that the House of Lords should read the Franchise Bill a second time, then wait till Redistribution Bill had come up to us, and should then proceed to deal with the Franchise Bill, giving it the precedence. I fail to understand the objection to this course. Perhaps the Government apprehend that we may use our hold on the Franchise Bill to force a Redistribution Bill unfairly Conservative upon them. If that is their fear it might be possible to come to some preliminary agreement as to what the Redistribution Bill should be, and then if we had found that common ground the Franchise Bill might be passed into law at once with Colonel Stanley's suspensory clause. In this way the apprehensions of both sides would be met. But I do not think the Prime Minister will be satisfied unless he can make the Lords pass through the Caudine Forks. . . ."

Sir Henry at once sent Lord Salisbury's letter on to the Queen, and the following correspondence ensued:

Sir H. Ponsonby to the Queen

ST. JAMES'S,
Oct. 29th, 1884.

I have sent Your Majesty a letter from Lord Salisbury, who repeats suggestion of Lord Cairns last

Session that the Lords might read Franchise Bill a second time and wait for Redistribution. May I suggest this to Mr. Gladstone?

The Queen to Sir H. Ponsonby

BALMORAL,
Oct. 29th, 1884.

Pray make the proposal you mention to Mr. Gladstone. I conclude Peers would undertake to offer no opposition to Redistribution Bill when sent up to them. C. Peel has gone to the Duke of Richmond to urge speedy settlement. You may stay on if of use.

Note by Sir H. Ponsonby of his letter to the Queen

Oct. 29th, 1884.

He is glad Peel has gone to the Duke of Richmond. He will make the proposal to Mr. Gladstone, though he fears that as this imperils the Franchise Bill, Mr. Gladstone will not accept. He hopes he may be of use though he is bound to say he cannot yet see the point of agreement.

Note by Sir Henry Ponsonby of his letter to Lord Salisbury

ST. JAMES'S PALACE,
Oct. 29th, 1884.

I sent your letter this morning to Balmoral.

The Queen will probably direct me to make the suggestion contained therein.

Is the enclosed right?

Personally, I share your doubt as to its acceptance

253

but refuse to allow the fate of Franchise Bill to be bound up with Redistribution Bill as this would do.

The object of Opposition is to prevent an interim Distribution Bill from being passed.

If Opposition leader desired to see provisions of Government Bill, I cannot but believe they would confidentially show it. Or if Opposition disliked asking, the Queen might show details.

I don't know, but believe Government would agree. If you approved, probably Lords would pass Franchise Bill without delay. If not, the Queen might fairly ask the Government to give fullest consideration to your criticism. In fact, I have hinted this to Her Majesty.

Who now hold the Caudine Forks? Will they make the same mistake as the Samnites did and take a middle course. Those who passed the Caudine Forks won, but not with honour. I hope neither parties will break their faith as the Romans did.   H. P.

Lord Salisbury to Sir Henry Ponsonby

20 ARLINGTON ST., S.W.,
Oct. 29th, 1884.

I have thought it better on the fly-leaf to give you Cairns' exact words, as they have more precision than mine. But if you prefer it you can take the shorter words I have written opposite, they mean practically the same thing. I am afraid your suggestion would not meet the consideration which I mentioned in my letter of yesterday. It would make it quite possible that there should be a dissolution after enfranchisement and before redistribution. We should therefore have no security for "a perfect measure".

My impression is that the suspensory clause is the only method that has any chance—and that not a very hopeful one—of leading to an issue.

Before the battle is over it would be presumptuous to say to whom the Caudine Forks belonged. But I think that the Government, from their point of view, have been awkward tacticians. They have staked everything on the chance that the majority of the Peers will give way. If on this point the count goes against them, as I think it will, they have left no policy open to themselves which will not do them more harm than it does to us. No harm whatever would have resulted to them from granting our very reasonable demands.

Yours very truly,   SALISBURY.

It is evident from these letters that Lord Salisbury, a shrewd tactician, had almost correctly gauged the hopes that had kept Gladstone adamant to the last. Balmoral, of course, was buzzing with messengers and rumours, as will be gathered from the following letters:

The Queen to Sir Henry Ponsonby

Oct. 28th, 1884.

Just received hopeful letter from the Duke of Argyll. Have telegraphed asking him to come here at once. I propose to entrust him with message to both sides. Hope I may still be able to do something if moderation is preserved.

255

Memo.—Sir Henry, however, did not think that the Duke of Argyll would have much influence, as he was hated by the Tories and distrusted by the Liberals.

By the next post, however, came the following letter from the Queen:

The Queen to Sir H. Ponsonby

BALMORAL,
28*th Oct.* 1884.

The Duke of Argyll cannot come. He is not strong enough for the journey north, but would go to London if necessary.

I have suggested his sending Lorne [1] here to take back message of my views to the Duke of Argyll.

There is no use in haggling about dignity and procedure and who is to blame as to state of affairs. The difficulty must be got over for the good and peace of the country irrespective of party. I have written to the Duke of Richmond.

The next day (October 29) Major A. Bigge (later Lord Stamfordham) wrote to Sir Henry Ponsonby from Balmoral:

MY DEAR SIR HENRY—We had a lively morning to-day and ended by packing off C. L. Peel to Gordon Castle, which he will reach sometime before midnight and get here again by dinner to-morrow!

He is to point out to the Duke [of Richmond] that the party must not be led against their convictions by Lord Salisbury, and come to terms—but this I suppose

---

[1] The Marquis of Lorne, afterwards ninth Duke of Argyll.

is the "snivel and drivel" you mention! I am afraid, judging from Trevelyan's face, when, by desire of the Queen, I showed him your cypher, that Lord Cairns' proposal will not be smiled upon by Mr. Gladstone. Peel, who was also consulted, thought perhaps there might be details in the proposal which, of course, you could not explain in a telegram, but which might make it more palatable to the Liberal swallow! I cannot quite see the objection to it, but Trevelyan asks how can we guarantee that the Conservatives won't throw out the Redistribution, then we shall have neither. He is very strong on resolutions being passed in both Houses in which would be stated broadly the lines upon which Redistribution Bill would be traced. This, I think, Peel will mention at Gordon Castle. Trevelyan is *praying* that there may be *no* dissolution, otherwise an accession of seventy Parnellites to House of Commons would ruin all chance of Renewal of Crimes Bill, which is perfectly indispensable for even the moderate amount of order that at present exists in Ireland.

Why won't Lord Cowper's plan satisfy both sides?

It is fair that Opposition should know the general principle of the Redistribution Bill and equally so that the Government should be credited with sufficient honesty to endeavour to carry through the Bill which would be laid on the table now—but which the Opposition seem to think would probably be thrown out by the Liberals themselves. (I was interrupted in this by a cypher to warn Lord Granville of the imprudence of allowing the French to extend themselves along the

Somali coast, as they seem to be flying their flag all over the place.) . . .

Lorne arrives at Ballater to-morrow morning. It would be a great triumph for the Queen if she could bring about a satisfactory settlement. Trevelyan says Lord S. and Lord R. C. are bent on dissolution. Very sorry for my mistake in cypher, curious you should hit on *asses* as substitute for right word.

Sorry you do not think Duke of Argyll will do as mediator. The Queen says he is most intimate with Gladstone. Would it not be better to have an outsider like him than a party man like the Duke of Richmond? The Prince of Wales has sent the Duke a letter from Goschen, who, recognising the situation exactly as you state it in your letter to me of yesterday, sees an only solution in Government "losing no time, as time is confessedly the chief difficulty" in introducing "Seats" directly F. is passed Commons and without waiting for latter to be finally passed Lords; then the latter would see Government mean business and that there will be parliamentary time enough for their plans to be carried out. He thinks Government might allow the sole tactical advantage which in his opinion Opposition will get, viz. "The power to transfer their opposition from one Bill to another and deceive country as to their real motives to force a dissolution either for party purposes or from hostility to F. Bill", to their opponents and yet be strong enough to maintain their present position. This does not seem to preclude Conservatives being stranded by F. Bill passing and "Seats" being afterwards thrown out by the Liberals and Irish so that they would have the election with increase of 2,000,000 electors with old areas. I don't quite see what he means about transferring opposition from one Bill to the other.

Yours of yesterday. In the last proposal from here the Leaders were asked to meet to agree to certain resolutions as to character of Seats Bill. I had no idea a meeting had been proposed so recently. Unfortunate my coming in just at this time, and the Queen very rightly says so many proposals in the last few months have become confusing! and I suppose she had forgot that such had been proposed and failed.

It is pouring, so we may not go to Kirk! but very mild.

Sir Henry Ponsonby was now instructed by the Queen to propose to Mr. Gladstone the suggestion that had been made to him by Lord Salisbury. His letter (October 30) runs:

DEAR MR. GLADSTONE—I am commanded by the Queen to make the following suggestion in the hopes that it may lead to an agreement, viz. that the House of Lords should read the Franchise Bill a second time, then wait till the Redistribution Bill reaches them. That thereon the Conservatives should not oppose the Government putting down the Franchise Bill for all its subsequent stages before the Redistribution Bill, leaving of course the House free to do what it pleases on those stages. HENRY PONSONBY.

Mr. Gladstone's reply was a blunt refusal to accept the suggestion, as will be gathered from the following letter from Sir E. Hamilton to Sir Henry Ponsonby (dated October 31):

SIDELIGHTS ON QUEEN VICTORIA

Secret.

10 DOWNING STREET, WHITEHALL,
31st Oct. 1884.

MY DEAR SIR HENRY PONSONBY—The Cabinet agreed with Mr. Gladstone in the opinion that the offer to concede the second reading of the Franchise Bill alone would make no substantial difference in the situation, and they could not see in the suggestion any hopeful means for an adjustment.

He has told Her Majesty that the Cabinet are really sensible of her efforts to bring about a settlement.

He has also mentioned to her the very confidential conversation which Hartington had the other day with Hicks Beach.—Yours sincerely,

E. HAMILTON.

Queen Victoria, now thoroughly alarmed at the seriousness of the situation, wrote four letters. The last of the four was to Sir Henry Ponsonby, and runs as follows (October 31):

I have seen Lord Lorne, and Mr. Peel returned last night. The Duke of Richmond has written to Lord Salisbury strongly urging the speedy compromise I so earnestly desire. I have written to-day to Gladstone, Salisbury and Northcote, pressing personal interview of leaders for exchange of views on assurance to be given of character of Redistribution Bill, and I have told Mr. Gladstone I believe that if these are not wholly inimical to Conservative prospects they would be accepted. I expressed the desire to Lord Salisbury that the question should be settled by Parliament. I suggested to Mr. Gladstone the Duke of Argyll as intermediator.

By the same messenger and a succeeding one came the following letters from Major Bigge to Sir Henry Ponsonby:

BALMORAL CASTLE,
31st Oct. 1884.

MY DEAR SIR HENRY—Peel returned last night. The Duke of Richmond will support the Queen's wish for immediate settlement, and will not be a party to prolonging the conflict. The Duke of Argyll says Mr. Gladstone will consent to passing resolutions as to character of Redistribution and acting on the idea evidently uppermost in Trevelyan's mind.

The Queen has written to propose a meeting of the leaders, and further suggests that it should be under the intermediation of the Duke of Argyll, for the purpose of discussing the nature of these resolutions.

H.M. has given Lord Salisbury to understand that the present Parliament should settle the question, so it is to be hoped he may see that his idea of forcing dissolution will receive no sympathy here. Mr. G. is told that the Government plans should be distinctly defined at the conference, and that if this is done, H.M. believes Opposition will concur.

I wonder if the leaders are to be brought together. If not, they might depute representatives. If this fails, Lorne suggests an invitation to Opposition Peers to abstain from voting, after the manner of William IV. (May 17, 1832), but surely things will never get so serious as to necessitate such a course.

Lorne seems to think Mr. Gladstone would consent to some plan to prevent the rural voters being swamped by the urban elements through the disenfranchisement of the small boroughs. I suppose he would group the latter.

BALMORAL,
1 *Nov.* 1884.

MY DEAR SIR HENRY—I send you the amended drafts of letters which went to Lord Salisbury and Mr. G. yesterday. I did not get them back in time for yesterday's messenger. It was proposed that H.M. should embody the draft submitted in one of her usual letters to Mr. G., which will perhaps explain its "stiffness".

As I told you, Trevelyan's face did not beam at Lord Salisbury's suggestion—your hint to the Queen that Mr. Chamberlain's resignation might follow an adverse vote of City shipowners was the cause of last night's inquiring telegram! Have you got reply and *Times* report this morning? Thanks for particulars of Lord R. Gower. As it is in the paper, the Queen will probably ask, so I shall be fully posted. . . .

I am very sorry I did not think of suggesting yesterday that a telegram should go to stop Lord Salisbury's proposal being submitted to Cabinet. Have sent telegram to say, "Queen hopes yesterday's Cabinet decision will not . . . interfere with yesterday's proposed acceptance, of which the Queen is most anxious".

The three leaders (Mr. Gladstone, Lord Salisbury and Sir Stafford Northcote) had now had time to consider the Queen's desire that they should meet and talk over their differences. Lord Salisbury accepted with a sneer; his letter ran:

Lord Salisbury, with humble duty, etc.

It will give him great pleasure to consult with anyone with whom Your Majesty wishes him to consult, and in obedience to Your Majesty's commands he will do all that in him lies to bring controversy speedily to a just and honourable issue.

While cheerfully complying with Your Majesty's wishes, he thinks it right to add that according to information he has received no danger attaches to the prolongation of this controversy for a reasonable time, and that there is no real excitement in the country in respect to it.

Mr. Gladstone pompously and lengthily refused,[1] whilst pointing out that Lord Hartington and Sir Michael Hicks Beach were already in touch with one another, and Sir Stafford Northcote said ditto to Lord Salisbury. Meanwhile, the Franchise Bill had been reintroduced into the House of Commons.

While, however, it was impossible for the moment to get Gladstone and Salisbury to meet, their respective lieutenants, Lord Hartington and Sir Michael Hicks Beach, were discussing ways and means of overcoming difficulties. It was known that Lord Hartington was in the fullest touch with Mr. Gladstone, but there was some doubt as to whether Sir Michael Hicks Beach could speak authoritatively for the Conservative leader, as the following letter from Major Bigge to Sir Henry Ponsonby shows (November 3):

---

[1] For text see *Letters of Queen Victoria*, vol. iii. pp. 564-6.

SIDELIGHTS ON QUEEN VICTORIA

MY DEAR SIR HENRY—Gladstone's reply to Her Majesty's last proposal is that already Hartington and Hicks Beach had met and would continue to do so and discuss general outlines of the Seats (Redistribution) Bill, but as it is necessary to ascertain whether H. B.'s views represent generally those of his party and if he is acting under mandate of his leaders, Hartington will find out and will be prepared to answer similar inquiries from H. B. Should these negotiations break down, Mr. G. will be ready to try some other plan on H.M.'s suggestions.

The Queen wired back her "greatest satisfaction" at these last hopeful letters. Northcote does not think things so serious as they are painted, but will see Lord Salisbury, who has not yet replied.

As far as I can make out, the Duke of Argyll wrote to the Queen and said that he had received a letter from Mr. Gladstone which made him more hopeful, whereupon the Queen at once wired to the Duke of Argyll to come. Lorne said telegram concluded, "Will send a carriage to meet you at Ballater", but even this did not get over the fact that Inveraray to Balmoral necessitated a night out, and when he said his gout prevented his doing so, Lorne was wired for. The letters which went to the leaders were by H.M.'s desire compiled by Lorne and me, the Queen having told the former that she thought the Duke of Argyll would be a suitable intermediary to bring about the meeting, and also that she thought the object of such an interview should be to agree upon resolutions. I had seen a précis of all the various moves on the board, but certainly did not recollect that a similar proposal had been made to the Triumvirate. Stupid of me, as, of course, it would have reminded H.M.

The Queen fancies Hicks Beach must be acting unbeknown to Salisbury and Northcote, as the latter does not refer to it. He has also written to the Duchess of Roxburghe and again suggests hanging up Franchise in Lords till Seats is through Commons, which we know Gladstone won't hear of, and he also suggests the same as Goschen that the Seats should be at once introduced when Franchise leaves Commons and the two Bills go on simultaneously in the two Houses, but this does not seem to make the Franchise much safer than in the "hanging up" scheme.

I have to write to Lorne and tell him of the H. B. and Hartington *pourparlers*, and that as long as they continue the Queen does not think further steps need be taken from Inveraray so far as concerns her last proposals. . . .

Hamilton and Knyvett write daily to ask that the appointment of the new peers may be pushed on. I have passed on both Hamilton's reminders, but really shall not bother the Queen any more, as she has already expressed astonishment at the hurry! I will make a note of Wyndham in case his application comes here. . . .

P.S.—Aberdeen papers startle us with reported fall of Khartoum and capture of Gordon.

For forty-eight hours it looked as if the Hartington-Hicks Beach *pourparlers* might bridge the gulf, but early in November the Conservatives surprisingly won a bye-election in Warwickshire which stiffened the Conservative attitude. On November 4 Lord Carlingford wrote to Sir Henry Ponsonby:

MY DEAR PONSONBY—I have just come from the House of Commons and have only time to say that things look as bad as possible, Lord John Manners having made a speech which was nothing less than a declaration of war, "no public or private communications possible", he said. What I wrote to the Queen was all true at the time, or apparently true, but alas! the scene has changed since then. How much the Warwickshire election has had to do with it, I don't know; certainly a good deal.—Yours very truly,

CARLINGFORD.

Lord Salisbury, however, was not quite so stiff, for on November 4 Major Bigge wrote to Sir Henry Ponsonby that Sir Stafford Northcote had replied "that Salisbury and he are ready to meet any of the Government on condition of secrecy being observed", but Major Bigge added, in his letter of that date to Sir Henry Ponsonby, "Mr. Gladstone feared secrecy was impossible. In the meantime he said a meeting was privately opened between Beach and Hartington."

Major Bigge's full letter runs as follows:

BALMORAL,
4th Nov. 1884.

MY DEAR SIR HENRY—Sir Stafford Northcote and Lord Salisbury have now both written and declared themselves ready to meet any member of the Government as long as secrecy is maintained, and Lord Carlingford is writing to Mr. Gladstone to beg that this condition may be strictly complied with.

Peel writes after long interview with Lord S. that latter quite concurs that it is important for interests of Conservative Party to settle the question and get it out of the way. This is satisfactory, but you will see Lord S., in his letter to H.M., does not see danger in prolonging the discussion. Peel says: "Salisbury would agree to anything which would prevent possibility of Election with new Franchise and old Constitution, but this is the great difficulty which *can only be solved by a meeting and free discussion*". We hope the underlined part is what Lord S. also thinks. Peel continues: "A clause in Franchise making it operative on passing of a Seats Bill would, of course, satisfy him". This we know the Government won't do. Both Lord S. and Northcote think dangers ahead are exaggerated. Peel thought result of meeting more satisfactory than he had expected, and that Lord S. will want greater security than resolution or promises which Government might be unable to carry out. That looks less promising, but it is a great point that they *will* meet. Here is copy of Lord Salisbury's letter.[1]

Two days later the following telegrams in cypher passed between Major Bigge at Balmoral and Sir Henry Ponsonby in London:

---

[1] See supra, p. 263.

Bigge to Ponsonby

Nov. 6th, 1884.

Queen wishes to know whether Salisbury and North-cote are aware of the Hartington-Beach negotiations —neither of their letters speak of it.

Ponsonby to Bigge

I do not know, but will try and find out. Since new departure I have not, of course, intervened.

Nov. 7th.

Saw Hartington, who said Beach only spoke for himself, but Salisbury and Northcote knew of his negotiations.

Saw Goschen—much alarmed at nature of Beach's proposals for redistribution.

Cabinet intend to ask Beach to bring Salisbury and Northcote with him to meet the Ministers they will send with Hartington. This will agree with the Queen's proposal.

Lord Granville doubts whether Mr. Gladstone and Lord Salisbury's meeting alone would conduce to settlement.

Nov. 7th, 1884.

Cabinet thought that Dilke and Hartington should negotiate with Beach and Salisbury, and both sides state more depending on these proposals.

Tory plan seems to give unlimited scope to principle of distribution by population.

The next day (November 8) Sir Henry Ponsonby returned to Balmoral, and met Lord Carlingford at Ballater, who told him that "the Duke of Richmond (the Queen said) was not aware of the Hartington-Beach negotiations. He saw no harm in a little delay in passing the Franchise Bill through the Lords if it was certain they would pass it when the Redistribution Bill came to the House of Commons."[1]

The Franchise Bill went quickly through the House of Commons, and on the first two nights conciliatory speeches were made on both sides, but on the 10th, and particularly on the 11th, the old bitterness was revived and Lord J. Manners spoke in warlike terms, he and Lowther denouncing compromise. The Queen asked the meaning of this—why her proposal for a meeting of the Chiefs was not proceeded with, and how the Hartington-Beach negotiations went on.

Mr. Gladstone answered that the Opposition showed hostile spirit and that the Hartington-Beach negotiations had come to an end; so he would now accept the Queen's offer of bringing about a meeting of the Chiefs.

He referred to the Queen's former letters, where she quoted "Lord Salisbury's readiness to consult with anyone whom Your Majesty wishes him to consult", and went on: "Mr. Gladstone humbly desires to express his willingness to meet Your Majesty's views for a direct interview, should Your Majesty still deem it expedient, between the leaders of the opposite parties".

Lord Granville wrote that it was a "pity to throw away any chance of meeting, but Lord Salisbury and Mr. Gladstone were not hopeful of the result".

In the Hartington-Hicks Beach conversations much

---

[1] Sir Henry Ponsonby's notes.

progress had been made with the details of the Redistribution Bill, and the conversations were only
broken off by the belligerent attitude of the Tory diehards, among whom were Mr. Harry Chaplin and Mr.
James Lowther. On November 12 Sir E. Hamilton
wrote to Sir Henry Ponsonby:

MY DEAR SIR HENRY PONSONBY—You will have got
my telegram. This sudden change of tone is very unfortunate and discouraging. My own belief is that the
Harry Chaplins and Jim Lowthers, just as they went
(as I know) last summer to Lord Salisbury and told
him that, if he did not fight, they would throw up the
sponge, so in like manner were now working, in consequence of rumours that an arrangement or accommodation was in the air. In their heart of hearts they
thoroughly dislike reforms, and what they want is a
row and dissolution, from which they think they can't
be worse off than they are now and may get some
advantage. The Warwickshire election has given them
heart; but they ought to know from experience that a
bye-election is a broken reed on which to depend.

There was a meeting this morning of the Tory
leaders in Arlington Street, and Cross told a friend of
mine on his way there that he did not consider all hope
of an arrangement at an end. This may be so; but the
conduct of the front Opposition Bench last night was
certainly not calculated to further this object.

The only chance now seems that the Government
should steadily pursue a course of conciliation, and
express their fixed determination not only to pass a
Redistribution Bill, but to pass one which will be ac-

ceptable to both sides of the House. By this means it is possible that not a few of Lord Salisbury's followers will put a pressure upon him to come to an arrangement on this understanding, sooner than run the risk of bringing down upon their heads the fall of their House.

Sir M. H. Beach has apparently behaved extremely well and honourably.

I greatly hope that Her Majesty's good offices, of which Mr. Gladstone is highly sensible, will not prove abortive.

A further idea of the causes operating against the Hartington-Hicks Beach conversations will be gathered from Mr. Horace Seymour's letter to Sir Henry Ponsonby dated November 14:

DEAR SIR HENRY—If the situation puzzles you, I can assure you it puzzles us a great deal more: nor can I give you more than surmise for a solution of what appears to be a change of front on the part of the Opposition leaders. Beach, I believe, gave his views on Distribution as his own, and without prejudice, but it is not possible that he could have approached Lord Hartington on the subject without the knowledge of some of his colleagues at least. Mr. Gladstone, as you know, made a most conciliatory speech on the second reading, and enunciated none but the *most* general principles, which embraced Beach's proposals. He carefully avoided giving a detailed outline for fear that he might include something to which the Opposition would take exception, or appear to give a pledge on a point which they would desire to modify. I take it from Cross's speech that he was aware of what was going on —but then something happened which caused a reverse movement, and, as you know, Lowther made a speech of an entirely opposite character from Cross, and Lord J. Manners also sounded the note for battle. Here comes in surmise. It is supposed that Lowther and Chaplin went to Lord Salisbury as they were reported to have done in August and threatened to "chuck up the sponge" altogether if he gave way; this, the Warwickshire election and Lord Salisbury's own inclinations may have combined to turn the tide. I believe Beach and Cross both expressed themselves in private as regretting extremely the tone adopted by Lord John Manners. However, the result of this tone was that Beach told Lord Hartington that fresh interviews would be unavailing. I expect the Tory Party are at sixes and sevens *re* this question. Anyhow, that there exists a party of conciliation will be seen by Mr. Gladstone's box of to-day to the Queen, but, alas! the effort has failed, as Lord Salisbury declines to negotiate on the basis of passing the Franchise Bill. There is, however, I believe, a considerable number of Tory peers who would be willing to pass the Franchise Bill if the Government were to introduce the Redistribution Bill in the Commons before the committee stage of the former Bill in the Lords, and this, as you know, Mr. Gladstone is willing now to do, *provided* the Franchise Bill is then passed into law. Our only hope lies in the Tory independent lords. If they will accept this, all will be well. If not, all will be very ill, and I think the Opposition, after all that has passed, and the unwillingness of the Government to carry the views of the Opposition into effect with regard to Redistribution, ought to give way and accept—but Lord Salisbury won't. On his head be the blood then.

Now that the Hartington-Hicks Beach conversations had broken down the way seemed clear for a meeting of Mr. Gladstone and Lord Salisbury, which Queen Victoria had suggested a fortnight earlier. Sir Henry Ponsonby's notes about this (dated November 12-14) are as follows:

November 12th, 1884.

The Duke of Richmond in reply to the Queen wrote that he was going to London (15th), so the Queen suggested I should go to Perth·to meet him, with a letter from her.

November 13th.

Mr. Gladstone cyphered that there was again a renewed possibility of coming to some understanding.

I telegraphed to Hamilton—November 14:

If cypher last evening does not alter suggestion contained in letter from Mr. Gladstone, please let me know does he propose to meet Lord Salisbury alone, or with others. If so, who? Is the condition of secrecy to be accepted? Private. I am going to meet the Duke of Richmond and urge him from the Queen that he should compel Salisbury to make agreement. Can I make any suggestion to him?

Sir E. Hamilton's reply ran as follows:

T

November 14.

There is decidedly more light again to-day. Can only suggest that communications from Lord Salisbury should be encouraged. Conversations could either be held alone or not, and would be secret. And for myself I fear that matters are again a turn for the worse.

That same day Sir Henry Ponsonby received the following letter from Mr. C. Peel:

WOODCROFT, CUCKFIELD,
14*th Nov.* 1884.

MY DEAR HENRY—I did not answer your letter in London to-day as I had nothing to add to what I said yesterday and I had to catch a train.

Richmond is to arrive in London with Lord Cairns on Sunday morning, and I have told him that I will go up on that day and tell him all I know before he meets his colleagues on Monday.

I am rather sorry that they are going to have a meeting of the party (Lords and Commons) on Tuesday, as I don't think party meetings generally tend to peace, internally or externally?

Time appears to be what is now wanted, as the number of moderate people on both sides who are anxious for a settlement appears to be increasing every day, and the Redistribution question is such a difficult and complicated one that it ought to be very carefully considered, and, if possible, arranged (at least as to its leading features) before it is launched. And this, I suppose, is what the Government feel, and what makes them anxious to ascertain the views of the Opposition on the subject. From Sir Stafford's letter, which I send you, I should rather doubt whether Sir M. Beach does not represent his own views more than those of the Opposition generally. If this be so, he is not a good negotiator, but I should hope that when new leaders of the Opposition have conferred together, they may find someone who can speak for them with authority and open a friendly negotiation with the other side. This, however, is only my own idea.

I had a talk with Mr. Trevelyan to-day and found him as anxious as we are for a settlement.

Always yours sincerely,   C. L. PEEL.

The following day Sir Henry Ponsonby wrote from Perth to Queen Victoria and Major Bigge (November 15):

I have seen the Duke of Richmond and Lord Cairns, who are hopeful and were anxious to carry out Your Majesty's wishes. They said Lord Salisbury had been expecting to hear more of proposed meeting as suggested by Your Majesty and was quite ready. They advised that Your Majesty should telegraph to Mr. Gladstone to proceed. The Duke of Richmond hopes that Lord Cairns may be associated with Lord Salisbury, but this must be left to Lord Salisbury.

To Major Bigge

They are both very anxious for agreement. In case of delicacy as to which side should first advance, perhaps the Queen would telegraph to Gladstone and Salisbury simultaneously, and if difficulty as to locality, perhaps ask Duke of Argyll to arrange matters.

Conversations now followed between Mr. Gladstone and Sir Stafford Northcote (November 14) at the house of a friend, and good progress was made with the principles of Redistribution. Then came a sudden peremptory message from Lord Salisbury that the Lords would not let the Franchise Bill go through unless they first had the Redistribution Bill sent up from the Commons. Negotiations were again broken off.

Gladstone not unnaturally felt indignant, and on November 16 he wrote to the Queen:

As it is useless proceeding with these private negotiations, since Lord Salisbury and Sir S. Northcote will only listen to the Franchise Bill being suspended in the House of Lords till the Redistribution Bill reaches it, the Government decided to make a public declaration.

The next evening (November 17) Mr. Gladstone moved a Declaration in the House of Commons which announced that the Government would pass the second reading of the agreed Redistribution Bill simultaneously with the Committee stage of the Franchise Bill in the Lords.

This undertaking converted a sufficient number of Lord Salisbury's adherents as to leave him in the lurch, and two great Tory leaders called on Lord Granville, eager and anxious to resume negotiations. The diehards, however, were still willing to lay odds that the Franchise Bill would not become law that year, as the following letter from Sir E. Hamilton to Sir Henry Ponsonby (November 17) shows:

My dear Sir Henry Ponsonby—It is impossible to write anything further on the general situation to-day.

We must await the result of the Ministerial declarations in Parliament this afternoon.

If the proposals made by Lord Granville and Mr. Gladstone are received by the Opposition in the same spirit in which they are offered, I should think it is very likely that there may then be a good opening for a meeting.

You will see by Mr. Gladstone's intended declaration that he has no wish whatever to force from the hands of the Opposition a "cut and dry" scheme for Redistribution. All he wants is some information in order to work their views, if possible, into harmony with those of the Government.

I am fairly sanguine now. All will depend on whether the responsible leaders of the Opposition, who are clearly anxious for a *modus vivendi*, will have the pluck to silence the more hot-headed members of their party like Harry Chaplin, who last night was ready to bet anyone a "pony" that there would be no passing of the Franchise Bill this year, and declared that he would expend his last breath in endeavouring to prevent a settlement.—Yours sincerely,

E. HAMILTON.

On that same day (November 17) the second reading of the Franchise Bill was moved in the House of Lords, and a few days later was passed.

Two days later, Lord Salisbury, now in a thoroughly negotiable mood, came with Sir S. Northcote to No. 10 Downing Street and took tea with Mr. Gladstone. The meetings went on—Lord Hartington, Sir Charles Dilke and Lord Granville also taking part. By

November 27 "the delicate and novel communications" between the leaders, without precedent in Parliamentary history, had resulted in complete agreement, and on December 1 the new Redistribution Bill was introduced with the assent of all parties. Four days later the Franchise Bill was read a third time in the House of Lords and passed.

The Queen, of course, was delighted and even considered giving Mr. Gladstone the Garter. Effusive missives passed between the two, and even Sir Henry Ponsonby came in for his share of the bouquets, for on December 1 Mr. Gladstone wrote to him:

In writing to acknowledge the important aid so "timeously" given by the Queen, I thought that my thanks to her should stand alone. But having allowed now a decent interval, I fulfil my intention and desire to record my sense of the tact, discernment and constancy with which you have promoted the attainment of an accord, and thus made an important contribution to political power where its preservation was of so much importance.

To this Sir Henry Ponsonby replied:

WINDSOR CASTLE,
Dec. 1st, 1884.

DEAR MR. GLADSTONE—You have honoured me far more than I deserve by the letter you have so kindly written to me.

In carrying out the Queen's commands I have found my duty greatly facilitated by the patient attention you always paid to what I had to say and the free and

GENERAL THE RIGHT HON. SIR HENRY PONSONBY, G.C.B.

open manner in which you spoke to me on the question under consideration.

I hope now that I may sincerely congratulate you on the agreement being complete.—Yours very truly,

HENRY PONSONBY.

The final letter of this series is from Sir E. Hamilton to Sir Henry who wrote on December 2:

MY DEAR SIR HENRY PONSONBY—Thanks for your letter.

I can assure you that Mr. Gladstone felt what he wrote to you. You have secured a very high place in Mr. Gladstone's estimation; and I often have the pleasure of hearing him sing your praises. The burden of his song is loudly re-echoed by those who work for him; and we all in Downing Street join in the chorus.

I am very glad indeed that we have a peace. I am glad on many grounds; but most of all for Mr. Gladstone's own sake. If he can once accomplish the task of settling the reform question, he may then be able to retire in glory; and an honourable retirement is probably what his friends ought most to desire.

I am afraid the Lubbock-Grey-Courtney Division are likely to give the Government much trouble with their new-fangled hobby of Proportional Representation. This, I think, promises to be the most serious difficulty ahead.—Yours sincerely,

E. HAMILTON.

CHAPTER X

MR. GLADSTONE'S RETIREMENT, 1894

IN 1894 Mr. Gladstone was eighty-five, and although his mind was as active as ever, certain defects of sight and hearing—slight, but sufficient to be a handicap in parliamentary work—led him to contemplate retirement. Such a decision was easily made, but the most serious obstacles were obvious when the question came to be considered as to who should succeed him as Prime Minister and Leader of the Liberal Party. He himself seemed to have expressed no opinion, probably because he was never asked to do so, but the intelligentsia of the Liberal Party supported Lord Rosebery, then Foreign Secretary, and a still larger body of Liberals were firmly of the opinion that a Prime Minister in the House of Lords was an anachronism in those democratic times—especially as it was the Liberal Party that was involved, and they, in turn, supported the claims of Sir William Harcourt, who held the post of Chancellor of the Exchequer.

The fact that Queen Victoria cordially disliked Gladstone is now well known: in fact she herself never made any secret of her antipathy to him in her later years. According to the late Lord Gladstone her relations with his father were of the most friendly description to begin with, and it was not until Disraeli appeared on the scene that she began to dislike him.

280

This, Lord Gladstone maintains, was entirely due to Disraeli, who poisoned her mind systematically against the Grand Old Man. Some people, however, thought this was owing to the fact that while Disraeli flattered and amused her, Gladstone lectured her and addressed her as if she were a public meeting.

Her opinion of Gladstone is very forcibly given in a letter which she wrote to Lord Lansdowne, when he was Viceroy of India, on August 12, 1892. The General Election of the preceding June had resulted in the overthrow of Lord Salisbury's Government and in the return of Mr. Gladstone to power with a majority of forty, which included seventy-two Irish Nationalists. The new Parliament met for the first time on August 4.

Her letter ran:

The Queen-Empress has to thank the Viceroy for his letter of the 27th June.

She feels more than ever at this painful, anxious moment when, by an incomprehensible, reckless vote, the result of most unfair and abominable misrepresentation at the elections, one of the best and most useful Governments has been defeated, how important it is to have so able and reliable a Viceroy in India.

The Queen-Empress can hardly trust herself to say what she feels and thinks on the subject. Apart from the pain of parting from some great personal friends and people whom she can trust and rely on, the danger to the country, to Europe, to her vast Empire, which is involved in having all these great interests entrusted to the shaking hand of an old, wild, and incomprehensible man of eighty-two and a half, is very great!

It is a terrible trial, but, thank God, the country is sound, and it cannot last. The Gladstonian majority is quite divided, and solely depends on the Irish vote.[1]

Rumours of Mr. Gladstone's retirement began to circulate in the January of 1894, which the usual official denial rapidly confirmed. Mr. Gladstone was then at Biarritz. He returned on February 10. "His colleagues", as Morley notes, "carried almost to importunity their appeals to him to stay; to postpone what one of them called this 'moment of anguish'." But Gladstone had by now made up his mind, although as he noted in one of his private memoranda a month later "Politics are like a labyrinth, from the inner intricacies of which it is even more difficult to escape than it was to find the way into them". His age and his infirmities brought him on February 17 to express a wish to see Sir Henry Ponsonby "not later than Friday" and "earlier rather than later". Two days later Mr. Gladstone wrote to Sir Henry:

If, as I understand, the Queen's coming up is fixed for Thursday, you, I conclude, will move from Osborne on that day, and perhaps you could make that the day for calling on me at any hour you like to name, as it will probably be a blank day at the House of Commons.

On February 24 Mr. Gladstone, as Sir Henry noted, "came to Buckingham Palace at eleven, and told me that his desire to see the Queen affected his retirement and that he did not want it to get out before Parliament was over. Could it be kept quiet?"

[1] Published in Lord Newton's *Life of Lord Lansdowne.*

That same day Sir Henry Ponsonby wrote to Mr. Gladstone, and kept the following rough note of his letter:

I repeated to the Queen the substance of my conversation with you. Her Majesty asked what was the message you desired to give her. I of course said I knew nothing. Her Majesty replied that she could not bind herself to preserve secrecy on a matter of which she knew nothing and asked for some hint. This I explained I could again get from you. Her Majesty observed that if it related to Parliament she could not promise not to consult several persons.

I did not feel capable of discussing this question, and I promised to repeat to you what Her Majesty had said.

On the same day Sir Henry also wrote to Sir Algernon West, who was then private secretary to Mr. Gladstone:

The Queen said she would not bind herself to any secrecy about matters where she must consult friends. Was it dissolution?—of course I would not say. All I could say was that I would ask him. She won't, she says, agree to keep secret some dark proposal he may make.

Mr. Gladstone's reply was as follows:

Thanks for your letter.

The very last thing I should pray for or claim is discussion on my notice or intimation. I should deem it wholly premature. For this reason I contemplated a letter and one not requiring acknowledgement.

If Her Majesty, on the other hand, enjoins a personal statement, which seemingly entails a day's delay, of course I will cheerfully obey.

If I am to write perhaps you will kindly let me know.

Friday now passed, and the Queen's fear that Mr. Gladstone might inveigle her into some sort of "secret discussion" had proved groundless. It was plain that she thought that if Mr. Gladstone had something to say to her of great importance there was no need why it should be treated so secretly, or why he should not beforehand give her some indication of his opinion. The next day Sir Henry Ponsonby wrote to Mr. Gladstone:

I could not get a very clear reply last night and indeed even now I cannot give a brief answer. The Queen said she feared that entering into a secret discussion with you might cause misunderstandings and that she would wish to be able to consult other friends.

I pointed out that in your letter you did not ask her to express any opinion and that you did not even ask for an acknowledgement, and therefore I asked whether a brief personal interview would not be best. The Queen said that if you did not expect her to do more in this matter than simply to listen, this might be so. But I should make it quite clear that Her Majesty should not be expected to discuss the matter. If so, the Queen could listen to you upon the subject when she sees you.

By this time, of course, the cat was well out of the bag. Everybody who was anybody—and a good many nobodies—knew that Mr. Gladstone was going to re-sign. Only Mr. Gladstone and the Queen seemed to be in any doubt as to the correct manner in which his resignation should be effected. The following day (February 27) the Queen wrote to Sir Henry Ponsonby:

The Queen hears from the Duke of Connaught (who asked her what it meant) that it is placarded every-where and is posted up at the clubs that Mr. Glad-stone is going to resign. Others have also asked and she only said she knew nothing, but thought there must be something "in the air".

Is the Queen not right in believing that when a Prime Minister resigns the Government is broken up? —of course, if one of them wishes to succeed him he must re-form and support the Government. This was done in '65 when Lord Palmerston died and Lord Russell was appointed.

The secret which Mr. Gladstone makes so much of, is constantly leaking out—in spite of all his great fuss and anxiety about secrecy.

The Queen had just sent this letter to Sir Henry when she received the following note from him: "Would Your Majesty wish to see Mr. Gladstone at 3 o'clock to-morrow?" "She had better see him to-morrow", replied the Queen, "but it would be more courteous to acknowledge his letter and say she would see him at three. What is the Queen to say to her family, who will ask her, and to Lord Rosebery and the Chancellor?"

Hardly had the Queen sent the note than she

received the following letter from Mr. Gladstone, which is dated February 27:

> Mr. Gladstone presents his humble duty to Your Majesty, and believes himself now authorised to convey to Your Majesty the preliminary intimation which he has thought it would be for the convenience of Your Majesty to receive.
>
> It is to the effect that, when the business of the present Session, and any matter immediately connected therewith, shall have been disposed of, he believes it will be his duty to tender to Your Majesty, on physical grounds, his resignation of office.
>
> As his present object is simply to inform Your Majesty, without asking or desiring even a formal acknowledgement of this letter, he reserves all explanation of particulars until the day, perhaps a very early one, when he humbly proposes to carry his intention into effect.

The next afternoon (February 28) Queen Victoria gave an audience to Mr. Gladstone, "who indirectly conveyed to the Queen what she might soon expect to learn from him". He afterwards told Mr. Morley (then Chief Secretary for Ireland) that he derived the impression that the Sovereign would not seek his advice as to a successor.

Meanwhile, the Queen feared that the formation of a new Government would interfere with her plans for a holiday, and that she would either have to curtail or abandon her projected visit to Florence. That day she wrote to Sir Henry Ponsonby:

BUCKINGHAM PALACE.

The Queen was asked no question about Lord Rosebery being unwilling, and on the contrary talked of future arrangements. If only it could be tided over till the Queen returns, or else the little rest and benefit she has looked forward to will be ruined; and this long-suffering and pain makes her very worn-out. If there is a change of Government it will take a fortnight or three weeks, and we ought to go on the 13th—Tuesday fortnight—and the day will be too short. Can Sir Henry not do something? To go so far for only three weeks would be useless almost.

The question as to who should succeed Mr. Gladstone had now reached a point when some definite decision should be made. The situation was aptly described by Sir Edward Hamilton, who had been private secretary to Mr. Gladstone, and who now wrote to Sir Henry Ponsonby on February 28:

I have generally troubled you with my remarks in times of crisis; so I hope you won't object to a few lines on the present occasion. They may be useful to you, for I think I know pretty well the lie of the political land; and I know you won't betray my indiscretion.

Everything would be quite smooth sailing if it were not for our great difficulty—I mean our big friend Harcourt; and as I am very much attached to him personally I regret more than I can say that he should constitute the difficulty. But for him, I am certain that every member of the present Cabinet would rally

287

round and joyfully serve under Rosebery. Rosebery is the only man really competent to be the Queen's Prime Minister. His colleagues (with that one exception) feel that; and he would inspire confidence among all right-minded citizens. But the two questions which have to be looked in the face are:

(1) Will Harcourt submit to serve under Rosebery, and

(2) If he would so submit, would Rosebery be content to take him as his deputy with the lead in the House of Commons.

I doubt if either of these questions can be answered in the affirmative; and there is no doubt that among the Radicals he will be strongly backed. They only know him as a fine fighting Parliamentarian. They have no experience of him as a colleague. This feeling enhances the difficulty of the situation.

It looks, therefore, as if the problem could only be solved in two ways, either by the supersession of H. in the House of Commons, which would be very awkward, or by the formation of the Government under another man than R., like Kimberley, who would be less frightened at having H. as leader in the Commons and be better able to pull with him.

This, I believe, pretty accurately describes the state of affairs.

There is one other point to which I should like to allude, and it is this: I take it that the man for whom, according to general expectation, the Queen will send, is Rosebery. But it occurs to me that in his own interests as well as those of the Crown it might be well that in the first instance the man sent for should be Kimberley as present leader of the House of Lords. He would be sure to say he must defer to Rosebery; and by this move it could not be said that Rosebery was selected as the Crown's nominee.

It is all very interesting; and I hope somehow or other the difficulties which I foresee may be surmounted and the right man be put in the right place.

The next day (March 1) Mr. Gladstone held his last Cabinet Council. His biographer, Lord Morley, describes the scene:

Mr. Gladstone sat composed and still as marble; and the emotion of the Cabinet did not gain him for an instant. He followed the words of acknowledgement and farewell in a little speech of four or five minutes, his voice unbroken and serene, the tone low, grave and steady. . . . Then, hardly above a breath, but every accent heard, he said "God bless you all" . . . and went out of one door, while his colleagues, with minds oppressed, filed out of the other. In his diary he enters: "A really moving scene".

A little later in the afternoon he made his last speech in the House, striking a "note of passion" and speaking "with rising fire". He sat down amidst the vehement plaudits of his followers, who were not supposed to know that this was his last speech as Prime Minister.

The next day Lord Rosebery received through the Prince of Wales a message from the Queen to the effect that she would like to see him at Windsor to ascertain whether he would be prepared to succeed Mr. Gladstone.

His reply to Sir Henry Ponsonby ran as follows:

FOREIGN OFFICE,
Secret. *March 2nd,* 1894.

MY DEAR PONSONBY—I have received the Queen's gracious message through the Prince of Wales. It would not be proper, I conceive, that I should address her on the subject of it, so I write to you with the intention that you should send this letter to her.

It would be affectation to deny that I have often seen it suggested that I might succeed Mr. Gladstone when he should retire. In view of that I have kept myself sedulously in the background. I have not made a speech or written a line for publication. I have done this deliberately to avoid this *damnosa hereditas.* And I delivered the only speech that I did make (that on the Irish Government Bill) in the full hope and expectation that it would put an end to any question of my leading a Liberal Government.

My reasons are these:

(1) I am altogether unfitted for the post, as regards capacity and knowledge.

(2) I am in an office where I believe I can do good work and where a change just now might do harm. Why then should I be taken out of a round hole and put into a square one?

(3) The House of Commons is justly jealous of the leadership of a Liberal peer.

The Liberal Prime Minister, if a peer, will be dependent entirely on the leader of the House of Commons. While the House of Commons is settling the affairs of the country under its leader, the Prime Minister will be shut up in an enemy's prison with an intrepid band of trusty followers.

The Radical cave announcement last night, though not, I believe, formidable in itself, is right in this—that a Liberal peer, as Prime Minister, is in a wholly false position. He cannot control the House of Commons or his representative there, he can only watch them from the Strangers' Gallery.

(4) I am very sceptical as to the apparent movement in my favour. It is, I believe, negative, and rises much more from dislike and distrust of one of my colleagues than from anything personal to me. In this anxiety to avoid him, they can see no issue or chance of safety but through me.

These are the objections I see and which I express without reserve, for I think it my duty to make the Queen aware of them.

Believe me, yours sincerely,   R.

We glory in our nebulous Constitution, but the question whether the Sovereign of this country acts on anyone's advice in the selection of a Prime Minister seems to have been skilfully avoided by constitutional theorists. Obviously, when a Prime Minister is hopelessly beaten at an election, his advice cannot be sought when the Opposition comes into power. The case is, however, quite different when the Prime Minister resigns and his party remains in power. The only question to be decided in that case is upon which

of his colleagues his mantle is to fall, and there can be
little doubt that he himself must be one of the best
judges.

Is this a case where possibly the Sovereign can do
wrong? The correct interpretation of this seems to be
that any minister can be selected who is able to form
a Government and who is therefore prepared to defend the action of the Sovereign in Parliament.

In the case of Gladstone, Queen Victoria had no
intention of asking his advice. Neither did he ever
imagine she would do so. Whether he would have re-
commended Rosebery, Harcourt or Kimberley must
therefore remain a matter of conjecture.[1] Harcourt had
strong claims, for he had been leader of the House of
Commons in Gladstone's absence and had borne the
great burden of the day. Some Liberals thought that
as he might refuse to serve under Lord Rosebery it
would be best to have Lord Kimberley or perhaps Lord
Spencer. Mr. Labouchere attempted to raise a revolt
amongst the rank and file of the Liberal Party against
a peer Prime Minister, and wrote a strongly worded
protest to *The Times*, urging Sir William Harcourt's
claims and questioning the Queen's right to make it
what he termed a Court appointment, but he received
little support.

On March 2, Mr. Gladstone, accompanied by Mrs.
Gladstone, was invited to stay at Windsor Castle by
Queen Victoria. As they drove to Paddington Station
from Downing Street they were affectionately greeted
by a large crowd, and on arrival at Windsor Station
they had quite an ovation. They dined with the Queen
that night, but probably the conversation was general
and nothing was said about the political situation.

[1] Lord Morley states that he would have preferred Lord Spencer.

The next day (March 3) a Council was held for the prorogation of Parliament. Mr. Gladstone was, of course, already at Windsor and the following Ministers were summoned from London: Lord Kimberley, Lord President of the Council; Lord Rosebery, Secretary of State for Foreign Affairs; Sir William Harcourt, Chancellor of the Exchequer; Lord Ripon, Secretary of State for the Colonies; and Lord Spencer, First Lord of the Admiralty. In addition to these, Lord Acton was present as Lord-in-Waiting. Lord Acton was a man of encyclopædic knowledge, but, like many erudite scholars, was inclined to be absent-minded—a circumstance which had a curious result.

Meanwhile, the secret as to who should be invited to follow Mr. Gladstone had been so well kept that apparently, with the exception of Lord Rosebery, none of the Ministers knew whom the Queen had selected. According to the usual procedure the Ministers were shown into one of the drawing-rooms, while the Queen waited in an adjoining room where the Council was to be held. The Lord-in-Waiting ushered in the six Ministers and the Council was held. At the conclusion, the Queen asked Mr. Gladstone to remain while the others retired, and he tendered his resignation, which (according to the Court Circular) was graciously accepted by Her Majesty.

His formal letter of resignation ran as follows:

10 Downing Street, Whitehall.

Mr. Gladstone presents his most humble duty to Your Majesty.

The close of the Session, and the approach of a new one, have offered Mr. Gladstone a suitable opportunity for considering the condition of his sight and hearing, both of them impaired, in relation to his official obligations. As they now place serious, and also growing, obstacles in the way of the efficient discharge of those obligations, the result has been that he has found it his duty humbly to tender to Your Majesty his resignation of the high offices which Your Majesty has been pleased to entrust to him. He desires to make this surrender accompanied with a grateful sense of the condescending kindness which Your Majesty has graciously shown him on so many occasions during the various periods for which he has had the honour to serve Your Majesty.

Mr. Gladstone will not suddenly burden Your Majesty with a recital of particulars. He may, however, say that, although at eighty-four years of age he is sensible of a diminished capacity for prolonged labour, this is not in itself such as would justify his praying to be relieved from the restraints and exigencies of official life. But his deafness has become, in Parliament, and even in the Cabinet, a serious inconvenience, of which he must reckon on some progress to an increase. More grave than this, and more rapid in its growth, is the obstruction of vision, which arises rom cataract in both his eyes. It has cut him off in substance from the newspapers, and from all except the best types in the best lights, while, even as to them, he cannot master them with that ordinary facility and dispatch which he deems absolutely requisite for the due dispatch of his public duties. In other respects than reading, the operation of the complaint
294

is not as yet so serious; but this one he deems to be vital.

Accordingly, he brings together these two facts, the condition of his sight and hearing, and the break in the course of public affairs brought about in the ordinary way by the close of the Session. He has therefore felt that this is the fitting opportunity for the resignation, which by this letter he humbly prays Your Majesty to accept.[1]

March 3rd, 1894

For the moment, Mr. Gladstone thought that the Queen was going to "break down", but she rallied herself, and there followed a conversation which was "neither here nor there". The Queen thanked Gladstone again for a little service he had done for her in the case of the Duke of Coburg—probably one of the smallest incidents of his four premierships. They spoke of oculists—and Mrs. Gladstone—but never a word regarding the successorship to the Prime Ministership. A halting moment or two passed, and then a "kind and warm farewell".

This is Gladstone's own account of the interview, related by him to Morley—but how true it is no one knows. Gladstone was over eighty, deaf, and going blind, besides being considerably upset at his farewell to public life. It seems almost inconceivable that the Queen should have talked of such trivial matters on an occasion like this—yet her account of the interview is missing: or perhaps was never written down.

When Mr. Gladstone left the room, a moment of intense and almost dramatic interest arose for the

---

[1] Published in Morley's *Life of Gladstone*, vol. iii. p. 388.

Ministers waiting in the anteroom, who were soon to see whom the Queen had selected to succeed Mr. Gladstone. The Queen now told Lord Acton to bring in Lord Rosebery, but she may have spoken low and he did not hear what she said, or possibly he may have been so sure she would send for Sir William Harcourt that he took it for granted that this was her choice. In any case he retired from the Council room and asked Sir William Harcourt to come in to the Queen. Naturally, Harcourt assumed that he was going to be asked to form a Government, and walked sedately into the Council Chamber. What Lord Rosebery's feelings must have been to see his rival summoned after he had been given to understand by the Prince of Wales that he was to be Prime Minister can better be imagined than described.

But his astonishment was nothing compared to the Queen's when having, as she thought, summoned Lord Rosebery, she saw Sir William Harcourt enter the room. Certainly most people would have found the situation most embarrassing, but not for a moment was she at all disconcerted. She merely said that there had been some mistake, and she hoped Sir William would retire again while she spoke to Lord Acton. Whether she told Lord Acton what she thought of him, history does not relate, but she asked him to bring in Lord Rosebery, who was thereupon offered and accepted the post of Prime Minister.

That evening Sir Henry Ponsonby wrote to Mr. Gladstone informing him that Lord Rosebery had been appointed Prime Minister in his place. Gladstone's letter in reply, written when he was dispirited and saddened by his eclipse, may well give the final touch to this chapter. Undoubtedly Gladstone would have preferred to have died in harness, and there is perhaps a touch of bitterness in his desire to be treated as " one of the public." His letter ran:

10 DOWNING STREET, WHITEHALL,
March 4th 1894.

DEAR SIR H. PONSONBY—I really was ashamed last night at your quickness in writing to me when you are under such pressure, locomotive and other, and when it is I who have been the means of bringing it upon you. Pray take no more trouble and let me take my chance as one of the public. Interesting as all intelligence is under the circumstances, it is probably better that for the time at any rate I should remain an extraneous person. And with many thanks for all your goodness and kindness, I remain, sincerely yours,

W. E. GLADSTONE.

INDEX

Aberdeen, Lord, 98
Acton, Lord, 293, 296
Adderley, Sir C. B. (Lord Norton), 250
Ailesbury, Lord, 129
Albani, Madame, 204
Albany, Duchess of, 242
Albany, Duke of. *See* Leopold, Prince
Albert Edward, Prince of Wales. *See* Wales, Prince of
Alberta, the, 1
Alexander II., Tsar of Russia, 65, 86, 130
Alexander III., Tsar of Russia. *See* Czarevitch, the
Alexandra, Queen. *See* Wales, Princess of
Alfred, Prince, Duke of Edinburgh, 75, 76, 77, 79, 119, 121, 125
Alington, Lord, 196 *n.*
Angeli, Heinrich von, 242
Argyll, Duchess of. *See* Louise, Princess
Argyll, Duke of, 156-7, 163, 164, 183, 202, 255, 256, 258, 261, 264, 275
Arthur, Prince, Duke of Connaught, 75, 77, 78, 119, 124, 125, 126, 285
Ashburton, Lord, 80

Baillie, Mrs., 134
Balfour, A. J. (afterwards Earl Balfour), 162, 169, 170
Balmoral, 1, 46, 195-6; the Pony Row at, 46-64
Baring, Edward (Lord Revelstoke), 80
Baring, Thomas, 81
Barker, Mr., 83
Barker, Rev. W., Rector of Cowes, 153

Baxter, W. E., 208
Beaconsfield, Lord, 88, 104, 142, 178, 193, 280, 281; and the Irish University Bill, 93-4, 95-8, 99, 100, 101, 102, 103, 104, 105, 106, 107, 108, 109, 110-11, 112, 113, 114-15; Colonel Ponsonby's interview with, 95-8; Gladstone and, 95, 96, 98-9, 100, 115, 155, 280-81; Queen Victoria and the influence of, 98, 165, 280-81; and the Queen's Speech incident, 155-7; and the extension of the franchise, 165
Beatrice, Princess (Princess Henry of Battenberg), 125, 126
Benson, Archbishop, 164
Beresford, Lord Charles, 17
Bessborough, Lord, 110
Biddulph, General Sir Thomas, 18, 52, 79
Bigge, Major (afterwards Lord Stamfordham), 165, 179, 256-9, 261-2, 263, 264-5, 266-7, 268, 275
Birch, Samuel, 72
Bock, Admiral Count de, 66, 68, 72, 74, 75, 81, 85, 86, 87
Boehm, Edgar, 47, 48, 49, 50, 51, 57, 58
Brand, Sir Henry Bouverie William (afterwards Viscount Hampden), 93, 202
Bright, John, 149
Brownlow, Lord, 212
Brunnow, Count, 66, 67, 80
Brunnow, Countess, 80
Buller, General Sir Redvers, 190

Cadogan, Lord, 184
Cairns, Lord, 164, 166, 167 *n.*, 173, 174, 175, 177, 178, 184, 199, 208, 209, 211, 219, 220 and *n.* 1,

299

221, 230, 233, 239, 248, 252, 254, 257, 274, 275
Cambridge, Duke of, 69, 76, 81
Campbell, Sir George, 208
Carlingford, Lord, 242, 266, 267, 269
Carnarvon, Lord, 241, 242, 243, 245, 246-7, 250 n.
Chamberlain, Joseph, 160, 168, 185-6, 187, 212, 228, 237, 238, 241, 242, 243, 245, 249, 262
Chaplin, Henry (afterwards Viscount Chaplin), 270, 272, 277
Childers, H. C. E., 140
Christian, Prince, 51, 52, 53-4, 62, 75, 125, 165 n.
Christian, Princess ("Lenchen"), 125, 126, 127, 165 n.
Churchill, Lady, 50, 64
Churchill, Lord Randolph, 160, 181, 182, 193, 198, 203, 212, 258
Clonmel, Lord, 17
Coburg, Duke of, 295
Codrington, Admiral Sir Henry John, 31, 33, 36
Cole, ——, junior, 70
Connaught, Duke of. See Arthur, Prince
Cook, ——, 77
Courtney, Leonard Henry (afterwards Lord Courtney), 279
Cowell, Sir John, 18, 120
Cowper, Lord, 189-90, 191, 193, 198, 216, 245, 257
Cross, Richard Assheton (afterwards Viscount Cross), 270, 272
Crystal Palace, the, 83, 85; the Shah's visit, 133-5
Czarevitch, the (afterwards Alexander III.), 119, 123, 132, 133

Dacres, Admiral Sir Sydney, 2, 3, 4, 5, 6, 7, 8, 9, 17, 19, 20, 28, 29, 30, 31, 32, 33, 34, 38
Dalhousie, Lady, 196
Dalhousie, Lord, 31
Delane, John, 109, 110
Derby, Lord (14th Earl), 98
Derby, Lord (15th Earl), 182
Dickson, Dr., 128
Dilke, Sir Charles, 160, 168, 169, 170, 174, 225, 228, 236, 268, 277
Disraeli, Benjamin. See Beaconsfield, Lord

Duckworth, Canon, 47, 48, 49, 50, 51, 52, 53, 54-5, 57-60, 61-3
Dudley, Lord and Lady, 86

Edinburgh, Duke of. See Alfred, Prince
Edwards, Major (afterwards Colonel Sir Fleetwood), 242, 249
Elfin, the, 1
Ellis, Lady, 72
Ellis, Lieut.-Colonel Sir Arthur, 66, 67, 68, 70, 119
Ely, Lady, 154, 195, 204
Emlyn, Lord, 212
Enchantress, the, 5, 6, 10

Fawcett, Henry, 246
Felix, M., 73
Fife, Lord, 195, 196-7, 199, 200, 204
Fisher, Lord, 6
Fitzgerald, Lord Otho, 16-17, 18
Forester, Colonel, 93
Forster, W. E., 43, 92, 138
Fowler, Henry (afterwards Viscount Wolverhampton), 208
Frederica, 133
Frederick, Empress (Victoria, Princess Royal of England), 127
Frogmore, 165 n

Gladstone, Helen, 196, 200, 201, 204
Gladstone, Lord, 280, 281
Gladstone, Mrs., 173, 195, 197, 199, 200, 201, 202, 204, 292, 295
Gladstone, W. E., 37, 98, 136, 159; and the incident of the Fatal Gun, 39, 45; the Irish University Bill and Disraeli's refusal to take office, 89-97, 99-117; the Queen's personal relations with, and opinion of, 88, 139, 145, 146, 185, 187-8, 190, 191, 195, 238, 278, 280, 281-2; Disraeli and, 95, 96, 98-9, 100, 115, 155, 280-81; and the affair of the Queen's Speech, 136-9, 141-55, 158; and the Franchise Bill, 159-69, 171-174, 177-81, 183-5, 190-94, 198-204, 207, 215, 216, 221-3, 225-30, 245, 246, 248, 249, 253, 257-60, 262, 265, 272; his attitude to-

INDEX

wards the House of Lords, 159,
161, 162-3, 164, 168-9, 170, 171,
186, 191-2, 194, 198, 205, 252,
255; his language alarms the
Queen, 161-2, 163, 167, 184-5,
229, 249, 250; asked to keep
younger Ministers in order, 168,
169, 170-71, 186, 187, 242;
opposes dissolution, 166, 171,
176, 202-3, 205; and the Queen's
intervention, 172, 173, 174, 179,
193, 194, 234, 237, 238, 239, 271,
278; his memorandum on the
situation, 190, 191-2, 193, 194;
conversations at Balmoral, 195,
196, 197-8, 199, 200-204, 213;
and attempts at discussions between Salisbury and Hartington,
234, 236, 237-8, 241; and Lord
Carnarvon's speech, 241; and
proposed personal meetings of
party leaders, 260, 261, 262, 263,
264, 266, 267, 268, 269, 273, 275,
276, 277; and Hartington-Hicks
Beach pourparlers, 260, 263,
264, 266, 271, 272, 273; meetings with Salisbury, 277-8; the
Queen considers giving him the
Garter, 278; he congratulates
Ponsonby, 278, 279; his retirement and the choice of his successor, 280, 282-97
Glynn, Sir George, 110
Gomm, Field-Marshal Sir W. M.,
73
Gordon, General, 191 *n.*, 265
Gorst, (Sir) John Eldon, 160
Goschen, G. J., (afterwards Vis-
count Goschen), and the Fatal
Gun incident, 2, 5, 6, 7-11, 17,
18, 19, 20, 21, 22, 23, 25, 26-8,
29, 30, 31, 32, 34, 37, 38, 39, 40,
41, 42, 43, 44, 45; and the
Franchise Bill, 163, 169, 193,
207, 245, 258, 265, 268
Gossett, Captain, 93
Gower, Lord Ronald, 262
Grant, Sir Francis, 81
Granville, Lord; and the Irish Uni-
versity Bill, 92, 110; and the
Shah's visit, 125, 126; and the
Queen's Speech incident, 143,
146, 147, 154; and the Franchise
Bill, 166, 167, 174, 175, 176, 177,
178, 179, 181, 183, 184, 190, 208,

209, 249, 257, 268, 269, 276,
277
Grey, Albert (afterwards 4th Earl
Grey), 199, 204, 205-10, 211-13,
215, 216, 279
Grey, General the Hon. Charles, 5,
6, 7, 90, 115, 119 *n.*1, 205
Grey, Edward, Viscount Grey of
Fallodon, 5
Grey, Sir George, 102, 103, 110-12
Grey, Henry George, 3rd Earl
Grey, 102, 103, 106, 212-13
Grey, Mrs., 76

Halifax, Lord, 37, 38-9, 40, 42, 43,
145
Hamilton, Sir Edward, 180-81,
186, 187, 213-15, 216-19, 224-8,
230-33, 236-7, 238, 250, 259,
260, 265, 270-71, 273, 274, 276-
277, 279, 287-9
Hamilton, Lady, 76
Hamilton, Lord George, 207
Hampden, Lord. *See* Brand
Hams, Captain, 81
Harcourt, Sir William Vernon,
110 ; and the Queen's Speech
incident, 141, 142, 143, 144, 146,
147, 148, 149, 154, 156, 158; and
the Franchise Bill, 179, 180, 182,
237; on Balmoral, 195-6; and the
Premiership, 280, 285, 287, 288,
292, 293, 296
Hardinge, General the Hon. Sir
Arthur Edward, his letters on the
Grand Duke Wladimir's visit,
66, 67-73, 74-87; on the Shah's
visit, 119, 120-24, 128-9, 130-35
Hardinge, Lady, 72
Hartington, Lord, and the Queen's
Speech incident, 142, 145, 146,
147, 148, 151, 152, 153, 158;
and the Franchise Bill, 176, 177-
178, 185, 224, 225, 229, 233 and
n. 2, 234-5, 236, 237, 238, 239,
240, 241, 260, 263, 264, 265, 266,
268, 269, 271, 272, 273, 277
Hekeem El Mema'lik, 120-21, 122,
124, 129
Helena, Princess ("Lenchen"). *See*
Christian, Princess
Hicks Beach, Sir Michael, 181,
182, 183, 202, 207, 212, 260,
263, 264, 265, 266, 268, 269,
271, 272, 273, 275

Hohenlohe, Princess, 22, 25
Holland, Sir Henry, 212
Hopetoun, Lady, 240
Hornby, Rear-Admiral Sir
 Geoffrey, 2, 3, 4, 6, 8, 10, 31,
 33, 35
Hussein Khan, H.H. Hajee
 Meerza, 119, 123

Inverness, Duchess of, 71

James, Henry (Lord James of
 Hereford), 197, 207, 221
Jones, Winter, 72

Kent, Duchess of, 165 n.
Kimberley, Lord, 288, 289, 292,
 293
Kingscote, Lady E., 76
Knollys, Sir Francis, 181
Knyvett, Cary J., 265

Labouchere, Henry, 152, 292
Lambert, Sir John, 228, 236
Lansdowne, Lord, 281
Leiningen, H.S.H. Prince, 2, 3, 4,
 5, 6, 7, 8, 9, 10, 15, 16, 17, 19,
 20, 21, 23, 25, 27, 28-9, 30, 31,
 32, 34, 35, 36, 38, 41, 44
"Lenchen" (Princess Helena), 125,
 126, 127, 165 n.
Lennox, Henry (Lord Henry Gor-
 don-Lennox), 81
Leopold, Prince, Duke of Albany,
 125, 126, 140, 141, 144, 147,
 153, 154, 155, 158
Lewis, Sir George Cornewall, 72
Lewis, Lady P., 72
Lonsdale, Lady, 199
Lorne, Lord, 256, 258, 260, 261,
 262, 264, 265
Lothian, Lord, 70
Louise, Princess, Duchess of Argyll,
 79, 125, 126, 127
Lowther, James, 269, 270, 272
Loyd-Lindsay, Sir Robert James
 (afterwards Lord Wantage), 212
Lubbock, Sir John (afterwards
 Lord Avebury), 279
Lumley, Augustus, 80
Lyons, Lord, 22
Lytton, Lord, 154, 156, 157

Macdonald, Admiral Sir Ronald
 Ian, 16, 17, 31, 32, 36

Malcolm Khan, H.E. Meerza, 119,
 126
Malmesbury, Lord, 202
Mandeville, Lady, 196
Manners, Lord John, 266, 269, 272
Mary, Princess, of Teck, 69
May, Sir Erskine (afterwards Lord
 Farnborough), 247
Melbourne, Lord, 98
Milward, Dawson, 193
Mitchell, John, 79
Montagu, Admiral the Hon. Victor,
 153, 154
Morley, John (afterwards Viscount
 Morley), 192, 199, 282, 286, 289,
 292 n., 295
Mundy, Admiral Sir Rodney, 4,
 31, 33, 36

Napoleon III., Emperor, 65, 68 n.,
 85
Nasr-ed-din, Shah of Persia, his
 visit to Queen Victoria, 65, 118-
 135
Norfolk, Duke of, 145
Northcote, Sir Stafford (afterwards
 Earl of Iddesleigh), and the
 Franchise Bill, 160, 177, 199,
 202, 207, 218, 223, 224, 241,
 242, 243, 245, 248, 260, 262,
 263, 264, 265, 266, 267, 268,
 274, 276, 277
Norton, Lord, 250
Novitzki, General, 68

Opura, Duke and Duchess d', 76
Owen, Professor, 71, 73

Paget, Alfred, 86-7
Paget, Lady Evelyn, 154
Palmerston, Lord, 98, 145, 285
Peel, Albert, 212
Peel, Sir Charles Lennox, 173,
 198, 199, 201, 253, 256, 257,
 260, 261, 267, 274-5
Peel, General Jonathan, 92
Peel, Sir Robert, 98
Pembroke, Lord, 212
Penzance, Lord, 242
Persia, Shah of, his visit to Eng-
 land, 65, 118-35
"Plon-Plon," 68
Ponsonby, General Sir Henry F.,
 90, 115; his memorandum on the
 question of the Fatal Gun, 12-16,

19; his letters to his wife, 16-19, 42-3, 195-6; private correspondence with Goschen, 22-4, 26-8, 37; correspondence with Prince of Wales and Prince Leiningen, 24-26, 28-9, 36; correspondence with Lord Halifax, 38-9, 40-42, 43; and the Pony Row at Balmoral, 47, 48-52, 54, 60-61; Sahl's letters to, 52-3, 55-7, 64-5; Canon Duckworth's letters to, 54-5, 57-60, 61-3; Colonel Hardinge's letters to, on Grand Duke Wladimir's visit, 66-87; and the Irish University Bill, 88, 90, 92-4, 107-108, 110; letter from Prince of Wales to, 91-2; his interviews with Disraeli, 93-4, 95-8, 104, 112; interviews with Gladstone, 95, 96, 98, 99, 100-101, 102, 104, 105-6, 109, 112; his memorandum of interview with Disraeli, 99, 100, 101, 102, 112, 113-14, 115; interviews with Sir George Grey and Lord Grey, 102, 103, 106; the Queen's thanks for his assistance, 106-7, 116-17; Sir G. Grey's letters to, 110-12; Colonel Hardinge's letters to, on the Shah's visit, 120-24, 129-35; and the affair of the Queen's Speech, 138, 139, 140-44, 145, 146-8, 149-151, 152, 153, 158; and the Franchise Bill, 163, 165, 167, 168, 169, 170, 171, 172, 174-5, 184, 186, 188, 193, 194, 200, 204, 246-247; sent to see Gladstone about the Queen's intervention, 165, 172, 173-4; misses messages of recall, 165, 167, 172; interviews with other Ministers and Lord Salisbury, 175-8; Lord Rowton's visit to Windsor, 179; Harcourt's letter to, 180; correspondence with Sir Edward Hamilton, 180-181, 186, 187-8, 213-19, 224-9, 230-34, 236-7, 238-9, 250-51, 259-60, 270-1, 273-4, 276-7, 278-279; sees the Prince of Wales, 181-182; and Gladstone's memorandum on the situation, 190, 191-2, 193, 194; the Queen to, on the misdeeds of the Government, 190-91, 238, 245-6; and the Queen's approaches to the Opposition, 193, 194, 200, 201, 202; conversations with Gladstone at Balmoral, 195-6, 197-9, 201-4; and Albert Grey's proposal, 205-13, 215, 216; and Duke of Richmond's letter, 219-21, 229-30; Gladstone's reply, 221-4, 225, 227; correspondence with Lord Hartington, 234-5, 237; and Lord Salisbury, 239-40, 251-2; and Lord Carnarvon's proposal, 241, 242, 243, 245, 246-7; further proposals to Salisbury and Gladstone, 251-5, 260; and suggested mediation of Duke of Argyll, 255-6, 258; correspondence with Major Bigge, 256-9, 261-2, 263-267, 268, 275; Lord Carlingford's letter to, 266; and party leaders' knowledge of Hartington-Hicks Beach negotiations, 268, 269, 271; Horace Seymour's letters to, 271-3; sees Duke of Richmond and Lord Cairns, 273-5; Charles Peel's letters to, 274-5; thanked by Gladstone, 278-9; and Gladstone's retirement, 282, 283-4, 285, 286; Hamilton to, on choice of Gladstone's successor, 287-9; Rosebery to, on his reluctance to accept Premiership, 290-91; Gladstone's letter to, after retirement, 297

Ponsonby, Lady, 53, 55, 56; letters to, 16-19, 42-3, 195-6
Ponsonby, Spencer, 120
Poulostioff, M., 69, 75
Prosser, Charles, 91

Raikes, H. C., 160
Ramsay, Sir John William (afterwards Lord Dalhousie), 31
Rawlinson, Sir Henry, 122, 128
Rendlesham, Lady, 73
Richmond, Duke of, 110; and the Franchise Bill, 164, 166, 172, 173, 174, 183, 193, 196, 198, 199, 200, 201, 202, 213, 216, 219-20, 221, 223, 229, 230, 233, 235, 239, 240, 248-9, 253, 256, 258, 260, 261, 269, 273, 274, 275
Ripon, Lord, 293
Rosebery, Lord, 177, 179, 222; and the Premiership, 280, 285, 287, 288, 289, 290-91, 292, 293, 296

Rothschild, Lionel, 76
Rowton, Lord, 164, 172, 173, 174, 176, 177, 178, 179, 186, 193
Roxburghe, Duchess of, 79, 265
Rupell, General, 68
Russell, Lord, 104, 285
Russell, Lord Charles, 93

Sadr Azam, Grand Vizier, 119, 123, 125, 126, 127, 128, 129, 130, 132
Sahl, Hermann, 48, 49, 50-51, 52-53, 54, 55-7, 58, 59, 60, 61, 62, 63-4, 242
Salisbury, Lord, and the Franchise Bill, 162-6, 167 n., 174-86, 193, 194, 198, 202, 212, 223, 225, 227, 229-41, 244, 245, 248, 250 n., 251-6, 258-77
Schouvaloff, Count, 66, 68, 75, 81
Scott, Colonel, 70
Seymour, Horace, 271-3
Shaftesbury, Lord, 182
Shah of Persia, his visit to England, 65, 118-35
Shaw, Captain Sir Eyre Massey, 79, 81
Sothern, E. A., 77
Spencer, Lord, 238, 292 n., 293; and the Queen's Speech incident, 137-8, 139-40, 141, 142, 143, 144, 146, 147, 149-50, 152, 154, 157, 158
Stafford, Lord, 78, 81
Stamfordham, Lord. See Bigge, Major
Stanhope, Hon. Edward, 160
Stanley, Arthur Penrhyn, Dean of Westminster, 76
Stanley, Colonel Sir Frederick Arthur (afterwards Lord Derby), 160, 252
Stephenson, H. F., 36
Stewart, Admiral Sir Houston, 31, 32, 34
Stockmar, Baron, 48
Stonor, Mr. and Miss, 196
Sturt, Hon. Napier, 196
Sultan of Turkey, 65
Sumner, Arthur, 17
Sutherland, Duke of, 77, 79, 83
Swan, Miss, the giantess, 73
Sydney, Lord, 67, 74, 76, 80, 110, 120, 121, 126, 129, 140, 141, 153-5

Taylor, E., 92-3
Teck, Duke of, 70, 81
Tholozan, Dr., 128
Torrington, Lord, 155
Trevelyan, Sir George Otto, 249-250, 257, 258, 261, 262, 275
Tryon, Captain, 38
Tussaud's, Madame, the Shah's visit to, 131-2

United Services Gazette, letter on "The Fatal Gun" in, 28, 29-36

Vane, Lord, 81
Vansittart, Captain, 31, 32, 36
Victoria ("Vicky"), Princess Royal of England (Empress Frederick), 127
Victoria, Queen, 65, 88, 98, 160; dislikes London, 1; and the incident of the Fatal Gun, 7, 11, 19-21, 23, 25, 26, 28, 37, 38, 39, 42, 43, 44-5; Goschen's letter to, 7-11, 26; her supremacy at sea, 12, 13, 14, 15, 16, 17, 23, 25, 37, 40, 41, 45; her letter to Goschen, 19-21, 26; and the Pony Row at Balmoral, 46, 47, 48, 49, 50, 51, 52, 56, 57, 58, 59, 60, 61, 63, 64; and the visit of the Grand Duke Wladimir, 65, 66, 67, 70, 72, 74, 76, 85, 86; and the Irish University Bill, 88-100, 103-9, 112-15; her personal relations with and opinion of Gladstone, 88, 139, 145, 146, 185, 187-8, 190, 191, 195, 238, 278, 280, 281-2; and Disraeli's perplexing refusal to take office, 94, 95, 96, 97, 99, 100, 101, 102, 104, 105, 106, 107-108, 109, 112, 113; the influence of Disraeli over, 98, 155, 165, 280-81; alleged to have refused to grant Disraeli a dissolution, 109, 110, 111, 112, 114; her thanks to Colonel Ponsonby, 116, 117; her description of the Shah's visit to Windsor, 124-8, 130, 133; and the affair of the Queen's Speech, 136-58; consults Beaconsfield on the constitutional position, 155-7; and the Franchise Bill, 161-75, 177-80, 182-5, 188, 189, 192, 193, 196-9, 203, 204, 216, 220-23, 229, 230, 234, 235, 237-40, 242, 245,

INDEX

248-51, 256-62, 264, 265, 268; and the position of the House of Lords, 161, 171-2, 185, 229; alarmed by Gladstone's language, 161-2, 163, 229, 249, 250; her efforts at intervention between the party leaders, 165, 172-174, 177-80, 182, 183, 189, 193, 194, 202, 223, 239, 240, 244, 249, 251-5, 258-65, 268, 269, 271, 273, 275, 278, 279; objects to language of younger Ministers, 168, 169, 170, 172, 186, 187, 242, 245-246, 249; will not be "the Sovereign of a Democratic Monarchy", 172; consults Lord Rowton, 178, 179; blames the Government for trouble at home and abroad, 190-91, 238, 245-6; and Gladstone's memorandum on the situation, 190, 191, 192, 193, 194; her consultations and correspondence with Duke of Richmond, 193, 196, 198, 199, 200, 219-20, 229, 233, 239, 248-9, 256, 260, 261, 269, 273; considers giving Gladstone the Garter, 278; her letter to Lord Lansdowne, 281-2; and Gladstone's retirement, 282, 283, 284, 285, 286, 287, 292; and Rosebery's succession to Premiership, 288, 289, 290, 291, 296; receives Gladstone's resignation, 293-5; summons Rosebery, 295-6

Victoria and Albert, the, 1, 2, 5, 6, 7, 10, 15

Villiers, Charles Pelham, 92

Wales, Albert Edward, Prince of (King Edward VII.), 47, 67, 155; and the affair of the Fatal Gun, 1, 5-6, 9, 10, 14, 15, 16-17, 18, 19, 20, 21, 24-5, 27, 28, 29, 31, 32, 33, 34, 35, 36, 37, 38, 39, 43, 44; and the Grand Duke Wladimir, 67, 68, 69, 70, 71, 74, 75, 76, 77, 78, 83, 86, 87; and the Irish University Bill, 91-2; and the Shah's visit, 119, 123, 124, 125, 132; and the Queen's Speech incident, 146, 147, 149; and the Franchise Bill, 177, 181, 182, 183, 258; and Rosebery's succession to the Premiership, 289, 290, 296

Wales, Alexandra, Princess of (Queen Alexandra), 78, 81, 86, 124, 200, 202

Warden, Rear-Admiral, 22

Wellesley, the Hon. Gerald Valerian, Dean of Windsor, 75, 117

Wellesley, Mrs., 75

Wellington, Duke of, 73

Wemyss, Lord, 164, 175, 177, 178, 180, 181, 183, 184, 211

West, Sir Algernon, 283

Westminster, Lord and Lady, 77-8

William I., German Emperor, 85, 146

William IV., King, 13, 261

Winmarleigh, Lord, 202

Wladimir, Grand Duke, his visit to England, 65-87

Wolseley, Lord, 191 n.

Wolverton, Lord, 179, 180

Wood, Sir David, 78

Wyndham, ——, 265

Yahya Khan, H.E., 119, 124, 135

Yorke, the Hon. Alexander Grantham, 154

THE END

Printed in Great Britain by R. & R. Clark, Limited, *Edinburgh.*

LETTERS OF
THE EMPRESS FREDERICK

Edited by
The Right Honourable
SIR FREDERICK PONSONBY, G.C.B., G.C.V.O.

With Portraits. 8vo. 25s. net

"No more poignant record of a tragic career has appeared in our time than the volume of the letters of the Empress Frederick to her mother, admirably edited by Sir Frederick Ponsonby. . . . The correspondence of the Empress covers the whole of her adult life and forms an effective substitute for an official biography. . . . On the main experiences of her life she poured out her heart, and we are in the presence of a living and palpitating human being from beginning to end."—*The Contemporary Review.*

"Few books published in recent years will interest the older generation more than these intimate and self-revealing letters of the charming and artistic Englishwoman who was destined for a tragic hundred days to become the German Empress. . . . These letters reopen many of the most controversial issues of another day, such as the attitude of Bismarck to the Emperor Frederick, the vexed question of Sir Morell Mackenzie, the unmannerly behaviour of young Prince William, and the subsequent intrigues of the Kaiser against his mother."—*The Spectator.*

"Sir Frederick Ponsonby has done his work very skilfully. The letters are allowed to speak for themselves ; his running commentary has, as he says, been 'reduced to the minimum,' but, with the brief yet—for the purpose—adequate account of the Empress's earlier years, this unobtrusive commentary sketches in the events and circumstances, domestic and political, of the Empress's life so neatly and exactly that the general reader can follow her story with as much interest as the student of history."—*The Times.*

"A book which is a valuable contribution to modern history."—*The Observer.*

"Apart from the political or historical value of this correspondence, it must have a particular interest as a human document, a self-revelation made to one from whom there could be nothing to conceal and with whom the relation of personal frankness had become a habit of life."—*Sir Rennell Rodd in The Empire Review.*

"Whether we regard the letters of the Empress Frederick merely as historical documents, or as a single 'human document,' their appearance is a matter of outstanding interest."—*The London Mercury.*

MACMILLAN AND CO., LTD., LONDON

A SELECTION OF NEW BOOKS

THE HAMWOOD PAPERS OF THE LADIES OF LLANGOLLEN AND CAROLINE HAMILTON. Edited by Mrs. G. H. BELL (John Travers). With Portraits. 8vo. 21s. net.

> A singularly vivid picture, probably unique in its intimacy and truth, of society in the eighteenth century.

JOHN LORD MONTAGU OF BEAULIEU: A Memoir. By Lady TROUBRIDGE and ARCHIBALD MARSHALL. With Illustrations. 8vo.

A SOLDIER'S NOTEBOOK, 1914–1918. By General A. A. BRUSSILOV. With Maps and Illustrations. 8vo.

ROOSEVELT: The Story of a Friendship, 1880–1919. By OWEN WISTER, author of "The Virginian," etc. With Illustrations. 8vo.

THE LIFE OF ROBERT OWEN. By G. D. H. COLE, author of "The Life of William Cobbett," "The Next Ten Years in British Social and Economic Policy," etc. Second Edition. With Portrait. 8vo. 12s. 6d. net.

A BOOK OF THE BASQUES. By RODNEY GALLOP. With Illustrations. 8vo.

ENGLAND IN THE AGE OF THE AMERICAN REVOLUTION. Book I. GOVERNMENT AND PARLIAMENT UNDER THE DUKE OF NEWCASTLE. By L. B. NAMIER, author of "The Structure of Politics at the Accession of George III." 8vo. 25s. net.

BRITISH FOREIGN POLICY, 1660-1672. By KEITH FEILING, author of "England under the Tudors and Stuarts," "History of the Tory Party 1640-1714, etc." 8vo.

THE CONCERT OF EUROPE. By R. B. MOWAT, Professor of History in the University of Bristol. 8vo.

MACMILLAN AND CO., LTD., LONDON